SEEKERS AFTER MATURE FAITH

SEEKERS AFTER MATURE FAITH

A Historical Introduction
To The Classics
of Christian Devotion

by
E. Glenn Hinson

With Special Psychological Commentary
by
Wayne E. Oates

BROADMAN PRESS
Nashville, Tennessee

© Copyright 1968 • Broadman Press
All rights reserved
Item code: 4265-31
ISBN: 0-8054-6531-6
Library of Congress catalog card number: 68-31113

To

Martha, Chris, and Elizabeth

PREFACE

I have written this book with a firm conviction that private devotion is essential to the life of the Church and that the devotional classics have much to contribute to private devotion. I do not agree with those who think Christians today are too "religious." They may be so in the superficial sense of the word. But in its true sense of commitment to God as revealed in Jesus Christ they are not. The chief problem in American Christianity, in world Protestantism, is shallowness. People attend Church . . . they don't worship God! They attend because it is expected of them and they want to maintain social respectability. The radical proposal of some contemporary critics that we do away with religious exercises will not solve the problem of shallowness. It will multiply it a hundred times. It will merely allow all of us to go our own selfish and inconsiderate ways, paying no attention to the demands of God or the needs of our fellow-men.

No, if the history of Christianity tells us anything, it tells us that we must go back again and again to the ABCs of religious experience. When its foundations are quivering from the combined tremors of social, economic, political, industrial, and scientific revolutions, the Church must strive to deepen the faith of its members. *Mature* faith is required. I underline the word "mature," for we have too often used "faith" tritely as the answer to everything. By mature I mean the kind of faith which can weather change and turbulence because it has reflected upon itself long enough to know where ultimate realities lie.

The devotional classics can offer some help in the shaping of Christian maturity. Not by themselves, of course. But studied alongside the Scriptures as guides in the quest of mature faith, they open up new avenues for our exploration. In teaching a course in the classics for the past several years, I have witnessed surprising reactions from students. With his permission, I relate the story of an exceptional student's dialogue with Augustine.

When he came to Southern Seminary, he came as a seeker,

not sure about future vocation, in fact, not sure about God or self. A philosophy major in college, he had imbibed fully of the main currents of modern thoughts. So, as he confided in personal conversations with me, he found that he could understand the nature of human existence either with or without a concept of God. He had no hostility to the idea of God, as many have; he simply could take it or leave it. He did not require the idea to live an upright moral life, to act kindly toward others, to devote himself to unselfish tasks, and to desire and work for the betterment of society. In his mind, the fact that he was a reasonable human being required these things.

We discussed many times the two poles from which one can interpret human existence. My own religious and intellectual experience has fortunately taught me that not every question has an answer and that those which do have answers may not have the same answers for everyone. The traditional arguments for God's existence, for example, carry weight only insofar as one has a prior disposition to believe in God. Whether or not he accepts God depends purely upon an act of faith, simple trust that there is a Supreme Being who is responsible for all existence, including one's own life. That fact was driven home to me early in my college career, when I was forced to admit that I could not answer the skeptic's question, "How do you know there is a God"? After months of sleepless nights tossing and turning, and in a moment of semiconscious inspiration, John 8:32 fixed itself upon my mind: "You shall know the truth and the truth will make you free." On the feeblest exegetical grounds—all I then possessed—I reasoned, "If Christ is truth, if God is truth, then no discovery I make ever will shatter that fact." At last, I was free. I resolved by an act of faith to "hold to Christ and for the rest be totally uncommitted," as Herbert Butterfield has stated so well.

In this student's case, then, I sensed that the best approach was to share religious experience, my own and that of others. I suggested to him that he read Augustine's *Confessions*. Gifted and thorough scholar that he is, he dug in, reading not merely the *Confessions,* but as many things as possible which would acquaint him with the great African theologian. Over a period of several months, I detected a change, a process of maturation. A slight catch in his voice disappeared. He became more outgoing and more deeply concerned about those around him. Within another year, he had resolved to become a pastor, and, whereas before he had been reluctant to engage in pastoral duties on a part-time basis even, now he sought such opportunities eagerly. He had "found" himself. One could not wish a man better equipped for the cure of souls.*

With some confidence about their value, then, I commend the Christian devotional classics to you. I have tried in this book to give a guide which will help serious Christians get started in what may become an exciting quest. Each chapter has been designed to fit the classics of a particular era into their historical context. In pursuance of this plan the general historical context of the era is sketched in sweeping strokes, the personal piety of the era discussed, and particular classics interpreted against the background of authorship and purpose. The book is essentially a *historical* introduction, therefore. However, Dr. Wayne E. Oates, Professor of Psychology of Religion at Southern Seminary, has furnished additional comments concerning the psychology of religious experience.

---

*As Dr. Hinson finds the classics ways to the self-realization of students, I have also found the little book by Lewis Sherrill, *The Struggle of the Soul,* to be a guide to their participation in the life of Christ. Sherrill uses the Book of Hebrews as a basic pattern of his development of the psychological understanding of faith and the emerging sense of selfhood. The student today tends to want to hear the word of Christ either from the "latest" in psychological idiom or the "oldest" in the wisdom of persons such as Augustine. David Roberts, in his book, *Psychotherapy and a Christian View of Man,* underwent psychotherapy and discovered afresh the great meanings of the Augustinian and Reformation view of the religious life. The reader will find that the convergence of the devotional life and the contemporary "search of modern man for a soul," as depicted in much of modern psychotherapy, to be an exciting way of bringing things both old and new out of Roberts' good treatment of worship and meditation. (W.E.O.)

Not everyone will agree with my choice of particular classics. Dozens of writings not mentioned have nourished the faithful through the centuries. Where I have omitted some favorites, perhaps the representative nature of my selections will help to counterbalance deficiencies. It was not possible, and would not have been helpful, to be exhaustive.

The word "piety" may bother some, since Protestants tend sometimes to associate it with superficial religious practice. I use it always in the *good* sense of genuine devotion and interchangeably with the word "devotion." I have found no satisfactory substitute for it.

I am particularly indebted to Dr. Oates for his contribution. His remarks are footnoted on various pages. My graduate assistant in Church history, Mr. Mark S. Caldwell, has prepared the index for the book and offered helpful suggestions. Dr. Eric C. Rust, Professor of Christian Philosophy at Southern, Dr. Marvin E. Tate, Associate Professor of Old Testament Interpretation, and Miss Barbara Thurman, a gifted theology student at the Seminary, have also helped by a careful reading. My wife, Martha, kept my sometimes flagging spirits cheered enough to get the book completed and typed the manuscript. Several classes in the Classics of Christian Devotion at Southern Seminary have helped to provoke my own thinking by their classroom energies and diligence. To all I offer heartfelt thanks.

I hope the classics will add to your life as many new insights as they have to mine.

Louisville, Kentucky   E. GLENN HINSON
April 1, 1968

CONTENTS

Preface   7

I THE CLASSICS IN A SECULAR AGE   15
   What Are the Classics?   15
   How to Use the Classics   17

II THE CLASSICS OF THE AGE OF THE
   FATHERS   25
   Personal Piety   29
   The Literature of Private Devotion   32
   Athanasius' *Life of Anthony*   35
   Augustine's *Confessions*   40
   Selected Bibliography   51

III THE CLASSICS OF THE AGE OF FAITH   55
   Personal Piety   60
   The Budding of Mysticism   67
   The Little Flowers and *The Mirror of Perfection*   74
   Selected Bibliography   80

IV THE CLASSICS OF THE AGE OF
   RENAISSANCE   85
   Renaissance and Personal Piety   88
   German and Dutch Mysticism   91
   The English Mystics   94
   The German Theology   96
   The Imitation of Christ   98
   Selected Bibliography   106

V THE CLASSICS OF THE AGE OF
   REFORMATION   111
   Reformation and Catholic Personal Piety   115
   Spanish Mysticism   117
   Reformation and Protestant Personal Piety   126
   Protestant Literature of Devotion   128
   Selected Bibliography   132

VI THE CLASSICS OF THE AGE OF DEISM AND THE ENLIGHTENMENT: PART I. ROMAN CATHOLIC CLASSICS 135

    Roman Catholic Personal Piety   139
    Quietism and Jansenism   140
    Francis de Sales' *Introduction to the Devout Life*   142
    Pascal's *Pensées*   147
    Brother Lawrence's *The Practice of the Presence of God*   156
    Selected Bibliography   161

VII THE CLASSICS OF THE AGE OF DEISM AND THE ENLIGHTENMENT: PART II. PROTESTANT CLASSICS 165

    The Development of German Pietism   166
    England and Puritanism   169
    Lancelot Andrewes' *Private Devotions*   171
    Jeremy Taylor's *Holy Living* and *Holy Dying*   174
    John Bunyan's *Pilgrim's Progress* and *Grace Abounding*   179
    William Law's *A Serious Call*   185
    The *Journals* of Fox and Woolman   191
    Selected Bibliography   195

VIII THE CLASSICS OF THE AGE OF REVOLUTION 201

    Personal Piety   207
    Kierkegaard's *Purity of Heart*   213
    Bonhoeffer's *Letters and Papers*   219
    Alfred Delp's *Prison Meditations*   226
    Teilhard's *Letters from a Traveller*   228
    Selected Bibliography   232

IX PERSONAL DEVOTION IN THE SPACE AGE 237
    Footnotes   243

THE CLASSICS IN A SECULAR AGE

What Are the Classics?

How to Use the Classics

I

The Classics in a Secular Age

What Are the Classics?

The devotional classics fall broadly into two categories—biographical and directive. The first group include confessions, personal letters, spiritual diaries, and interpretative biographies or autobiographies—all of which offer unusually intimate glimpses into the lives of saints. A Christian who has struggled arduously, often frantically, to find meaning in life, bares his inmost soul for others to examine. Like the Psalmists, who, incidentally, probably furnished the prototype for this type of biography, he owns up to his sin and weakness and calls upon God for help.

The second group of classics customarily furnish prescriptions for religious conduct and private worship. They give, as it were, directions for finding the oases in life's deserts. Based on the experience of weary travellers, who have wandered the same paths until they found a resting place, they try to leave some tracks or guideposts for others to follow.

Neither the biographical nor the directive classics chart only one path, however. On the contrary, in reading them one perceives quickly how diverse personal religious experience is.[1] Although ultimately they have the same quest, the true understanding of the encounter between man and God in general and of their own encounter in particular, they approach it from a hundred

---

*Asterisk footnotes throughout the book: Special Psychological Commentary by Wayne E. Oates.

different directions. Their creators or inspirers range intellectually from giants like Augustine and Pascal to near illiterates like Francis of Assisi and Teresa of Lisieux, the famous Roman Catholic mystic of the nineteenth century. They present the whole spectrum of human contrasts—young and old, rich and poor, male and female, gay and morbid. Their numbers include both laymen and clerics, churchmen and rebels. They exhibit all sorts of personalities and reflect fully their individuality in the classics they penned.

But, someone will ask, what constitutes their "classic-ness," then? Surely they have something in common to give them such far-reaching impact. I agree. But their classic-ness does not stem from stereotyped religious answers. Quite the contrary. It is generated by the *depth* in which they lived their lives and experienced and articulated their struggle. Recall, for instance, what Bunyan said about Luther's commentary on Galatians: "I found my condition in his experience, so largely and profoundly handled, as if his book had been written out of my heart: . . ."[2] That was Augustine's and Wesley's sentiment, too, though they did not say it in so many words. The classics rang true! They said what we have felt but could not say so exactly.

And here is a point to be noted with special care. The men and women who wrote these works did not have an experience of a completely different type than our own. If they had, we could lay them aside and forget them. Later generations, on the contrary, have read and reread and treasured them precisely because they did ring true to the life of every man.

Because that is true, I forewarn you, reading the classics produces sometimes a disquieting experience, like Augustine's in hearing the story of the monk Anthony. The story snatched him rudely from his hiding place and compelled him to see himself as he really was. So others have also found. The classics hold before us a mirror in which we may see ourselves both as we really are and as we ought to be. Pointedly, then, they ask, "Will you resolve to put off the old image and put on the new"?

We look to the classics, therefore, as our guides. Not all will be equally suitable for everyone. This depends really on what route we have chosen to travel through life. But placing ourselves under their direction, be assured, we will find them pointing out things we may not have realized about our route or about ourselves. They will share with us their knowledge of the way, not asking servile acceptance, but engaging us in a dialogue about life. The classics were written in order that we, too, might share the rich lives and experience of the saints.

How to Use the Classics

The diversity and historical conditioning of the classics oblige me to spell out certain suggestions for their profitable use. A careful observer will note how closely these suggestions correspond with the modern day rules for biblical interpretation. Such correspondence is not accidental. Although an overly critical attitude may stifle the devotional use of the Bible or the classics, an anti- or non-critical attitude may overtax one's credulity so much that he will not profit from reading them. In fact, it may cause him to reject them entirely.

The best approach in our day, therefore, is an historical one. The historian tries to balance objectivity with sympathetic insight. In line with this, even if he rejects certain recorded events or ideas as unlikely in view of contemporary experience, he will still be willing to ask, "What did this mean to the person who recorded it"? A case in point are the miracles associated with Francis of Assisi and his followers in *The Little Flowers* and *The Mirror of Perfection*. Today, an objective historian does not dismiss Francis's miracles out of hand because they are difficult to believe, as some critics of the nineteenth century would have done. Rather, while admitting that one simply cannot know what actually occurred, he accepts the fact that something happened and is content to examine the effect such things had on Francis's followers and on Francis himself.

With this in mind, I offer the following "rules" for using the devotional classics, based on my own experience and the experience of others.

MAKE A CHOICE. First, make a choice. Not every writing will offer satisfying fruit for everyone. Some of the classics, of course, have *broad* appeal; but none has *universal* appeal.

The choice depends to a large degree upon one's personality, religious interest, and background. Those who have a critical turn of mind will probably like the *Confessions*, the *Pensées, Letters and Papers from Prison,* and *Letters from a Traveller.* Those who have a greater preoccupation with questions of morality may feel drawn to *The Rule and Exercises of Holy Living and Holy Dying, The Pilgrim's Progress,* or *A Serious Call to a Devout and Holy Life.* The pietists may find companionship with the *Imitation of Christ,* with one of the mystics, or with *The Practice of the Presence of God.* To my surprise, though the choice was quite logical, two young ladies in my class on the classics chose as their favorite *The Little Flowers* and the *Mirror of Perfection.* In the end, the selection will have to be a personal one.

Making a decision obviously requires perusing much literature. And, although this book is intended as an aid in selection, one will deprive himself of an enriching experience if he does not range far enough afield. Who can tell, after all, what will strike his fancy in this plush garden of flowers? The way to make a satisfying selection is to spend time looking and sampling.

RECONSTRUCT THE CONTEXT. When the selection has been made, the second step is to reconstruct the context. The aim, of course, is to engage in a dialogue with their author. This can only happen if we take pains to place them in their setting in life. Three background features require particular attention.

1. *The times in which they were written.* It hardly needs saying that much of the diversity of these writings stemmed from the

fact that they were written at different times. The age of Francis was not that of Augustine, the age of Bonhoeffer not that of Pascal. If we hope to grasp the abiding values of the writings of each, we must learn all we can about the era in which he wrote.

2. *The author.* Equally important is the person who wrote. How vastly different are the intellectual preparations, temperaments, and skills of Brother Lawrence and Jeremy Taylor. How vastly different the religious pilgrimages of Pascal and Bunyan. Without knowing such things about them we cannot hear them as accurately as we ought. As in any personal dialogue, understanding will deepen as one comes to know the person better.

3. *The specific context of the writing itself.* We cannot always recover the specific context for these writings, but all that we can learn will help us to absorb their truths. The *German Theology* and the *Imitation of Christ,* for example, are particularly obscure. Yet, even in the case of these, we can deduce from information concerning German and Dutch mysticism and concerning the "Brothers" movement what created the impetus for them. To know specifically that Pascal's *Pensées* are notes written at various times in preparation for an apology for Christianity, on the other hand, greatly increases our appreciation of its astounding disarray. In either case, the more specifically we can reconstruct the context, the more we will gain from reading the classic.

READ CRITICALLY AND YET SYMPATHETICALLY. As regards the actual reading of a writing, we must read critically, but in sympathy with the author. The tendency will be to forget one or the other of these rules. Some, overawed by the thought of a saint, may try to force themselves to believe everything they read. The result would be intellectual nausea in some cases and discarding the work in others. Consider again the extreme example of *The Little Flowers of St. Francis.* Written in an era of unbelievable gullibility, no modern could possibly accept as fact everything they relate. But they still contain many "flowers" worth picking. Above all, they hold up to our eyes Francis's wonderful ideals of poverty, obedience, and love of God.

The other approach may be extreme skepticism, forgetful of the context in which a classic was written just as much as the overly sympathetic reader. We may just as well settle the matter here and now—some questions simply can't be answered. Then, why boggle so long that we have no time left for picking the fruits? Who can say, for·instance, exactly how much Augustine or Bunyan exaggerated their sense of sin when they wrote? Do we have to answer that question to see the point each was trying to make—viz., no matter how unworthy we may be, God still loves us and seeks our redemption?

To appreciate and benefit from the classics, therefore, we must hold criticism and sympathy in balance. Having reconstructed carefully the context in which they were written will aid immensely. But, in the last analysis, the best aid will be ordinary common sense.

READ LEISURELY AND REREAD. Once you have made a choice of classics, read those selected in a leisurely manner, and reread them periodically. In a day of intense speed and frenzied activity, this will not be easy. But it is essential, if genuine conversation is to take place. The great ideas of the classics need time to fallow and germinate before they produce fruit in us.

Besides reading in an unhurried manner, we ought also to reread the classics, or certain portions of them. Literature that runs deep deserves this consideration. At every reading, certainly, new and fresh insights will pop up, as in the reading of the Bible. Yet we ought not to reread the whole of certain classics every time, no more than we ought to reread the whole of the Scriptures every time. Like all literature, the classics have arid and unfruitful sections. For that reason, we ought to mark certain luxuriant parts and return to them when we have a few moments for reflection.

Marking favorite passages will have some by-products, too.

The pastor will undoubtedly want to share them with his congregation from time to time. Others will want to share them with friends. Quite often, we can introduce a third party to share our conversation, no other than one of the great saints.

EXPAND THE RANGE OF SHARED EXPERIENCES. This comment offers an appropriate opening for me to add a final suggestion concerning the use of the devotional classics. Beginning with our own reading, we need to expand the range of our experience by sharing with others. With this in mind, we have formed "cell groups" of twos and threes in our class at Southern Seminary, pairing off according to interest in a particular classic on which the group would lead class discussion. The practice has benefited the class in several ways. First of all, it is a good pedagogical device, helping the student to master the material more readily. Second, it stimulates questions which can be addressed to the classic and to one another. Third, it lets people speak candidly when they know their problems have kinship with those of the saints. Fourth, it often creates the context for the development of lasting Christian friendships which will remain throughout life.*

What is to prevent the forming of such cell groups within the churches today? Or on the college campus? Or in homes? Or in offices and factories? There is no use forming such groups with-

---

*The small group has been studied technically by many persons. One of the most comprehensive studies is a volume entitled *Small Groups: Studies in Social Interaction.* (Edited by Paul Hare, Edgar F. Borgatta, and Robert E. Balles). A briefer paperback survey is entitled *The Small Group* by Michael S. Olmsted (New York: Random House, 1959). The dynamics of a small group are in themselves a searching of the "here-and-now" relationships of people to each other. If we can keep searching for the appearing of the Holy Spirit in the gathered community, the group does not become as morbidly introspective nor superficially social as it would if this were not the spoken and unspoken prayer of the group, as a group, and the members as individuals.

out a nucleus to revolve around. Lack of one has all too often resulted in failure. The classics could form the nucleus for however long or short a period is desired. No matter what classic one prefers, he will profit immensely from sharing with others.

From time to time, Christians have tried this with genuine benefit. Surprisingly, we seem so easily to forget what the Moravian and Wesleyan societies did. Wesley's Aldersgate experience took place, in fact, in a Moravian meeting as the preacher read the preface to Luther's commentary on Romans. Such meetings laid the foundations for the evangelical revivals of the eighteenth century.

In our own day, also, churches have experimented profitably with cell groups which focused their discussions around the classics. In one Louisville church, for example, a group of young men and women, some seminary students, employed the following pattern as they met each Sunday evening for about a year. In round robin fashion, they read a selected portion from one of the classics. The reader raised a point for discussion. The dialogue proceeded from there, as the group brought their varied knowledge and interests to bear on the point at issue. The result was increased spiritual maturity for some and serious soul searching by all. As in the Seminary classroom, the classics helped to clear the air, to produce frank and open discussion, and yet to weld the group together as seekers of mature faith.

Conclusion

For many centuries, the devotional classics have held an esteemed place in the life of the Christian Church. But their finest hour has always been in the ages of turmoil. In an age that demands mature faith—in our age—we need again to take the classics from the book shelves and to ask the saints to guide us and to share with us their knowledge of the way. Who knows but what an Augustine, a Bunyan, or a Wesley is about to be stirred to see himself and to follow Christ, to remold his life and to hearken to Christ's call.

THE CLASSICS OF THE AGE OF THE FATHERS

Personal Piety
The Literature of Private Devotion
Athanasius' Life of Anthony
Augustine's Confessions
Selected Bibliography

II

The Classics of The Age of The Fathers

The age of the Fathers, the second through the sixth centuries, furnished a fertile field for devotional writings, for it tested and refined men's faith in the crucible of change. Although there were intervals of quiescence, it was on the whole a time of ferment. Politically, socially, economically, and intellectually it seethed with revolution. In a word, the age of the Fathers was an age not unlike our own.

The political story is well-known. The Roman Empire had, like a huge colossus, extended its sway all around the Mediterranean and into the inhabited lands that bordered on it. It reached its apogee in the time of Hadrian (117-138). But however proficient the Roman genius for administration, it could not hold such a vast and far-flung dominion forever. Revolts flared again and again. Now the Jews, now the Persians, now the Barbarian tribes rose up to hack at the sides of the colossus. For four centuries, it held firm, losing a little ground here or there, but winning it back again. But then, weakened from internal disorders and from gradual socio-economic and moral deterioration, it could resist no longer. The Barbarians of Europe, many of whose kin now made up the larger part of the Roman army, pressed southwards, little by little whittling away the incredible Roman domain. First one tribe, then another, dashed in to kill, plunder, and retreat. Within a hundred years, 376 to 476, Rome had lost half her holdings and the Empire that remained was only Roman in name; in substance, it was Greek.

Throughout its imperial history, of course, the major problem was the unity of the Empire. With so many diverse elements, Rome's cohesiveness was always touch and go. The Emperors worked hard to keep the giant from falling apart. That was the aim of provincial administrative organization, of the vast network of Roman roads, of a postal system, and of the increasing centralization of authority. It was the cause of the persecution of the Christian Church, for the Church threatened to sever the ties that bound Rome's citizens tightly to her. It was the reason also, whether the main reason we cannot say, of Constantine's adoption of Christianity. But by the time this happened, it was too late. Rome had begun to come apart at the seams; it could not withstand revolt within and attack from without.

Rome's political decline was accompanied and assisted by social and economic upheaval. For a long time, the Empire had thrived on the rich prizes it had seized by conquest. But when the wheels of expansion ground to a halt, the economy slowed down too, almost imperceptibly at first, but then more noticeably as the reserves from conquest drained away. At the heart of the political and social upheaval, of course, was the institution of slavery. The Roman economy and the Roman society had become very dependent upon slaves. For the ruling classes, slaves operated the magnificent villas, managed the homes, cared for the estates, tutored the children. When the supply of slaves dwindled, then, it left Roman society impotent. Rome had no middle classes to take up the slack and the upper classes were not ready to accept change of status.

By way of contrast, the lot of the large mass of people within the Empire was usually a hard one. They owned no slaves who could do their work. They eked out a minimal existence on small plots of ground, or in arts and crafts. With little or no education, they were at the mercy of those who could read and write. Taxes laid an additional heavy burden upon their straining shoulders. They had too many children and not enough to feed them. What could they do but expose them on a rubbish pile or sell them for slaves to willing buyers? Housing was incredibly bad in large, crowded cities like Rome. In spite of great Roman advances in technology—water systems, central heating, solid buildings—the conveniences which might have eased the burdens of daily life hardly filtered down to the impoverished masses.

Moral decay was evident everywhere. Moralists like Seneca (*ca.* 4 B. C.-A. D. 65), the gifted Emperor Marcus Aurelius, and other intellectuals, deplored Roman manners and customs in terms no less severe than those of Christian preachers. They, too, lacerated the masses for infanticide, prostitution, marital infidelity, brutality, and corruption of all kinds. Marcus Aurelius (161-180) strove mightily to effect a moral reformation of the Empire along the lines of his Stoic philosophy as the means of saving it: His efforts proved unavailing in the long run. So did the efforts of many succeeding Emperors.*

What we see, therefore, are vast contrasts—contrasts that weakened Rome internally and made her vulnerable externally. Nowhere is this more evident than on the intellectual plane. On one level stood the intellectual elite, and on the other, far below, the great majority of the people.

---

*The social context in which we worship shapes not only the mood but the nature of our devotional life. Jesus, in His contemplation, wept over Jerusalem and her corporate sin in stoning the prophets and persecuting those who were sent to them. The Christian era dawned, and the fledgling new fellowship of "those of the Way" grew from infancy into childhood against the background of the decadence of Rome, who had appointed herself the guardian of peace of the world, and who had sworn to do so even if it had to enslave every opponent and kill off every rebellious population. The blood of the martyrs became the seed of the Church in this growth process.

Today, we have socially sensitive and ethically prophetic psychologists, not the least of whom is Erich Fromm. During World War II, Erich Fromm published his book, *Escape from Freedom,* in which he pointed out how the Third Reich of German Hitlerism was the result of the people relying dependently upon dictatorships

In the era of the Fathers, as is well-known, the prevailing intellectual current was what we call Hellenism, a composite of many and diverse antecedents. Broadly, it consisted of an amalgam of Graeco-Roman and Oriental elements. There was certainly no "pure" stream of any, but it is possible to single out within the variegated composite a few dominant philosophical schools—Neo-Platonism, Stoicism, and to a lesser degree, Neo-Pythagoreanism, and the Academy (Aristotelianism). I will make specific explanations of these only insofar as they bear on certain classics; it suffices here to reiterate that, like existentialism today, they both exercised the Christian intellectual and offered him an occasion to develop an apology for his faith.

The mind of the unlettered man, though sometimes hearing the Stoic or Neo-Platonic sage, operated on a far different wave length. What bothered him, even a cursory glance at Christian or pagan writings of this era will show, was his fear of demonic powers. Even the supposedly enlightened sometimes shuddered before demons. They were believed to be everywhere, inhabiting the statues of the gods, producing sicknesses and diseases, causing widespread calamities, exacting vengeance for wrong, and opposing what was right. In our day, we can hardly comprehend

---

in order to escape the demands of freedom, the disciplines of personal responsibility. In the Fifties, David Reissman wrote his book, *The Lonely Crowd,* in which he averred. that the *inner* sense of direction of the American people had been lost in the search for conformity in the outer-direction that comes from compulsively seeking the approval of those around us at the expense of our own integrity as persons.

The devotional life represents the "quest for inner direction," as one explores the "inner world" and seeks to define his own destiny. As he does so, he arrives at an awareness of his own selfhood and calling in life. Amid the collapsing structures and worn-out "solutions" of ambitious world rulers, we are driven back upon our own inner resources in God and ask that He search and try us, for we are men and women of unclean lips, and we dwell in the midst of a people of unclean lips.

how great was the ancients' dread of these. They carried magic charms, learned secret formulas, consulted oracles and soothsayers, invoked the gods, offered sacrifices, built memorials, kept household deities, and attached themselves to one or more religions—all in the hope of averting sudden disaster from these unseen powers, which, they thought, governed their world.

Naturally, many offered help. Magicians sold secret spells and amulets, wise men tried to instruct, scores of religions promised redemption. Perhaps most assuring among these were the so-called mystery religions, syncretistic compounds of oriental and Greek religions, Greek philosophical thought, and popular superstitions. They attracted droves with rites and ceremonies that dramatized the plain man's hope of salvation. But over all— magician, philosopher, and priest—Christianity triumphed. Why? For many reasons, perhaps. But one fundamental reason was the personal piety of its members. So, let us examine what the Church offered in terms of personal piety.

Personal Piety

The early Church was quite conscious of the challenge posed by belief in demons and responded accordingly. It gave firm assurance that Christ had vanquished the prince of demons once and for all. One who belonged to him need have no more fear, for the very name of Christ is dreadful to the fiercest demon. In its baptismal ceremony, the Church had the initiate renounce Satan and his works and pronounced over him a formula of exorcism. The Holy Spirit given in baptism, he was assured, would cause demons to flee in haste.

Yet, even after baptism, the Church had to guide tremulous souls in the battle against demon-inspired temptations. To do so, it armed them with the name of Christ and the sign of the cross. Tertullian, for example, could confidently promise his flock that, if they made the sign of the cross, on all occasions the Devil would hasten away from them. Some things of this sort bordered closely on pagan fetishism certainly, and many barely planted

Christians undoubtedly carried their charms and amulets long after baptism. Consequently, the Church had to tutor them more deeply in the rudiments of Christian piety.

At the center of this piety, of course, stood public worship. The pious Christian's regimen included both daily and weekly gatherings for Bible reading, prayers, homilies, the observance of the Lord's Supper, and so on. The sermons of Origen, Chrysostom, and Augustine reveal that there were both shirkers and enthusiastic attendants, even as today.

There were also diverse attitudes and practice regarding private devotion. Some applied themselves with zeal to fasting, giving of alms, prayers—care of the poor, sick, widowed, and orphaned. They guarded their behavior so as to be without reproach from friend or stranger. Others, again as today, did little to cultivate personal devotion. They would refuse to discharge even the minimal obligations to which Christ called them, and the Church often had to prod and plead.*

The truly devout Christian's private schedule would include prayers as often as six times daily—upon arising, at nine o'clock, at noon, at three o'clock afternoon, at bedtime, and at midnight.[1] The Lord's Prayer was recited three times daily. That prayer in fact constituted the very hub of personal piety, as is proven by classic commentaries on it by Tertullian, Cyprian, Origen, and Gregory of Nyssa.[2]

---

*Today we have psychological evidence as to the collapse of both public and private rituals of worship that are commonly understood and accepted. For the Early Patristic worshipers these were "means of grace" which brought relief from guilt on a corporate basis. Today, the fasts and festivals have turned into "dieting" and "gourmet eating" respectively. The alternating anxiety with which people attend to eating too much and resort to crash diets is a commentary on the emptiness of our inner lives. The person afflicted with alcoholism, as a compulsive drinking pattern, often complains about trying to "fill up a great emptiness." Whereas specific rituals and practices *can* be meaningless in and of themselves, we know that a

The Christian ideal came eventually to be projected in the monk. Although it could claim numerous antecedents in Jewish piety and elsewhere, Christian monasticism first blossomed as persecution diminished in the second half of the third century. Somewhat inaccurately, perhaps, Anthony (251-356) is hailed as its founder. He did become its chief exemplar. Denying self, as literally as possible, the earliest monks took up Christ's challenge to the rich young ruler. Then, they proceeded to a solitary place and devoted themselves entirely to fasting, Bible reading, prayer, and the conquering of the demons which tempted them. They interrupted their routines only to take care of the minimal bodily necessities. Soon, others came and communities formed. Out of this natural tendency for solitaries to live in close proximity to one another grew cenobite (communal) monasticism—the first known monastery founded by the Egyptian Pachomius around A.D. 320.

The monk exercised a profound influence upon the average Christian in the age of the Fathers. An admiring biographer tells us, for instance, that kings and princes crouched at the foot of Simeon Stylites' pillar, "hoping to catch, as if they were precious pearls, the vermin that dropped from his body." Simeon (ca. 390-459) spent thirty years or more perched atop a pillar in the desert near Antioch, laden with chains. What created such admiration? The fact that the monk, more than anyone else, fulfilled the scriptural injunctions for self-denial and unswerving

---

structured devotional life that follows a well-known and repeated pattern of spiritual disciplines can go far toward giving the spiritually famished and fretfully dependent person security. Even the Quakers, who reject the whole idea of specific rituals in corporate worship, such as Baptism and the Lord's Supper, have planned patterns of meditation such as the enforced period of silence, or the "compline," when no word is spoken for a period of twelve hours. Thus they develop the nonverbal depths of communication with each other in the family as well as prayer with God. What kinds of specific plans do you have for a devotional life? Any?

devotion to God. So significant was this kind of dedication that Augustine, the foremost leader of western Christendom, organized his clergy under a monastic rule. Thenceforward, asceticism became the ideal of the priest as well as the monk.

The Literature of Private Devotion

Enough has been said to give a general impression of personal piety in this era. But what about devotional literature? What role did it play in the cultivation of spiritual maturity? The answer is, a very important role.

Besides the Bible, already discussed in the last chapter, accounts of the lives and deaths of saints and martyrs assumed a substantial place in the Christian's devotional thoughts. Beginning with the second century, indeed, a kind of fetish was made of martyrdom. Stories of martyrs' deaths were embellished with purported miracles and signs from heaven. Christians who lapsed in persecution sought letters of reference for readmission to the Church from martyrs about to make their last confession. Eventually, the Churches commemorated their deaths in the Christian calendar along with great events in the life of Jesus and the Apostles. From the fourth century on, a pious Christian would not easily forget the deeds of the saints and martyrs.[3]

Like certain martyrologies, the numerous fictional "gospels" and "acts," composed by devout but simple souls for the edification of their brethren, will today be received with surprise and amusement. Perhaps with good intention but quite erroneously, they tried to uphold the Christian faith by filling in the blank spaces in the life of Christ and the Apostles, or other saints, with imaginary feats, sayings, and travels. In a certain *Gospel of Thomas,* for example, "Thomas" relates "miracles" from Jesus' infancy—how he fashioned twelve birds out of clay on the Sabbath, and when rebuked by Joseph for breaking the Sabbath rule, put them to flight; healed a man who had sundered his foot with an axe. There are fictional letters supposedly exchanged between Jesus and Abgar, King of Edessa in Syria, letters of

Paul not included in the New Testament, and so on. Such works possess almost no historical value. Moreover, they probably had limited influence even in the more credulous early centuries.[4] Tertullian's report that the pious Asian presbyter, who wrote the *Acts of Paul and Thecla* "out of love for Paul,"* was defrocked by the bishops would indicate clearly the official pressures to keep such literature from the hands of the laity.[5]

Somewhat more consequential, particularly in view of the influence of the monks, were the monastic biographies and collections of maxims usually referred to as "The Sayings of the Fathers." In this day, "lives" and "sayings" undoubtedly were treasured because, as indicated above, the devout Christian, cleric or lay, looked to the monk for his ideal. Insofar as he was able, he emulated his example. How frequently in these accounts, the

---

*A psychologically trained person would reflect upon the *motivation* of the pious Asian presbyter who wrote a work about Paul and Thecla "out of love for Paul" that got him into such trouble with his bishops. The whole situation seems a bit *ambivalent.* Ambivalence is a word from contemporary psychology which could be defined with the word from the book of James, "double-mindedness." Today, it means "the simultaneous attraction for and repulsion from the same object or person." The pious Asian presbyter must have had such mixed feelings toward Paul, although one can only surmise that he had. However, it does bring to mind the ways in which devout men often do their own cause great harm. They actually feel hostile, and in the name of "love" will do something that is understood by others as a damaging act. As one would put it in the modern idiom, if Paul had *friends* like the pious Asian presbyter, he didn't need enemies! We often damn each other with faint praise.

The devout person who contemplates before God has trouble accepting the fact that he has *both* loving and hostile feelings toward God, man, and himself. The motives of man are never unalloyed but are universally ambiguous. Prayer, in this sense, is an exercise in letting our *mixed,* contradictory feelings come into clear consciousness just as they are before we express them in word or action. The genuinely prayerful person never underestimates his own capacity for ambivalence, *if* he can help it!

person seeking the help which evokes the wisdom of the Fathers is simply a nameless Christian. The following narrative from the *Sayings* sums up well the Christian's quest:

A certain man asked the abbot Anthony, saying, "What shall I keep, that I may please God?" And the old man answering said, "These things that I bid thee, do thou keep. Wherever thou goest, have God ever before thine eyes; in what thou dost, hold by the example of the holy Scriptures; and in whatever place thou dost abide, be not swift to remove from thence.* These three things keep, and thou shalt be saved.[6]

Another prolific source of devotional literature was the writings by or about the Church's outstanding leaders and thinkers. They included almost every type of writing—biographies, letters of spiritual counsel, sermons, commentaries, theological treatises, and so on. Not many achieved the rank of classics, to be sure, but in their own day they guided hundreds of the faithful along their chosen routes of faith. Often, the writings answered a pious layman's or clergyman's request. Thus it was that Origen produced his *Commentary on the Gospel According to John* and numerous other works. A certain pious Alexandrian named Ambrose, who later was ordained a deacon, equipped Origen even with a secretarial staff to facilitate his work. In like manner,

---

*The admonition, "in whatever place thou dost abide, be not swift to remove from thence," strikes the pastoral counselor of today with force. We call this the "geographical solution." A person plagued with alcohol addiction blames it on his "bad company" and tries to solve it by hastily "removing from thence." The couple with marital troubles "pack up and leave." The rebuked child jumps up and runs out of the room. The unhappy pastor starts looking for another church just when he is on the verge of breaking through the resistance of problems from which each previous pastor has run. Yet, these are the times when all such persons are prone to pray hardest and be most desperate. They are times of great revealing from God. God reveals to us our own true purposes in life. He reveals to us our weaknesses, our dependence upon others, our true identity as persons. These are times of great "opening" of

hundreds of other treatises, some devotional or semi-devotional, supplied comfort, offered spiritual advice, answered questions, rebuked, cajoled, pleaded, and inspired the army of simple saints who lived in the age of the Fathers.

In all of this vast array of literature, only a few stood the test of time. Two, Athanasius' *Life of Anthony* and Augustine's *Confessions,* warrant specific comment. Though not everyone will desire to read the *Life of Anthony* today, it so stamped its mark on later saints and classics that it will be profitable to devote particular attention to it here. The *Confessions* is, of course, pre-eminent among all classics.

Athanasius' Life of Anthony

Times and author. Composed about 357, the year after Anthony's death, in response to the request of "certain brethren in foreign parts," the *Life of Anthony* reflects to a degree the turbulence of the tumultuous fourth century.[7] Ironically, in this era the problems of the Church matched, or even exceeded, those of the Empire. After having emerged scarred but safe from the persecution of Diocletian and Maximian (303-311), it was rocked in north Africa by the Donatist schism, a division of the Church over the question of the validity of the ministries of clergymen who had lapsed during the persecution, and then

---

the self. Consequently, the admonition of "the Sayings of the Fathers" is remarkably appropriate. John Bunyan's *Pilgrim's Progress* later depicts Christian and Pliable in the Slough of Despond. Naturally, they were both anxious to get out of there. But Pliable was *swift* to remove from thence. He got out first. Christian stayed in longer. The difference was that Pliable got out the way *he* knew: the way nearest the City of Destruction. Christian waited until he learned from God the way he did *not* know: the way nearest the Celestial City.

Prayer in this sense, then, is the struggle with the temptation to use the "geographical solution" too quickly rather than to wait for some deeper revealing of God of new ways through, not out of, our difficulties.

throughout the Empire by the heresy of Arius, who denied the true divinity of Christ. Constantine scarcely realized when he made his peace with the Church between 313 and 323 what a dangerous alliance he had entered into.

The life of the author, Athanasius (*ca.* 296-373), so integrally interwoven into the fiber of these ecclesiastical struggles, conveniently furnishes the highlights needed to grasp the character of the times. Born and reared in Alexandria, he probably obtained his training in the catechetical school there. A bright youth, he was ordained a deacon and became secretary to Bishop Alexander. In this capacity he accompanied the latter to the Council of Nicea in 325 and led the supporters of Alexander to victory over the Arians. Thereafter, he was destined to play a fateful role in the life of the Church. Although a very young man at the time, his keenness of mind, determination, and unpresuming mien gained the respect of the orthodox and the hatred of Arians. On becoming Alexander's successor in the see of Alexandria in 328, he soon found himself the target of Arian attacks. Five times he suffered deposition and exile. Nevertheless, he remained stedfast in his resolve to defend the decision of Nicea against Arian plots and political compromises.

Regardless of Athanasius' striving to prevent it, the Arians, by various manipulations, gained virtual control of the Churches only five years after Nicea and held it for more than thirty years. Their success was due largely, it would seem, to Constantine's deep disappointment that Nicea had not produced the unity he had sought for Church and Empire. Then, too, after Constantine's death, his sons divided their loyalties—Constans and Constantine II, the western rulers, upholding Nicea, Constantius, the eastern ruler, favoring Arians. The death of Constantine and later of Constans in 351 opened the floodgates for Arianism, for now Constantius reigned alone.

So distressing was the conflict between Arian and Nicene Christians that Constantius' successor, Constantine's nephew Julian, undertook to revive and restore paganism. He reigned less than two years (November, 361-June, 363). Yet, even if he had not met an untimely death in a military campaign against the Persians, it is doubtful whether he would have succeeded in so radical a plan. Notwithstanding its disagreements, the Church had planted itself so firmly in Roman soil that not even the destruction of the Empire a century later could uproot it. The legendary statement ascribed to Julian on his death, "You have conquered, O Galilean," is a fitting epitaph for a dying paganism.

Athanasius lived long enough to witness the partial excision of the Arian "cancer" from the Body of Christ, though Arianism remained a potent force apart from the Church for several centuries more. He fought, too, against its offshoot, Macedonianism, which denied the true divinity of the Spirit rather than the Son. And, finally, he paved the way for the rejection of Apollinarianism, the reverse of Arianism, which negated the humanity of Christ by saying he did not possess a human mind or rational soul.

The book. The specific context for the writing of the *Life of Anthony,* Athanasius' flight to the deserts of Egypt (356-362) in order to escape arrest on the order of Constantius, helps us appreciate its character. It is not biography, as moderns conceive of biography. Rather, it follows the pattern of the Greek *encomium* or eulogy. But there is a difference. Biographical data are employed not so much to praise the man as to edify the readers who admire his example, like certain Psalms of the Old Testament. Thus, Anthony teaches lessons of faith. Athanasius has Anthony himself sum these up in his reply to certain monks who came to seek his advice. What is the hermetic life? they inquire. Love and trust the Lord, avoid bad thoughts and fleshly pleasures, disdain a full stomach, be humble, pray continually, sing the Psalms, memorize the commandments of Scripture, hark back to the deeds of the Saints, avoid anger, examine yourself (ch. 55).

Why Athanasius chose Anthony for his model of piety is clear enough. First, because he, like many others, knew and loved him deeply. But more important still, Anthony had lived a remarkable life.* "Really," says Athanasius, "for monks the life of Anthony is an ideal pattern of the ascetical life."[8]

Upon the death of his parents during his eighteenth or twentieth year, Anthony had responded to Christ's command to the rich young ruler by selling his extensive possessions, distributing the proceeds to the poor, and devoting himself to a life of self-denial. He first took up residence with an aged ascetic in a neighboring village and studied the habits of other ascetics (chs. 1-4). Having proved himself master of demons in many skirmishes (chs. 5-10), at about age thirty-five he resolved to find even greater solitude to wage his spiritual warfare, and with that aim in view, he moved across the Nile River to the desolate region around Pispir, the "outer mountains" (chs. 12-13). So many sought his counsel and aid, however, that he left his place of retirement now and again to help them get started on a monastic career (chs. 14-15). When he failed to acquire the martyr's crown during the persecution under Maximin Daja (311) (chs. 46-48), he fled to a still more secluded place, the "inner mountains," which looked across the Red Sea toward

---

*Anthony was chosen by Athanasius because he knew him and loved him. Anthony was a "model" with whom Athanasius *identified*. The psychological dynamic of such a choice is known as "identification." Identification is that process in which a person is changed into the likeness of the one whom he loves and knows, the one whom he trusts and likes, one whom he feels he can safely become. The process is more unconscious than conscious, more of a transformation that comes from deep love and trust than an imitation that comes from a conscious mimicry.

Erik Erikson, in his book *Identity and The Life Cycle,* calls this "leadership polarization," in which a growing person is enabled to identify himself as a person by choosing and committing himself to a leader. The possibilities of disillusionment here are great, because we are prone to give ultimate and absolute place to another

the Sinai Peninsula (chs. 49ff.). There, except for occasional journeys back to Pispir or other places to lend counsel and aid, he lived out the remaining years of his life. At his own request, he was buried in the soil of his beloved "inner mountain" (chs. 89-95).

At the very heart of the fervent admiration of contemporaries for Anthony lay his ability to do battle with and overcome demons. Athanasius records repeated bouts with them throughout Anthony's entire lifetime (chs. 5-10, 12-13, 51-53). His miracles (chs. 56-64, 83-88) involved the defeat of demonic beings. Even Anthony's refutation of certain Greek philosophers used the proof that Christ's name and the sign of the cross vanquished all demons! (chs. 72-80). Whatever else Anthony's life might have said to the people of his day, it taught that Christ comes not in word but in power.

What was Anthony's answer to demons? The name of Christ, the sign of the cross, prayer, and fasting. "Indeed," he boasts, "they dread ascetics for their fasting, their vigils, their prayers, their meekness, calmness, contempt of money, lack of conceit, humility, love of the poor, almsgiving, freedom from anger, and, most of all, their loyalty to Christ" (ch. 30).[9] And in that you have the ideal Christian of the fourth century.

---

human being in our lives. This is idolatry in its most subtle form. Yet, the possibilities of spiritual growth, even if it involves disillusionment and heartbreak, are greater than not to make the choice at all. Therefore, the injunction of Hebrews 13:7: "Remember your leaders, those who spoke to you the word of God; consider the outcome of their life and imitate their faith." This is what Athanasius did in choosing Anthony.

Prayer, then, seen from this vantage point, is the serious, reflective, and decisive consideration of the lives of people who have gone before us in the faith of Christ. We look for Christ in them. We worship the Christ and love the people who reflect the power of Christ to us. As we worship Christ, we are "changed into his image" (II Cor. 3:18); at the same time we are able to appreciate the weaknesses of our leaders if we pray for them.

Augustine's Confessions

Times and author. Like Athanasius, Augustine of Hippo (354-430) played such a signal role in the life of Christendom that we can most easily depict the times by sketching succinctly the major facts of his life, for the moment passing lightly over the period covered in the *Confessions* (354-388).

The son of a pagan father and a devout Christian mother, he distinguished himself sufficiently in local schools that his father, with considerable strain on meager family resources, packed him off to Carthage to study when he reached age sixteen (2.3.5-6). Augustine's fancy inclined to rhetoric, so he trained to become a teacher. Always searching for truth, he became an adherent of the Manichaean sect then flourishing in Carthage (Book 4). After completing his formal studies, he taught in Thagaste one year (375-376), but he went back to Carthage following the unexpected death of a dear friend, an event which unhinged his soul from whatever had held it firm (4.4-7). During this seven year stay in Carthage (376-383), he had great difficulties controlling his sexual urges and finally entered into liaison with a woman who bore him a son (4.2.2).

In 383, taking his common-law wife with him, Augustine left Carthage, already discontented with his Manichaean faith (Book 5), and made his way to Rome to seek a chair of rhetoric. He stayed only a year, however, before accepting a similar post in Milan (5.8-13). Although still skeptical regarding the Catholic Church when he arrived (5.14.24), his three years there proved to be the crucial ones for his conversion. As a result of numerous influences*—his mother Monica; friends like Alypius, Nebridius,

---

*Identification, as was discussed in relation to Athanasius' choice of Anthony, is more than a one sex choice. Augustine received much of his likeness from his mother, Monica. This points to one of the great struggles of the soul in the "quest for identity," as it is now called in psychological literature. C. G. Jung calls the masculine principle within us the *animus* and the feminine principle within

Simplicianus, and Pontitianus; Ambrose, Bishop of Milan; Neo-Platonic philosophy; and the *Life of Anthony,* among many—he avowed his allegiance to Christ and received baptism.[10]

About a year later Augustine left Milan, along with his mother, Monica, and his son, Adeodatus, to go back to Africa. Monica died *en route* at Ostia (*Conf.* 9.11). So Augustine and Adeodatus continued the journey together. When his son, "begotten carnally from my sin" (9.6), died the next year, Augustine's grief was compounded. The whole chain of events in preceding years led him to take up a monastic regimen along with some companions (388-391).

The year 391 opened a new chapter in his life. A "certain good, God-fearing Christian," having heard of his reputation, attracted Augustine to Hippo by vowing to renounce worldliness if only he might hear the famous man preach. When Augustine granted his wish, he so awed the Catholics of Hippo that they immediately ordained him a presbyter.[11] Soon Augustine, revealing again the stamp of Anthony on his life, established a monastery within the church of Hippo. The Bishop, the aged Va-

---

us the *anima.* We are not to become "one-sided" in excluding either of these from us. Is it a "threat to one's manhood" to have the gentleness and patience of a Monica? Is it a "loss of femininity" to become a Joan of Arc, an Amelia Earhart? Augustine apparently spent many years of his life in striking a balance between the demands of his mother as over against those of his father. The principles of aggressiveness and passivity, the traits of strength and gentleness are involved in the wholesome life of the total person, quite apart from whether one is a man or a woman. One can be both and should be both, but this comes by much inner reflection and personal devotion.

This points to the value of a husband and wife praying together. Each can infuse the strength of the one into the other. The harshness of the husband is mellowed into patient strength; the indecisiveness of the wife is matured into resoluteness of mind. Could it be that through the mystery of love and marriage this is what takes place in order that they may truly be "one flesh"?

lerius, perceiving the conspicuous gifts of his new presbyter, urged Augustine to preach or hold discussions even in his presence.[12] In 395 he prevailed upon him to be consecrated co-adjutor Bishop. Though contrary to regular custom, this assured that Augustine would succeed him on the episcopal throne[13] when he died in 396.

From the time of his ordination as a presbyter until his death in 430, Augustine skillfully piloted the ecclesiastical ship in north Africa through one storm after another. Although these occupied the Church simultaneously, Augustine's writings as well as Possidius' biography show that he concentrated on them one after the other. First, until about 400, he occupied himself with the undermining of his old faith, Manichaeism.[14] Then, for the next eleven years, he mounted a crusade against Donatism,[15] which resulted in a Catholic triumph at Carthage in A.D. 411. Thereafter, Donatist influence seems to have dwindled until the Islamic invasions dealt the death blow to the weakened north African Church. Augustine refuted Arians, too, now and then,[16] but their influence in north Africa was probably negligible by this time.

The remaining years of his life, A.D. 412-430, were taken up primarily with Pelagianism, which emphasized man's free will so radically as to exclude the operation of divine grace in man's salvation, and pagan attacks on Christianity. Possidius states that Augustine labored ten years against Pelagians. Actually it was for more years than that, but his main anti-Pelagian writings were published between 412-421.

Simultaneously, though, political circumstances started him on the road to his *opus magnum,* the *City of God.* The latter appeared in installments over a thirteen-year period, 413-426, occasioned by the revival of pagan charges that Christianity had brought the fall of Rome. Not long after the sack of Rome by Alaric in A.D. 410, in fact, the Vandals, led by Alaric, and the Goths moved southward and crossed into Mauretania from Spain, laying waste the land and the Church. Carthage, Hippo, and Cirta held out until after Augustine's death. But he lived to see the siege engines erected at the wall of his beloved city. His last acts concerned the preservation of his people and his Church, counselling flight from persecution for laymen and strengthening the fainthearted, but warning the clergy to be cautious about fleeing, lest they be thought cowards or leave the flock without shepherds.[17] Mercifully, he died August 28, 430, a few months before the Vandals breached the walls.

His letters, his sermons, his essays, and his biographer, Possidius, make quite clear that Augustine was a man intensely sensitive to life—the struggles of man, of the Church, and of the world. He knew what life was all about, for he had quaffed deeply at its many streams. But no work of his illuminates this so brilliantly as the *Confessions*.

The book. Though obviously in debt to many predecessors, among them Anthony of Egypt, Augustine outstripped them all in the *Confessions*. None perceived and told half so profoundly the human quest for the meaning of life. Augustine even borrowed the style of a memoir or autobiography,[18] but the substance was his own, "the record of a seeker after God," as R. L. Ottley labeled it.

The *Soliloquies* of Augustine, in the form of a dialogue between Augustine and his own reason, written in Cassiacum during his final quest, furnish a clue to the *Confessions*.* Bidden by his reason to pray, he pleads, "O eternal God, let me know myself. Let me know you. That is my prayer" (*Sol.* 2.1.1). Relentlessly throughout the *Confessions*, Augustine probes and

---

*The soliloquy—from Augustine to Dag Hammarskjöld's *Markings* —has been and remains the way in which people "keep in touch" with themselves. The life of prayer reminds us that in our feverish performance of the various "roles" expected of us—worker, husband, wife, father, mother, citizen, etc.—we lose touch with our selves. The soliloquy, then, becomes a "lower form of prayer" which enables us to encounter what Meister Eckhardt called the Self within the

searches within to understand himself. Who am I? he wants to
know. His own history tells him. From childhood until conversion he discovers a sordid picture. He confesses to God what the
Psalmist had confessed long before:

For I know my transgressions, and my sin is ever before me. Against
thee, thee only, have I sinned, and done that which is evil in thy
sight, . . . Behold, I was brought forth in iniquity, and in sin did
my mother conceive me.[19]

Why hang these dirty rags on the line? ". . . Not because I
love them," says Augustine, "but in order that I may love Thee,
O my God" (2.1). Not a few have quibbled and found fault
with Augustine's confession of his sins. Why, for example, does
he make such a to-do about stealing pears in his youth (2:4-9)?
Was it that serious, or was Augustine exaggerating his guilt for
rhetorical emphasis? Admitting some legitimate room for exag-
geration, I would say that such criticisms reflect a failure to
understand Augustine's main point. In his mind, the pear stealing incident assumed an equal proportion with offenses such as
his youthful and adult fornications because both symbolized the
Augustine who did not know God—reckless, wanton, profligate,
corrupt, useless to himself or others. "A pioneer in the science of
experimental psychology,"[20] he made an extraordinarily probing
analysis of himself. Petrarch phrased exactly the experience of
many *Confessions* readers, saying, "Whenever I read your Confessions, I experience two contrary affections—hope and fear,
sometimes not unmingled with tears; since I account myself to

---

self, the image of God within us. At the intersection of all our roles,
we stand as selves searching for the Self, God. Augustine's *Confessions* are both soliloquies and prayers, in that the conversation bursts
forth from autobiographical musing into direct address to God. This
kind of praying is often left out of our "programmed" prayers,
both privately and corporately. The capacity to "converse with
oneself honestly" is the foyer of prayer.

be reading the narrative, not of another man's pilgrimage, but of my own."[21]

Augustine had such a purpose in mind, too, when he wrote. Relating in Book II his "foul deeds of the past and the carnal corruptions of my soul," he asks rhetorically, "To whom am I telling these things?" And replies:

Not to thee, O my God; rather, I tell them before Thee to my own kind, to the human race, no matter how few men may happen upon these pages. For what reason? So that I, and whoever reads this, may realize out of what depths one must cry unto Thee. What is closer to Thy ears than a heart that is penitent and a life founded on faith? (2.3.5).[22]

Thus the Confessions had a dual aim, each of which would come to fruition in the other. By baring his soul before God, Augustine praised him. By praising God, he bared his soul for all to see.

So the other half of the epigram is inseparably annexed to the first—"Let me know myself—Let me know Thee." Augustine knew existentially how difficult of fulfilment both were, but he pressed on relentlessly. Doubtless the most quoted statement in the Confessions is the pithy comment on the central desire of man. "Thou dost bestir him so that he takes delight in praising Thee: for Thou hast made us for Thee and our heart is unquiet till it finds its rest in Thee" (1.1.1).[23] Where does this rest come from? Who will grant it? "Who will grant unto me that Thou wilt come into my heart and inebriate it, so that I may forget my evils and embrace my one Good, Thee?" (1.5.5), Augustine asks repeatedly. Then, he beseeches, "Narrow is the household of my soul, for Thou to come into: let it be enlarged by Thee. It lies in ruins: do Thou rebuild it. It has things within it which offend Thine eyes: I confess and know it. But who will cleanse it?" (1.5.6).[24] The answer? None but God, my God, the God of mercy and compassion. "Rest is indeed with Thee, and untroubled life," Augustine concludes after relating the pear incident. "He who enters into Thee enters into the joy of his Lord, he

shall not fear and he shall be best situated in the Best Being. I
myself slipped away from Thee, my God, and in my youth I
strayed too deviously from Thy firm support, and so I became
a barren desert unto myself" (2.10.18).[25]

In his account of the death of his cherished young friend,
Augustine shares with us the essence of his opulent religious discovery—that in God alone, in Him who "came down here and
took up our death and slew it with the abundance of His own
life" (4.12.19),[26] rests "the fulfilment of every aspiration, the
answer to every perplexity, the 'fresh springs' which make all
human beings new."[27] With his soul's grief uncontrollable, he
confesses:

I knew that it had to be lifted up to Thee, O Lord, and to be made
well, but this I neither would nor could do, especially because Thou
wert, in my thoughts, nothing substantial or stable. For Thou wert
not Thyself but an empty figment of the imagination. My error
was my God. If I attempted to rest my soul on this, so that it might
find repose, it would slip through the emptiness and again fall back
on me. For myself, I continued to be an unhappy place, where I
could not stay and which I could not leave. For, to what place
could my heart flee from my heart? Where could I get away from
myself? Where elude my own pursuit? (4.17.12).[28]

To those probing questions, he replies, In Him. Where is He?

He is in the depths of the heart, but the heart has wandered from
Him. Return into your heart, O sinners, and cleave to Him who
made you. Stand with Him and you shall stand firmly; be at rest
in Him, and you shall be rested (4.12.18).[29]

Herein lies the synthesis of knowing God and knowing self.
As long as man is without knowledge of God, he is without
knowledge of self.[30] Without knowledge of either, he cannot ascer-
tain whether his is a dying life or a living death. The route to
Reality has to be that given by God. In the period of turmoil
and confusion just before his conversion, Augustine confides,

. . . I entered into my innermost parts under Thy guidance.* I was able, because Thou didst become my helper. I entered in and saw with the eye of my soul (whatever its condition) the Immutable Light, above this same eye of my soul, and above my mind . . . (7.10.16).[31]

Neo-Platonism gave Augustine the philosophical base he sought. His conversion to Christianity, in fact, involved primarily the personalizing of certain Neo-Platonic tenets by the gospel of Jesus Christ.[32] But in spite of that the conversion process took a long time. After breaking with the Manichees in 383, he first taught rhetoric in Rome and afterwards in Milan. There he came under the sway of the eloquent Bishop Ambrose. Ambrose's highly stylized preaching answered most of his objections to the literary qualities of the Bible. At the same time, Simplicianus,

---

*This passage from *The Confessions* is one of the first purposeful uses of what has come to be known as the psychological method of *introspection*. Augustine, in another writing, *Concerning the Trinity*, gives one of the earliest empirical descriptions of the human person found in Christian writings. An earlier one than this was Aristotle's *Concerning the Soul*. Augustine found what he called a vestige of the Trinity in the soul of man. Charles N. Cochrane says that Augustine "provides a vindication of what may be called the primitive and original values of selfhood, the sense of existence, of awareness, and of autonomous yet orderly activity which constitute the native endowment of man." (*Christianity and Classical Culture*, New York: Oxford University Press, 1944, p. 400.)

A Jewish doctor, Sigmund Freud, used this same method of introspection, coupled with the method of free association, to explore the nature of personality through the study of his own dreams, as well as the dreams of others. He emerged with a "secular trinity" of the id, the ego, and the superego.

The "structure" as well as the function of the human spirit has been a source of psychological interest until now. The person who engages in prayer will ask practical questions like: "Is this really God revealing himself to me, or is it just my own desire. Am I being 'selfish' or am I for the first time discovering who my real self really is?" Augustine decided that there is a "triune character of

Ambrose's tutor, helped Augustine philosophically by relating to him how the Neo-Platonist philosopher Victorinus had become a Christian. This left only the moral hurdle and it was here that the *Life of Anthony* came into play.

In the summer of 386 while Augustine was staying at Cassiacum with his friend Alypius, a fellow African named Ponticianus narrated to them the story of the "father" of Christian monasticism, the hermit Anthony, and how two Roman civil servants had resolved to forsake all things for Christ, even their fiancées, after reading the story. Ponticianus' narrative made a deep mark on Augustine's mind, which was already ripe for conversion. For the first time, he really had to face up to himself as a human being without flinching.

---

selfhood," to use Cochrane's phrase: existence, knowledge, and will. Augustine says: "I would that men would consider these three in themselves . . . for I am and know and will." (*Confessions,* xiii, xi, p. 12.) In another work, *The City of God,* he says: "We both exist, and know that we exist, and rejoice in this existence and knowledge. In these three, when the mind knows and loves itself, there may be seen a trinity—mind, love, and knowledge—not to be confounded by any intermixture, although each exists for itself and all mutually in all, or each in the other two and the other two in each."

The central spiritual exercise the devout worshiper should draw from the reading of Augustine's *Confessions* is that "the self" refers to the total being of Augustine and not to a moralistic idea of selfishness. Here is a connecting link with the concerns of the worshiper and of the contemporary theorist of personality. When we love our neighbor as ourselves, we are made to ask: "How do we love ourselves?" Paul answers and says that no person "hates his own flesh, but nourishes and cherishes it as Christ does the church." (Eph. 5:29) The reader will take me seriously then when I ask that both you and I reappraise in our own prayers what our basic attitude toward our self is. Is it in keeping with the facts? Ask God. Augustine asked God and found the "spangled heavens of the inner being of man" as an answer.

But thou, O Lord, all the while that he was speaking didst turn me back to reflect upon myself; taking me from behind my back, where I had heretofore placed myself, whereas I had no list to observe mine own self: and thou now settedst me before mine own face, that I might discern how filthy, and how crooked, and sordid, and bespotted, and ulcerous I was. And I beheld and abhorred myself, nor could I find any place whither to flee from myself. And if I went about to turn mine eyes from off myself, he went on telling his tale; and thou thereupon opposedst myself unto myself, and thrustest me ever and anon into mine own eyes, to make me find at last mine own iniquity and to loathe it. I had heretofore taken notice of it; but I had again dissembled it, winked at it, and forgotten it.[33]

The point of crisis had been reached.* A short time later, he made the final step after reading Romans 13:13f. in response to what for him was a divine oracle, a child's voice saying, "Take up, read." He was baptized on Easter eve, 387. Christendom had enlisted at long last one of its greatest saints.

Before closing this study of the *Confessions* I must add an often neglected fact about Augustine which the *Confessions* did not intend to be forgotten. Although Augustine had a deep personal experience of God, he was devoted to the Church. More than any other Christian great, in fact, he welded together the

---

*Augustine's personal history built a system of warring forces within him. Each of the great influences of his life presented a claim for mastery. He struggled to gain hold of a consistent vision of the unified spirit. These "warring forces" represented different value systems, ideals and goals. Augustine finally decided which was the *real* Augustine.

One of the most provocative and inspiring psychologists in this century is little known outside the world of professional psychologists. He has never made newspaper headlines, been publicized in any way, or received the consideration that he deserved for the hard work of the few short years he lived. He is Prescott Lecky. Lecky is the psychologists' psychologist when they become contemplative. He said that the whole thrust of the human spirit is toward a consistent, coherent, and communicable set of values. He said that

three elements of religion—the intellectual, the experiential, and the institutional.[34] How could it have been otherwise? Even during his most skeptical moments, Augustine still went to Church, at his mother's urging if for no other reason. And, when his doubt finally turned to faith, he discovered that the Church, with all of its faults, proved to have the truth found in Jesus Christ.

If from the vast store of religious literature, the Bible excepted, I had to choose only one for the edification of the Church, without a moment's hesitation I would choose Augustine's *Confessions*. By it, indeed, a "classic" could well be defined, for it penetrates so deeply and directly the heart of the human enigma as to leave others far behind. Scarcely any book has had a more hungry acceptance and made a more lasting imprint upon Christian intellectuals. Yet it is not simply a book for intellectuals; it belongs rather to all mankind. It expresses for all a universal longing and a universal hope.

"any value entering the system which is inconsistent with the individual's evaluation of himself cannot be assimilated; it meets with resistance and is likely, unless general organization occurs, to be rejected." Prescott Lecky, *Self-Consistency: A Theory of Personality* (New York: Island Press, 1945, Copyright by Kathryn Lecky), p. 82.

Augustine experienced that "general reorganization" of his life as the Lord turned him back to reflect upon himself, taking him from behind his back, where he had heretofore placed himself. Lecky's psychological description describes what happened to Augustine. Yet, our temptation is to say that if a thing can be understood and described, this in some way detracts from the depth of the encounter with God. Far from it. To understand oneself, as John Calvin said, aids in meeting God and vice versa. It is a reciprocity.

Selected Bibliography

Personal Piety and the Literature of Private Devotion
   Bouyer, Louis. *The Spirituality of the New Testament and the Fathers.* Translated by Mary P. Ryan. (London: Burns & Oates, 1963). A learned treatment, thoroughly conversant with critical questions.

The Life of Anthony
   Life of St. Anthony by St. Athanasius. Translated by Sister Mary Emily Keenan, S.C.N. *The Fathers of the Church,* vol. 15, edited by Roy J. Deferrari, *et al.* (Washington, D. C. The Catholic University of America, 1952)
   St. Athanasius, The Life of Saint Anthony. Newly translated and annotated by Robert T. Meyer. *Ancient Christian Writers,* No. 10, edited by J. Quasten and J. C. Plumpe. (Westminster, Maryland: The Newman Press; London: Longmans, Green & Co., 1950)

The Confessions
   The Confessions of St. Augustine, Book VIII. Edited and translated by C. S. C. Williams. (Oxford: Basil Blackwell, 1953). Offers valuable background study of the influences on Augustine, pp. vii-xxvii.
   Saint Augustine, Confessions. Translated by Vernon J. Bourke. *The Fathers of the Church,* vol. XXI, edited by Roy J. Deferrari, *et al.* (New York: Fathers of the Church, Inc., 1953). An idiomatic modern translation.
   Ottley, R. L. *Studies in the Confessions of St. Augustine.* (London: Robert Scott, 1919). The most incisive study of the *Confessions* in English.

THE CLASSICS OF THE AGE OF FAITH

Personal Piety
The Budding of Mysticism
The Little Flowers and The Mirror of Perfection
Selected Bibliography

III

The Classics of The Age of Faith

Although it was the heir of the great bishop of Hippo, the age of faith gave birth to few classics, devotional or otherwise. It was not the age of classics because of a lack of the "stuff" from which classics are chiseled, but rather in the tools to chisel them. Bound by easy acquiescence to traditional doctrines of the Church, it allowed little room for the doubt which had brazed and polished Augustine's *Confessions* in the previous age.

The reasons for this state of affairs lie concealed in the strange history of Europe during the millennium following Augustine's death. Already, as he wrote his great philosophy of history, the *City of God,* the actors who played the first act for it, the barbarians, were coming on stage. Moving gradually southwards, they put an end to Rome's long dominion in Europe and north Africa. The period of their own rule, 476 on, was a gloomy one for Latin Europeans, for they brought little culture to replace that which they destroyed.

Meanwhile, the followers of Mohammed introduced the second act in the European drama. After their leader's death in 632, they initiated their unparalleled drive to vanquish the world for Allah. Within a century they had conquered Palestine, Egypt, all of the north African littoral, and most of Spain, but they were finally halted by Charlemagne's grandfather, Charles Martel, at the famous battle of Tours.

Although the Muslims have retained most of this territory to the present day, the Frankish tribes which stopped them opened the third act. Many years previously, the Franks had united to

55

build their hegemony in Gaul (France) under the Merovingians. The Merovingian power passed into the hands of their "mayors of the Palace," the family of Charlemagne, the Carolingians. Martel and then his son Pippin routed their major rival, the Lombards. Because of distinguished service in protecting Rome, and as a reward for a grant of the "Papal States" in 754-756, Charlemagne's father, Pippin the Short, received the title "patrician of the Romans."

Building on the foundation laid by his forebears, Charlemagne (781-814) proceeded to forge a small empire in western Europe. By the time of his death his holdings included most of modern day France, Germany, and Italy. The papacy had both helped and been helped by him, for Charlemagne used the Church to consolidate his power, to assist in the education of his people, and to legitimize his claims to be "Emperor of the Romans." On Christmas day, 800, in recognition of his service, a grateful pope placed the imperial crown upon his head.

Not long after Charlemagne's death his "empire" fell to pieces. His grandsons made a three-way division in the famous treaty of Verdun in 843. Of the three, only the German part remained strong during the Norse invasions of the tenth and eleventh centuries. After a long reign by Louis the Pious, vigorous Saxon dukes, Henry I and Otto I, seized the kingdom. Between 919 and 962 they reconquered much of the former kingdom of Charlemagne. Pope John XII, acknowledging the Saxon power *de facto,* placed the imperial crown upon Otto's head in 962. The so-called Holy Roman Empire had begun.

This Empire, in reality a German kingdom, lasted almost eight and a half centuries, and was destroyed finally by Napoleon in 1806. Long before its fall, however, it engaged in several fierce contests and saw the boundaries of Otto changed many times. The Empire was torn frequently by civil wars. The Vikings struck during the tenth and eleventh centuries, leaving most of England and Europe in the confusion of feudalism. New kingdoms emerged as the crusades brought new and powerful social, economic, political, and intellectual forces into play. France, England, and Naples (southern Italy) began to surmount the divisiveness of the feudal system in the twelfth and thirteenth centuries and to acquire a sense of national unity. By the time of the Protestant Reformation, other European states had been formed.

In the midst of this political turmoil, there loomed a universal power in the one Roman institution which the barbarians had not destroyed, the Roman Church. By parlaying one contender against the other, astute popes managed to make Rome an effectual third force in European politics. The zenith of power was reached by Innocent III, who virtually ruled Europe during his pontificate (1198-1216). This great power was not merely spiritual either. By the latter half of the Middle Ages the Church had amassed vast fortunes and owned gigantic estates in every country. The monasteries in particular boasted fabulous manors in France, England, and Germany; in all but name, the monks had become powerful medieval barons.

Without feudalism the Church could hardly have held sway as it did. This social and political system enabled it to exert a ponderous influence amidst the quarreling and fighting of other contenders for power. Until the Renaissance, the awe accorded the Church by the masses helped popes to enforce their views with considerable success. The threat of an interdict, frequently employed by Innocent III and his successors, threw fear into the stoutest princes, for the halting of religious services such as marriage or burials could easily throw their kingdom into utter confusion.

Although feudalism helped the Church, it did not help the masses. It created vast contrasts in wealth, manner of life, freedom, provisions, and status, similar to those of the Roman era. A few, the feudal lords, lived in luxury—the multitude of serfs in hopeless poverty. The lords had freedom—the serfs slavery; the lords rich foods—the serfs meager ones; the lords palatial homes—the serfs rotten hovels; the lords supreme rights according to power—the serfs no rights. In brief, the peasant was a chattel, a piece of property, which the lord could use as he desired.

An extreme case illustrates the situation well. A certain serf married another without securing his master's permission. To avoid the lord's wrath, he and his bride took refuge in the village church. The parish priest interceded with the lord that he not separate them, for they were very much in love. Incensed, but unable to get his serf back without agreeing, the lord consented. But when he laid hands on the pair, he buried them alive in a single grave. The priest managed to arrive on the scene in time to save the groom; the bride had already suffocated.[1] Feudalism did not exist in this form throughout the Middle Ages, nor was it always so malicious as this story might indicate. Ecclesiastical lords were probably more temperate than others. Some lords acted compassionately towards their serfs. On the whole, however, feudalism did little to engender the consideration for human life taught by the gospel. Its evils, in fact, sowed the seeds for numerous revolutions and planted several which sprouted, along with others, in the Protestant Reformation. The Church, ensnared inextricably in the feudal net, suffered from the revolts along with the nations.*

Quite apart from feudalism, the Middle Ages were hard in

------

*The vast wealth of feudal lords and the abject poverty of the masses reminds one of the present-day crisis of conflict between the poverty-stricken ghetto dwellers and the more affluent suburban dwellers. Just as in the "age of faith," or the "age of assent," as Professor Hinson calls it, the chasm existed between lord and serf, it exists today between ghetto and suburbia. The same kind of desperate difference prevails. Also, the young people of our day "break out" of the confines of their affluent parents' authority and adopt the ways—morals, clothes, and unemployment—of the poor. We called them "bohemians" in the thirties, "beatniks" in the fifties, and "hippies" in the sixties of the 20th century.

Yet, the devotional life, particularly of Protestants, does not make

many ways. There were few conveniences such as we possess to-day. Famines, plagues, and natural disasters occurred with regularity. The lower classes always suffered most, of course, but calamity is no respecter of persons. The Black Death which swept across Europe during the fourteenth century (1347 and after) decimated the entire population. Some villages were wiped out entirely; large cities lost half of their population. So great was the devastation, in fact, that the monks and clergy refurbished their thin ranks by appointing boy priests, a factor which some have stressed as the principal cause for the terrible decline of the Church before the Protestant Reformation. Be that as it may, the harshness of these centuries leaves us with little wonder regarding the multiplicity of fears and superstitions of the average man and concurrently of the powerful role the Church played in his life.

The dominant role of the Church in society generally applied particularly to the intellect. Indeed, it is for this reason that the Middle Ages have been called the age of faith. "The age of assent," G. G. Coulton has insisted, would be more accurate. For, even though the masses accepted the Church's pronouncements through these centuries, they did not necessarily commit themselves to them. Instead, they retreated into the sanctuary of silent acquiescence.

In general, one must divide medieval thought into two broad

---

room for this "break out" nor give it a distinctly Christian meaning. Also, drugs become a way to adventure for young people. The consciousness is expanded through the use of LSD, not prayer and contemplation. The need of young people to adventure and "learn the hard way" through brute personal experience is denied them. No provision is made for it. They become "programmed" people, looking for a programmed God. They attempt to leap the chasm between the affluent and the poor by taking on the less desirable dimensions of poverty. The Scripture says, "Blessed are you poor, for yours is the kingdom of God." With Professor Hinson's analysis of feudalism and my discussion of the "hippies" as a background, what does this mean?

categories—academic and popular. Academic thought was built upon Augustine's magnificent, though not systematic, theology. The idea which gripped the medieval mind especially was that of the two cities—the city of God and the city of man. The popes did their best to implement the supremacy of the city of God over the city of man. To their minds, though they certainly did not go unchallenged, the ideal city of man would be that which received its governance from the city of God, the Church. More pointedly, the ideal city of man should receive its power and direction from the Roman pontiff, who stood in Christ's place as head of the Church. The law of the Church, in as many respects as possible, should become the law of the state. Whereas the temporal ruler is due the allegiance of his subjects, should any conflict arise between Church and state, the latter owed final allegiance to their spiritual ruler.

The systematizing of Augustine's theology took shape gradually via Pope Gregory the Great (590-604) in the medieval universities. Whereas, Gregory had given a rather popular version, the "schoolmen" developed a full-blown academic structure. Thomas Aquinas fashioned the final synthesis and even supplanted Augustine as the foundation for Roman theology. This scholastic synthesis is, of course, too intricate to permit exposition here. What must be made clear is that it was primarily the *academic* side of medieval thought. Beside it stood two other important streams—popular piety and mysticism—both of which furnished the soil for the classics of Christian devotion.

Personal Piety

Three things ruled the medieval everyman's world of existence —the Church, his lord, and demons. The three were closely bound together. But because the Church determined his *final* destiny, it probably had the edge over the other two. Sometimes it was his friend in the struggle against one or both, sometimes not. If he had any ultimate hope, however, it lay in the Church he adhered to.

The medieval man's modern counterpart cannot comprehend such slavish attachments because he is not dominated by any of the three powers.* Education has helped him to cut away the bonds which made all three so potent. But education was something the medieval man lacked. Whatever education he might obtain was given by the Church, for the Emperor Justinian had closed the doors of the last pagan school in 529. Thereafter, the monasteries or the cathedral schools provided *all* education. Obviously such training was confined almost solely to theology, ecclesiastical business, or personal piety. Understandably, it was not until Charlemagne insisted on a liberalizing of education that many besides monks and clerics took advantage of these schools. Yet Charlemagne's efforts to liberalize and expand education were a mere drop in the colossal sea of ignorance. The real advance came several centuries later in the founding of the great universities—Paris, Bologna, Oxford, Cambridge, and others. By the thirteenth century these began to show their worth as learning experienced a "rebirth" on a grand scale.

Meantime, for about eight centuries, roughly 500 to 1300, the Church held an envious position in Europe. Even when the popes did not fare well in international politics, the local parish

---

*The modern pastoral counselor wonders if this is really so. Has not the State taken the place of the Church today in our "everyman's existence"? Also, W. H. Whyte, in his book, *The Organization Man,* leaves us with the clear impression that the company has taken the place of the "lord" of a feudal society. Continued interest in demonology by psychiatrists today causes us to conclude, also, that complexes have replaced demons. Complexes, says C. G. Jung, are active parts of the contents of the unconscious portions of one's being which behave autonomously. "The . . . complexes . . . come and go as they please. . . . They have been split off from consciousness and lead a separate existence in the unconscious, being at all times ready to hinder or reinforce the conscious intentions." (C. G. Jung, *Modern· Man in Search of a Soul.* New York: Farrar, Rinehart, 1939, p. 70.) A Catholic priest, Victor White, writes of this in his book, *God and the Unconscious,* and com-

or monastery did. Through the generosity of wealthy landowners, burdensome ecclesiastical taxes on all of the faithful, and astute business management, clerics and monks erected great cathedrals, churches, and cloisters, thousands of which stand today as monuments to the age of faith. The Church, as explained above, became the wealthiest and most powerful institution in the western world, a station undermined at last by the Protestant Reformation.

Just as it could compel support of its financial enterprise, the Church could compel attendance at its many functions, levying fines and exacting discipline of those who refused. The average man's calendar was an essentially religious one, studded with holy days and church festivals. The medieval Church calendar, of course, represented an elaboration of the earlier version and played a very important role in the instruction of the illiterate faithful. What the latter could not learn for himself by reading, the Church taught through sight or activity. The average peasant must have relished the festival as relieving him of the tedium and humdrum of daily life.

The principal day for public worship was the Lord's day, i.e., Sunday, as it is today. On that day the faithful crowded the parish churches, the clergy or monks in the choir, the section

---

pares the medieval concept of "devils" with the modern concept of complexes. Gregory Zilboorg, in his *History of Medical Psychology,* contrasts the medieval practices of "diagnosing" demons with the contemporary psychiatric care of the mentally ill.

When one works with the seriously disturbed mentally ill person, one repeatedly finds himself becoming more and more contemplative. He spends time in meditation, often silence, with a mute patient who has trouble putting into words his inner perceptions. He also gets vistas of insight into the way in which the illness of the person is really his attempt to be "autonomous," to have a freedom that is his own.

From this point of view, healthy prayer life should be the "cultivation of inner freedom" in order that one may have access to *all* that God has made him, so that no *part* of him my cast aside to "live a life of its own" to his detriment and that of those about him.

behind the sanctuary, the great lords and ladies in the front of, or on a balcony, of the nave, often seated in elegant boxes, the lesser dignitaries immediately behind, and the artisans and serfs taking up the places that were left. The whole arrangement gave a rather precise type of the medieval concept of the Church— the clergy and monks piloting and the others passengers in the ecclesiastical ship (nave) which bore them all through the waters of life to the golden strand. The services provided a similar picture. The clergy gave—the faithful received. It would hardly have been any other way, for they alone knew the language of the mass, Latin, and the entire service was in that language. In fact, as the ages hastened on, many clergy, too, had little knowledge of Latin, often stumbling through the rubrics of the mass without comprehension of the words of institution: "This is my body . . . This is my blood." Roger Bacon illustrated parrot-learning with the analogy of the manner in which "clerks and country priests recite the Church services, of which they know little or nothing, like brute beasts." Even Thomas Aquinas complained that many priests were "so ignorant that they cannot even speak Latin."[2]

If many of the clergy had difficulty, one can readily understand the impatience of pious laymen who had no grasp of Latin and no way to acquire it. Their impatience expressed itself, beginning about A. D. 1000, in sectarian movements in which the laymen themselves took the lead. By 1200 there were over one hundred of these sects all over Europe, seeking the plain man's pathway to salvation. They varied widely, of course, in specific character, but all made common protest against the Church's grievous faults: (1) the radical and unbiblical distinction between clergy and laity, as reflected in worship, dress, withdrawal of the cup from the laity, and so on, (2) immorality and ignorance among the clergy of all ranks, (3) the cupidity of church officials and of the whole ecclesiastical system, (4) superstitions connected with relics, festivals, pilgrimages, and various observances, (5) the obscurity of public rites and preaching, (6) the incomprehensi-

bility of theology, and (7) the burdensome character of ecclesiastical taxes, fines, and the like.

The proliferation of these sects and the vehemence of their
protest manifested clearly how far the gap between the hierarchy
and the masses of the faithful had widened. Even the faithful
monks, for many centuries the lay Christian's ideal and themselves
originally laymen, failed to bridge the chasm. After long years
of selfless missionary labor and self-denial, they too had taken
refuge and waxed fat in the luxury of institutional security.
Several times some had managed to rediscover the fountainhead
of the monastic ideal and to forestall the process of institutional
obesity; Benedict of Nursia did it about 529, Cluny about 900,
and the Cistercians about 1100. But this time, institutionalized
monasticism failed, and a new type, the mendicant or "begging"
orders, took its place.

In the two most influential mendicant orders, Franciscans
and Benedictines, both founded shortly after 1200, the initial
purpose of bridging the gap between the hierarchy and the masses
soon ran afoul. They set out to preach and ended up persecuting.
By 1232 the Dominicans were placed in charge of the dreaded
inquisition and were wringing "saving" confessions from the
theologically illiterate masses. The inquisition operated on theological hairsplitting. In the end, it did little to effect a reconciliation of the disaffected masses; the reconciliation was never accomplished, although a military crusade finally thinned the ranks
of the "heretics" enough to allow the Church to regain some of
its former power. But the blow came later. New and powerful
forces, not in the hands of the illiterate masses this time but in
the hands of a new liberated group, were in ferment. Within
another century the Church heard the death knell sounding for
its control of men and society in the Protestant Reformation.*

---

*The next few pages of this manuscript will reveal graphic stories
of the way in which people within the "system" which Dr. Hinson
has described did in deed and fact rebel. Conformity may be the

What has been said here must not leave anyone with the impression that personal piety was a negligible thing in the age of faith, however. Quite the contrary. The truth is, the center of piety was in flux during this period. For some time, as in the age of the Fathers, the monks and clergy provided the ideal. In time, though, the Church's temporal power and wealth, once seemingly a boon, proved too much, and, assisted by human frailty, greed and avarice laid powerful hands on those called to live by the gospel. More than one critic of the Church leveled an accusing finger at its wealth as the root of all evil. Even the gentle Piers Plowman, who lets his love of the Church be clearly understood, accused priests of seeking leave of their bishops to dwell in London, "To synge there for symonye, for silver is swete."[3] The Lady Meed (Bribery), he added, "in the popis paleis . . . is prevy" (2:18; p. 77). She labors with Falsehood, Simony, Envy, Lechery, Usury, Covetousness, Avarice, Sloth, Wrong, and other sins to destroy the Church (2.79-105). She "apoisonide

---

conscious intention of ecclesiastics in their rule over people, but their "system" has a way of producing forms of religious life which in themselves are socially acceptable and understood means of rebellion. Furthermore, the way in which earlier rebels become the "waxed fat" conservatives of a later generation is described in the above comments of Dr. Hinson. Why is it, one wonders, that the mendicants would become in their later years "fat" and overfed? Could it be that their previous contempt for their rulers was the side-long glance of their envy?

Prayer, from this point of view, would be the examination of our violent criticisms of the "system" around us, whatever it is. If we, put in the place of power, would act in the same way, then are we not like cups, the outside of which is clean and the inside of which is dirty? This is called by psychologists "a reaction-formation," i.e., a violent expression of the exact opposite set of feelings consciously, which in turn obscures in the unconscious the real motive. Today, the rabid atheist may be tomorrow's religious leader; the most pious ones who protest too much about their goodness may be the lascivious ones of tomorrow.

[poisoned] popis, apeiride [tainted] holy chirche" through her gifts (3.115; p. 87).

With this state of affairs the average layman looked elsewhere for his example. Quite often he found it among his own kind. Allowing the usual number of religious pikers, and the Middle Ages had neither more nor less than any other era, the personal devotion of many laymen in this era is truly astounding. Besides the previously mentioned evidence of zeal in Church architecture, one must reflect with some awe upon the faithful amassing of relics; erection of shrines; pilgrimages to Rome, the holy land, or other holy places; fasting; prayer; vigils or watches; and participation in church activities. The crusades, discounting all the false and self-serving motives which brought them about, bear eloquent testimony to a deeply rooted piety even in the very centuries when the hierarchy was most corrupt. To be sure, it may have been a superstitious piety. The "Children's Crusade" of 1212 reveals incredible naiveté, but it also reveals incredible faith in the Almighty, who had manifested Himself in Jesus Christ.

As the religious climate changed, then, it is not surprising to find King Louis IX of France among the saints, canonized less than thirty years after his death. Thoroughly indoctrinated with love for Christ and the Church by a devout mother, who would rather "that he were dead than that he had done mortal sin."[4] A frail body and arduous struggles in early life added to his sense of dependence on God.[4a] From early youth to death he exemplified the medieval ideal of piety. His contemporary, Jean de Joinville, himself no mean saint, depicts throughout his *History of St. Louis* what the ideal was and sums it up in Louis's deathbed letter to his son, Philip, written from Tunis in 1270. The "testament" exhorts Philip to love God with his whole heart, to receive adversity with patience and prosperity with humility, to confess his sins often, to attend worship diligently, to maintain good in the kingdom and not to be covetous, to love and support the Church, the clergy and the religious (monks), to hearken to God's word and prayer, to let no one lead him into sin, to thank God often, to judge righteous judgment, to restore property belonging to another, and to lead a virtuous life.[4b] "This holy man," says Joinville, "loved God with all his heart and followed his example: as appeareth in that even as God died for the love He bare His people, so put he his body in jeopardy many times for the love he bare his people; . . ."[5]

The Budding of Mysticism

Undergirding and directing personal piety throughout the Middle Ages was mystical theology, which budded and blossomed in monastic soil. Its seed represented a cross-fertilization of Jewish piety as reflected in the Psalms, later Platonism, and the rich piety of the New Testament, particularly Paul and John. Before looking at the cultivation of mystical thought, it will be of value to attempt a definition.

Broadly speaking, the word "mysticism" designates the belief in and search for direct experience of God, or, as Dean Inge phrased it, *"the attempt to realise, in thought and feeling, the immanence of the temporal in the eternal, and of the eternal in the temporal."*[6] "Mystical theology" attempts to describe the experience of the mystic and to formulate in some systematic fashion what it is and how it is achieved. Christian mystical theology differs from mystical thought in general in that the experience is formulated in terms of God's self-revelation in Jesus of Nazareth.

While admitting considerable diversity in the records and interpretations of Christian mystical experience, we can still set forth a basic pattern. In most cases Neo-Platonism provided the warp and woof upon which the mystics wove the Christian design. This philosophy, which incidentally developed concurrently with the development of Christian theology and probably was influenced somewhat by it, viewed the world as resulting from a series of emanations from the One, the World Soul or Mind

(*Nous*). Unity represents perfection, diversity imperfection. The greatest diversity produced matter. Thus, says the Neo-Platonist, there is an eternal striving for reintegration into the One, from which all things derived.

Man is a duality. He consists both of body (matter) and soul. The soul was usually subdivided further into animal and rational soul (*nous*). The rational soul or mind is a spark of the world Soul or Mind. In accord with the principle that all things seek reintegration, the human soul or mind strives for reintegration with the World Soul or Mind, the One. It is restless until it finds rest in the One.

The union of human soul with divine will take place naturally at death. However, the soul's restless desire will not allow it to wait, and even now its desire need not be frustrated. Already the mind may wing its way to God, "the flight of the Alone to the Alone," in Plotinus's famous phrase.[7]* This "flight" involves

---

*Early Christian mysticism drew heavily upon Plotinus. The emphasis was and is, among mystics, upon the expansion of consciousness, the diffusion of the self, and the blending of the self with the One or the All. Modern Western Christianity has moved just the opposite in terms of a non-mystical, narrowed and pinpointed consciousness, and the separation of the self from all else in uniqueness. Yet the need for religious experience of a personal, mystical kind is somehow at the heart of the renewal of the vitality of religion. As Huston Smith, Professor of Philosophy at Massachusetts Institute of Technology says, ". . . religion cannot be equated with religious experience, neither can it long survive in its absence." (Huston Smith, "Do Drugs Have Religious Import?" *LSD: The Consciousness Expanding Drug.*, ed., David Solomon, New York: G. P. Putnam, 1966, p. 169.)

From the beginning of modern scientific psychology, efforts have been made to treat the disorders of the human spirit through various ways of expanding the consciousness of persons—first hypnosis, then the sodium amytal release interview, and now the use of LSD, both on a blackmarket and a medically supervised basis. This is one direction our culture goes in attempt to make up for the nutritional deficiencies in our religion due to the absence of intensely personal

mystical contemplation, for the One fills, or rather *is* all things and "has its center everywhere, but its circumference nowhere." The One is present, therefore, we merely need to be aware. Awareness does not come from the intellectual process, however. Rather, "we must eliminate all knowing and all association, all intellection whether internal or external." "In sum," counseled Plotinus, "we must withdraw from all the external, pointed wholly inwards; no leaning to the outer; the total of things ignored, first in their relation to us and later in the very idea; the self put out of mind in the contemplation of the Supreme;[8] . . ."

Borrowing this philosophical backing, Christian intellectuals wove into it the Christian belief in a personal God who revealed Himself in Israel, Jesus, and the Church. They distinguished their work from that of philosophical Neo-Platonists in etching

---

religious experience. The other direction is a blending of Christian concepts today, not with Neoplatonism, but with the wisdom of Oriental religions and their disciplines of "getting in touch with the Universe as a whole." Contemporary psychologists and psychotherapists show great interest in Oriental religions: Karen Horney embraced Hinduism as her faith before she died. Gardner Murphy has experimented extensively with extrasensory perception and says that no psychology is complete unless it comes to grips with man's place in the cosmos as a whole and his feelings of loneliness in it.

All this suggests to the activist Christian who would "deepen" his spiritual life: you cannot do so unless you are willing to *widen* your perceptive capacities. Do you practice prayer with listening to the various sounds, tones, and noises around you? Do you practice the presence of God by relaxing your whole being consciously? Do you remove yourself, as did Jesus, from the crowd of people around you and spend much time in meditation alone? What place does prayer have in your going to sleep and your waking up? You do not have to go to an Indian *guru,* or wise man, or learn this in Bombay or Calcutta. Nor do you have to use drugs, be hypnotized or have psychotherapy. You can begin to do these as a praying Christian where you are. They are one form of "opening the spirit" to God.

with bold thread their belief in the divine transcendence, on the one hand, and His personal nature, on the other. Many made contributions to the finished product—Clement and Origen of Alexandria, the desert fathers, Gregory of Nyssa, Augustine and Pseudo-Dionysius, to mention only a few. But it was Augustine and the obscure late fifth or early sixth century Christian, Dionysius, who got the tapestry ready for medieval use. Enough has been said about Augustine in the previous chapter, so we can limit our discussion here to Pseudo-Dionysius.

Dionysius was thoroughly Neo-Platonist up to a point. Where compelled by Christian faith to trace a different line, he chose to follow the Old Testament and Gregory of Nyssa in the view that God is utterly unknowable in His transcendence. Figuratively this means that He dwells in darkness. Thus the true initiate, the mystic, proceeds from light to darkness in his quest of union with God, just as Moses proceeded to the darkness of Mt. Sinai. What he sees is not God Himself, but the place where He dwells —the place of utter unknowability. His route of ascent must be by way of negation, like a sculptor chipping away the excess in order to bring to light the image hidden in his block of stone. In order to experience the Transcendent One, one must lay aside all sensible knowledge. When he ascends the mountain to its peak, his mind "will be totally dumb, being at least wholly united with Him whom words cannot describe."[9]

Augustinian and Dionysian mystical theology put forth shoots in the theology of John Scotus Erigena, a brilliant ninth century scholar at the court of Charles the Bald. It was in the twelfth and thirteenth centuries, however, that it truly budded. In those centuries two great representatives, Bernard of Clairvaux (1090-1153) and Hugo of St. Victor (1096-1141), surrounded by a host of lesser buds, began to produce the plants from which sprang all subsequent medieval mystical thought. Bernard, unquestionably one of the most influential men in Europe in his day, cross-pollinated a host of earlier lines to bring forth an essentially new plant; Hugo outlined more clearly than others before him the *method* of the mystical quest. Others did so little to alter their products that we need not comment on any but these two.

In his systematic work *On the Steps of Humility,* Bernard divided the way to Truth into three stages. The first stage involves traversing in reverse the steps of pride by which man lost the divine image and alienated himself from God; in other words, it involves the learning of humility. The second stage is more positive and forms the very core of Bernard's theology. In this stage one advances in love via four steps: (1) love of self for self's sake, (2) love of God for self's sake, (3) love of God for God's sake, and (4) love of self for God's sake. At first glance Bernard's ladder startles, seeming much too egocentric.

But Bernard was a man of great practical wisdom.* Only if one learns first to love himself properly, he contended, will he learn how to love God. He who loves himself as he ought will love God in the realization that He can be of worth only because of God. He who loves himself as he ought will also love his neighbor, in whom he will see himself. Thus he will advance

---

*In deed and fact Bernard's "staging" of the phases through which love goes can well be said to anticipate much of the modern psychological understanding of the development of the capacity to love. The view of human nature he expresses is realistic: we cannot love until we have been loved. People of the churches of the Great Awakening—Baptists, Disciples of Christ, Cumberland Presbyterians, etc.—put it in terms of salvation: they say that we cannot be saved except by grace, i.e., by the free gift of love from God. This we have in Christ.

However, Bernard helps us to be much more precise and clear in our thinking. The process he describes is accurate concerning the normal development of persons from infancy to adulthood in the scientific sense of those terms. The infant, in the first place, is helpless and "loves itself for itself's sake"; this is *survival* love. The child, in the second place, loves God for his own sake; this is the *prudential* love of a smart child. Any smart person knows that it is the clever thing to do to love other people, but his motive for doing it is for his own good. The young person, in the third place, learns

from selfish love to that love of self which asks that God do with
him as He pleases. When he has reached this point, probably
attainable only in the resurrection, he will be ready for the third
step, the vision of God. Even though the full beatific vision lies
in the future, the Abbot of Clairvaux believed on the basis of
first-hand experience that one can have a momentary vision
even now because both God and man's soul are spiritual. The
Word of God serves as intermediary, linking the soul, which has
perfect love with God, and erasing the distinction between love
of self and love of God.[10] In his *Sermons on the Canticles* delivered to his fellow monks Bernard depicted his personal experience of the "bridegroom's," i.e. the Word's, "comings" to his
soul, a passage worth quoting at length:

> But now let me try to tell you of my own experience, as I set out
> to do. I speak as a fool, and yet I must admit that the Word has

to love others for their own sake, and to love God because God is
love. This is *unselfish* love. The adult, in the fourth place, if indeed
he has really become an adult, loves others and God quite above
and beyond whether it enables him to survive, whether it is the
wise thing to do, or whether it is particularly unselfish. This is
unconditional love. The works of Harry Stack Sullivan in his *Interpersonal Theory of Psychiatry* (New York: W. W. Norton, 1953),
taken apart from a theological reference to God, are remarkably
compatible with this interpretation.

The person who reads Bernard of Clairvaux devotionally will
find a clue to more effective prayer in one particular way. He will
find himself not being satisfied with saying he loves God or his
neighbor. He will be at the work of prayerfully assessing the *quality*
of his love. It is not enough that I say that I love my wife, my students, and my God. I really pray best when I move on into asking
"how" I love and what is the quality of my love. This analysis of
love calls for considerable honesty. The Apostle Paul prays for us
appropriately, then, when he says: "And it is my prayer that your
love may abound more and more, with knowledge and all discern-
ment . . ." (Phil. 1:9) What Bernard of Clairvaux has done is to
describe very accurately the "abounding" process, the stages through
which love goes.

come even to me, and that many times. But never, when He has thus entered into me, have I perceived the actual moment of His coming. I have sensed His coming in advance. But never have I been aware of the particular moment when He came or went. Whence He came from my soul, whither He goes on leaving me, or by what road He enters or departs, I know not even now. . . .

You ask, then, how I knew that He was present, since His ways are past finding out? Because the Word is living and effective, and as soon as ever He has entered into me, He has aroused my sleeping soul, and stirred and softened and pricked my heart, that hitherto was sick and hard as stone. . . . Thus has the Bridegroom entered into me; my senses told me nothing of His coming, I knew that He was present only by the movement of my heart; I perceived His power, because it put my sins to flight and exercised a strong control on all my impulses. I have been moved to wonder at His wisdom too, uncovering my secret faults and teaching me to see their sinfulness, and I have experienced His gentleness and kindness in such small measure of amendment as I have achieved; and, in the renewal and remaking of the spirit of my mind—that is, my inmost being, I have beheld to some degree the beauty of His glory and have been filled with awe as I gazed at His manifold greatness.

But when the Word withdraws Himself from me, it is as when a fire is taken from beneath a boiling pot; my fervour and devotion languish and grow cold, and that is how I know that He had gone. My soul is then inevitably sad, till He return and my heart kindle in me once again.[11]

Whereas Bernard spoke and wrote with the intensity of personal experience concerning the divine-human encounter, his contemporary Hugo, Abbot of St. Victor, made his contribution as a systematic thinker who had pondered the experience of others, Bernard included. His chief concern was to describe for others how one may go about achieving the vision of God through contemplation. Prayer, he explained, proceeds upward in three stages: (1) thought (*cogitatio*), (2) meditation, and (3) contemplation. Like Bernard, he made love the key. Love is God's road to man and conversely man's road to God. God is love. It is His gift to those whom He loves. If one lacks love, he does not have God. He will find God by examining nature—plants, animals, and man himself—and above all by looking in-

ward at himself, where God has poured *His* love. Hugh summed
up his prescriptions concerning the soul's journey to God with
the usual reference to the Canticles.

Certainly that one who comes to you is your Beloved. But He
comes hidden, unseen, and imperceptible. He comes to touch you,
not to be seen by you; to admonish you, not to be beheld. He comes
not to give Himself entirely, but to present Himself to your awareness; not to fulfill your desires, but to gain your affections. He
offers the first and certain signs of His love, not the plenitude of
its perfect fulfillment! In this especially is there evidence of the
pledge of your espousal, for He who in the future will permit Himself to be contemplated and possessed by you forever now presents
Himself to you that you may know how well-disposed He is. Meanwhile you are consoled in His absence, since by His visits you are
continually refreshed lest you grow weak. My Soul, we have now
said many things; but after all these words I ask you to acknowledge
Him only, love Him only, pursue Him only, take Him only, and
possess Him only.[12]

The Little Flowers and the Mirror of Perfection

Bernard and Hugo of St. Victor had a host of followers and
imitators of their brand of mystical theology among intellectuals.
But in the same era in which they propounded their theology
less sophisticated types of piety were springing up as well, offering to satisfy the religious hunger of the masses. The Church
trampled most of these underfoot, labeling them heresies and
doing its best to keep them from spreading. But one wild plant
miraculously survived the censors for a time and turned out to
be the Church's most popular saint in all ages: Francis of Assisi.

The Life of Francis. Francis began life in plush surroundings
in the quiet, lovely village of Assisi, which lies midway down
the Appenine mountain range in Italy. His rich merchant father,
Pietro Bernardone, could afford to dress him in fine clothes,
entertain his friends with lavish banquets, and keep him atop
the social ladder. For the first two decades of his life Francis
reveled in such "vanities." However, a year in prison, a conse-

quence of his participation in the campaign of Assisi against the neighboring city of Perugia, turned his thoughts to more serious considerations. Although he returned momentarily to old haunts after being set free, a sustained illness caused him "to muse on other than his wonted thoughts," says Thomas of Celano. Trying to shrug off an increasing sense that God's hand was turning him to new things, he joined a new military expedition—this time against Apulia. But as he outfitted himself with the trappings suitable for a noble's son, he had a nocturnal vision. Afterwards he refused to go to Apulia and instead took up the rugged life of a hermit, pondering what it was God willed for him. Through intense prayer, meditation, and reading of Scriptures, he learned what it was—to marry Lady Poverty. How costly that decision!

His avaricious father soon disinherited and disowned him. Thinking him mad, he at first locked Francis in a dark room. But when that would not dissuade him, he pronounced the dread formal renunciation. Without wincing Francis stripped off his clothes and, save for the kindness of the bishop, would have gone away stark naked.* Shortly thereafter, robbers waylaid and beat him, and his former friends derided his misfortunes. In time, however, the depth of Francis's religious com-

---

*The holy unrest of Francis was engendered in the fierce heat of his rebellion against his father. The plush opulence of Francis' early life would call for a reaction of deep proportions if his father did not, with all the wealth he had, maintain an unconditional love for his son that was understood to be so by his son. This apparently did not happen. Psychologists who look upon religion as *always* and in *every* case being a conformity of child to parent simply have not read the biographies of persons such as Francis. Here, religious experience was the "method of operation" of the rebellion against his father. However, when psychologists point to the integral relationship between our attitudes toward our parents and our religious attitudes, they have firsthand evidence of this in Francis of Assisi. Whereas Francis did not rebel *against* religion but *by means* of religion, he did reject his father's way of life.

The discipline of prayer and devotional searching is hereby il-

mitment began to show and to be voiced abroad. Others took the vow with him.

Francis and his little band, which eventually reached the number twelve, went about begging and doing good—just as Jesus had done. They repaired dilapidated churches, preached, healed the sick, cared for the needy, and did whatever they could to fulfill Jesus' command. After about five years, Francis ventured to seek papal sanction for his band of *poverello*. With acute suspicions of another heresy or sect the shrewd and powerful Pope Innocent III gave reluctant and somewhat ambiguous consent. His consent spelled disaster for Francis' vision. Within a few more years his "rule," no more than a collection of Scripture verses, was revised once, and then again, and the Franciscan Order was born. Francis, his health failing from rigid ascetic exercises, became a member of an organization he had no intention of founding.

The Biographies. Francis died in 1226 at age 44. In the two decades following his conversion about 1206 he had imprinted deep tracks in the sands of time. Like every great man, a product of his times and yet transcending his times, he so impressed the religious of his generation that the Church canonized him less than two years after his death and thousands of the faithful still

---

luminated: is our interest in and devotion to God and the godly life simply a *means* of shaking loose the shackles of parental tyranny? Or, is it an end in itself, and is the freedom it gives of idolatry of our parents simply a by-product and not the main intention of our spiritual devotion? When we face up to this squarely, we not only will be purified in our love of God, but also we will be more objective and less irrational about our parents. Without some such insight we will fall back into another kind of bondage which not only degrades us but dishonors our parents. Francis' life, though lived in alienation from his father, nevertheless was never a disgrace but was always an honor to his father. There is a difference between honest rebellion against parents and a way of life chosen to dishonor them.

visit the shrine where his body is buried in the luxurious surroundings he disowned. So great was his contemporaries' awe of Francis, in fact, that a modern can only speculate about what actually happened in his lifetime. The most accurate story is Thomas of Celano's two *Lives.* The first written in the year of Francis' canonization, the second sixteen or more years later. They portray simply and powerfully the saga of a remarkable man.

The *Little Flowers* and the *Mirror of Perfection,* which somewhat surprisingly have become the "classics" rather than Celano's works, both consist of compilations of the words and deeds of Francis and his early followers. The work of unknown Franciscans of the second or third generation, they borrowed from Celano's two lives and various other sources. *New* material is composed chiefly of the legends about Francis' disciples and oral stories handed down through a half century. The *Little Flowers,* in fact, consists of two relatively distinct parts: chapters 1-38 being stories about Francis and his initial followers, chapters 42-52 about friars of a later date. Chapters 39-41 are an aside on Antony of Padua and Simon of Assisi. The *Mirror of Perfection* was compiled about 1312, the *Little Flowers,* about 1373.

The late date and obviously prejudiced character of these writings raise the issue of reliability. Can one believe the stories? The stories themselves do little to increase confidence in them. Filled with accounts of miracles, they cause the modern to suspect the whole lot. Quite frankly they look like nothing more than the pious speculations of later generations about the saint and his disciples. Furthermore, these late accounts go considerably beyond the early ones given by Francis' contemporary Thomas of Celano. Certainly no historian would employ them without exacting criticism in writing a biography.

Whoever reads devotionally will also want to read critically. One who has had some training in critical method will spot quickly many historical inaccuracies. The only certain judgment he will wish to make is that Francis made a remarkable impact on his generation. I personally reserve judgment about Francis' visions, levitations, stigmata, and various miracles. The hyper-credulous temperament of his day allowed people to interpret spiritually in a way we now find impossible. Yet, dogmatic judgments either for or against the occurrence of certain recorded miracles should not be made even today. The stigmata perhaps illustrate best the need for caution on all sides.

The early accounts reveal a process of development in the story and reveal, incidentally, that already in the years immediately after Francis' death some doubted whether he had had them. In his *First Life,* Thomas of Celano made the point that Francis kept his wounds concealed and only gave reluctant consent to Brothers Elias and Rufino to see the nail prints in his hands and feet and his pierced side. In the *Second Life,* however, Francis was stripped naked as he lay dying, so that all could see. Bonaventure, penning a new official biography in 1260, felt constrained to explain at greater length how the detailed story of the stigmata came to be known: it was told by Francis himself to one brother who discovered the secret. A century later, the *Little Flowers* included a whole section devoted to the occurrence. Further doubt is cast on the event by the obvious attempt of biographers to draw a parallel between the lives of Francis and Jesus. Francis is only slightly more human than the Lord himself. Ecclesiastical dogma barely sufficed to save him from deification. That he would share even the passion could have been his biographers' design, just as were certain other stories from his life.

Despite such critical questions, the stigmata have strong attestation. Could they have occurred? Present-day knowledge of the mutual interaction of mind and body would favor the *possibility,* though not the probability. It is not hard to believe that Francis so fixed his mind on emulation of Jesus and sharing in His passion that he did in fact begin to experience in his flesh what he thought were the visible signs of Jesus' suffering. This was, as a matter of fact, the point Thomas of Celano made in his *First Life*. To his associates the stigmata verified the intensity with which Francis followed the Lord.*

Whatever one decides finally concerning the critical questions, the life and devotion of Francis of Assisi offer a compelling example. What other Christian has exceeded his commitment to live by the gospel, as he understood it? Yet the works *about* Francis point up dramatically why the "age of faith" produced such a paucity of genuine classics. Easy acquiescence did not foster serious reflection on the *meaning* of Francis's vow of poverty; later generations have had to do that reflection for the Middle Ages. It took a more skeptical era—the Renaissance and Reformation—to get beneath the surface of assent and to probe into the recesses of faith. Francis, Bernard, Hugo, Bonaventure, and many others stood on the threshold, but they were not prepared to step across.

---

*Considerable research has been done in modern psychiatry to be more specific about the signs of the body concerning the state of the whole being of the person. The psychophysiological states of unhealth and disease are ordinarily spoken of as *real* bodily changes that have no infection, lesion, trauma, or growth as their explanatory cause. The explanation is in the *function* interference and bodily appearance. For example, blushing is a common example of an apparent psychophysiological state. Some cases of the hives would be another. The stigmata of Francis cannot be placed under the rigorous diagnostic equipment that medicine uses today to determine their cause. Such things are within the realm of possibility, however, and yet one cannot speak dogmatically about the experience of a person of another era concerning such physiological changes. Diagnosis is hard enough and often impossible when the person is in the clinic before the physicians. When he is not and eight centuries of time separate us from him, all anyone can do is to conjecture and surmise.

Selected Bibliography

General Background and Personal Piety

Cannon, William Ragsdale. *History of Christianity in the Middle Ages.* (New York & Nashville: Abingdon Press, 1960.)

Deanesly, Margaret. *A History of the Medieval Church, 590-1500.* 8th ed. (London: Methuen & Co., Ltd., 1954.)

Coulton, G. G. *The Medieval Scene.* (Cambridge: University Press, 1960.)

————. *Life in the Middle Ages.* 4 vols. (Cambridge: University Press.)

Knox, Ronald A. *Enthusiasm.* (New York: Oxford University Press, 1961.)

Mysticism

Gilson, Etienne. *History of Christian Philosophy in the Middle Ages.* (New York: Random House, 1955.)

Inge, W. R. *Christian Mysticism.* (New York: Meridian Books, 1956.)

Underhill, Evelyn. *The Mystics of the Church.* (New York: Schocken Books, 1964. Reprint.)

James, M. R. *The Varieties of Religious Experience.* (New York: Collier, Co., 1961. Reprint.)

Butler, Edward C. *Western Mysticism: The Teaching of Saints Augustine, Gregory and Bernard on Contemplation and the Contemplative Life.* 2nd ed. (London: Constable, 1951.)

Zaehner, R. C. *Mysticism: Sacred and Profane.* (Oxford: Clarendon Press, 1957.)

Petry, Ray C. *Late Medieval Mysticism.* LCC, vol. XIII. (Philadelphia: Westminster Press, 1957.)

Dionysius

The Mystical Theology and the Celestial Hierarchies of Dionysius the Areopagite. By the Editors of the Shrine of Wisdom. The Shrine of Wisdom, 1949.

On the Divine Names and the Mystical Theology. Translated by C. E. Rolt. (London: S.P.C.K., 1920.)

Bernard of Clairvaux

On the Love of God. Translated by Rev. Terence L. Connolly, S. J. (London: Burns Oates & Washbourne Ltd., 1937.)

On the Song of Songs. Translated and edited by A Religious of C.S.M.V. (London: A. R. Mowbray & Co., Ltd., 1952.)

The Steps of Humility. Translated with introduction and notes by George B. Burch. (Cambridge, Mass.: Harvard University Press, 1942.)

Gilson, Etienne. *The Mystical Theology of Saint Bernard.* Translated by A. H. C. Downes. (London: Sheed & Ward, 1940.)

Hugh of St. Victor

Selected Spiritual Writings. Translated by a Religious of C.S.M.V. (London: Faber & Faber, 1962.)

The Divine Love. The two treatises *de Laude caritatis* and *De amore sponsi ad sponsam.* Translated by a Religious of C.S.M.V. (London: A. R. Mowbray & Co., Ltd., 1956.)

Soliloquy on the Earnest Money of the Soul. Translated by Kevin Herbert. (Milwaukee, Wisc.: Marquette University Press, 1956.)

On the Sacraments of the Christian Faith. Translated by Roy J. Deferrari. (Cambridge, Mass.: The Medieval Academy of America, 1951.)

Bonaventure

The Works of Bonaventure. Translated by José de Vinck. (Paterson, N. J.: St. Anthony Guild Press, 1960.)

Gilson, Etienne. *The Philosophy of St. Bonaventure.* Translated by I. Trethowan. (New York: Sheed & Ward, 1938.)

Francis of Assisi

Thomas of Celano. *The Lives of S. Francis of Assisi.* Translated by A. G. Ferrers-Howell. (London: Methuen & Co., 1908.)

Bonaventure. *The Life of St. Francis.* Everyman's Library. (New York: Dutton, 1910.)

The Little Flowers of St. Francis and *The Mirror of Perfection.* Idem.

Moorman, John R. H. *The Sources for the Life of S. Francis of Assisi.* (Manchester University Press, 1940.)

Petry, Ray C. *Francis of Assisi, Apostle of Poverty.* (New York: AMS Press, Inc., 1964. Reprint.)

Sabatier, Paul. *The Life of St. Francis of Assisi.* Translated by L. S. Houghton. (New York: C. Scribner's Sons, 1894.)

Cuthbert, Father, O.S.F.C. *Life of St. Francis of Assisi.* 3d ed. (London: Longmans, Green & Co., 1925.)

THE CLASSICS OF THE AGE
OF RENAISSANCE

Renaissance and Personal Piety

German and Dutch Mysticism

The English Mystics

The German Theology

The Imitation of Christ

Selected Bibliography

IV

The Classics of The Age of Renaissance

The Renaissance of the fourteenth, fifteenth, and sixteenth centuries supplied the raw materials for a cornucopia of classics. Politically, socially and economically, intellectually, and religiously it was an unsettling, searching time. Old institutions began to sway and then topple in order to make way for new ones. Old kingdoms fell before new ones. Old classes lost their hold on society. Old ideas gave way to fresh ones and purveyors of old ideas to purveyors of new. It was a time when the European was once again compelled to reexamine the basic questions of human existence.

The reasons for this reexamination of old issues are multitudinous. The twelfth and thirteenth century crusades played a major role, for they dredged out some of the long silted up channels between East and West. Through these newly opened channels flowed a potent stream of ideas which had once irrigated western thought but had been turned to other channels. The main part of the stream brought with it the fruitful topsoil of ancient Greece and Rome. Once again, attention was focused on the "greats" of the pre-Christian era. These, in disfavor since Christianity's triumph in the era after Constantine, found a host of imitators and disseminators. In doing so, they broadened immensely the horizon of European culture.

One effect of this new spirit was to make westerners more adventurous. The Latin countries—Italy, Spain, and Portugal—sent explorers around the globe in search of new riches, lands, and places to trade. Discovery meant new wealth, and the influx of wealth increased the power of great medieval cities. The agrarian feudal society began to decline. Nationalism flamed up and overturned the old balance of power. In place of the dominance of Church and Holy Roman Empire, other powerful principalities and states came into being—France, England, Spain, and Portugal. While popes and emperors played their deadly game of power politics, these looked to their own interests. When at last the former took note of what was happening, it was too late; the die was cast.

Meanwhile, tragedy struck the once powerful Byzantine Empire. Harassed constantly, but still standing firm against invasions from the East from the seventh century on, the Emperors had begun to plead for assistance from their Christian brothers in the West, whose star was now rising. The first crusade, in 1095, brought some relief. But Christians of East and West discovered that as a result of separation since 1054 they understood one another poorly. Subsequent crusades proved less beneficial and even resulted in feuding among the crusading armies. Finally, in 1204 the Westerners attacked their former ally and captured and sacked the capital city, Constantinople. Fatally weakened, although strong enough to repulse the western conquerors in 1261, the Empire made an easy prey for the still advancing Turks. Constantinople fell to the Ottomans in 1453.

Subsequently, the West centered its attention on defense of itself against the Turks and on its own mounting problems. Discoveries, new trade routes, new sources of income, nationalism, and many other factors started to rot away the foundations of feudalism. The cities provided a place of refuge for the peasant and manufacturing helped to free him from his servitude. Those who remained on the soil expressed their intense dissatisfaction —first vocally and then with violence. One insurrection after another agitated further an already unsettled situation. Political, social, and economic factors ripened for the great revolution which came to a head in the revolt of Martin Luther.

Notwithstanding its significance in preparing for the Protestant

Reformation, however, the Renaissance was essentially an intellectual movement. The classics, rediscovered as a result of fresh contacts with the East, opened up again the Greek way of looking at human existence, viz., from the presupposition that man is the measure of all things. In the age of faith the Church had provided the measure; now the individual provided it. This radical change in the locus of norms for human life brought in its train a radical reappraisal of all cultural values. Classical art forms, architecture, literary genres, fashions, and interests replaced those prized in the ecclesiastically dominated Middle Ages. Criticism supplanted credulousness. Concern for exactness of language took the place of concern for theological preciseness. In a word, man had decided to take over the reins long tightly controlled by the Church.*

The new flower of learning blossomed first in Italy. Sponsored by opulent and powerful noble families, like the Medici, and sometimes by the popes, it got a strong grip on all aspects of life. Though its spiritual glow has long since faded, we may still see the indisputable effects of it in the art and architecture of all the great Italian cities—Rome, Venice, Florence, Pisa, and Milan. Concern for the dignity of man is etched ineradicably in the matchless nude sculptures of Michelangelo, in the paintings of da Vinci, Raphael, and a multitude of other greats.

From Italy the humanistic draughts blew across the rest of Europe. They reached the Netherlands and Germany in the late fourteenth and early fifteenth centuries, fanned especially by the Dominican preachers who formed the Brothers of the Common Life. From the Netherlands humanism was carried to

---

*During the Renaissance, one might add, the distinction between science and religion began to emerge. The idea of a *psychological* vs. a *spiritual* interpretation of man would have been unthinkable by people of the beginning of this era. Today we take it for granted because the humanistic study of man as man has so thoroughly separated itself from the distinctly religious interpretation. Consequently, we today must be disciplined in *both* points of view to see things steady and see them whole.

England and popularized there at Oxford and Cambridge by the distinguished scholar Erasmus of Rotterdam. It blossomed late in France and Spain, too late really to have much impact before sides were taken regarding the reformation of the Church. But in both England and Germany it sank its roots deeply enough that it became the handmaiden of reform; the result in those countries was the triumph of Protestantism.

Renaissance and Personal Piety

In Italy the Renaissance had a negligible effect on the piety of the common man. That was true because leading Italian humanists—Petrarch, Boccaccio, Valla, Dante, Marsilius of Padua—concerned themselves only incidentally with religion and morality. Boccaccio's famous *Decameron*, for example, consisted of a collection of short stories designed to teach moral truths, but one has the impression in reading them that Boccaccio was more interested in style than in ethical maxims. The preponderance of labor was expended on classical studies, literary criticism, political theory, and the fine arts; in short, the Renaissance in Italy involved largely a renewed interest in classical learning.

In the Netherlands and Germany, in rather sharp contrast, the Renaissance aided religion. Whereas the Italian literary critic Lorenzo Valla restored classical texts and proved the Donation of Constantine spurious, for example, the Dutch scholar Erasmus produced a critical edition of the Greek New Testament. Or, whereas Michelangelo, Raphael, da Vinci, Perugini, and other Italian artists and sculptors aped the Greek greats by using classical models and subjects, Holbein, Kranach, and Dürer chose biblical subjects and avoided nudes.

Northern humanism differed in other ways, too. Being about two centuries later in time and aided by the invention of moveable type in 1456, it had broader appeal. Its impact was not confined to the educated and wealthy, and its sponsorship did not come from the popes or the Medici. On the contrary, the newly founded schools and universities assured a general diffusion, even to the common people. This later movement, therefore, put itself at the service of the masses and took an interest in the common man's aspirations and hopes, including the religious ones.

The tie-in of humanism with religion came through forcefully in a multitude of criticisms aimed at the Church. Even after he severed his ties with Rome, Luther never excoriated with greater élan the faults of the institutional church than his humanistic precursors and contemporaries. Ulrich von Hutten's *Letters of Obscure Men,* a satire on the clergy, was read with relish by humanists everywhere.* Purporting to be letters *from* the clergy, they poked fun at the papacy, the hierarchy, and common clerical ignorance, laziness, cupidity, ineptitude, and immorality. In the fourth letter, for example, Hutten set forth and commented on things found in three's in Rome:

Three *ridiculous* things: the example of the ancients, the papacy of Peter, the last judgment.
Three things in *superabundance*: antiquities, poison, ruins.
Three *articles kept on sale*: Christ, ecclesiastical places, women.

---

*The use of wit and satire against the establishment of religion is a hallmark of the emerging "scientific" interest in life. The popular conception of the psychologist and psychiatrist today is that they could have *no* interest in religion, at all, if they are in these professions. In turn, "psychologist" and "psychiatrist" jokes run the rounds: "Have you heard the one about a psychiatrist who. . . ." These jokes are often done in pure humor without the aim to hurt. Often they are told in derogation of the professions who are the butt of the joke. Medical doctors, and psychiatrists in particular, are receiving many of the same criticisms today which were levelled at the church in the period being discussed in the present chapter.

Yet one needs to ask himself as he disciplines his devotional life: Have I examined my use of humor? Is humor a means of grace, or is it a means of hurting other people? When I tell a joke, is it at other people's expense and aimed to make them "squirm," or is it a way of poking fun at myself? Do I take myself too seriously and others too lightly? What *is* consecrated laughter?

Three things *painful to Romans*: the unity of the princes, the growing intelligence of the people, the revelation of frauds.

Three things *Romans disliked most to hear about*: a general council, a reformation of the clerical office, the opening of the eyes of the Germans.

Three things *held most precious*: beautiful women, proud horses, papal bulls.

Hutten's more famous contemporary, Erasmus, engaged in a comparable critique of popular morality, manners, and religion in his *The Praise of Folly*. "Folly" charged that men's minds were preoccupied more with appearances than with reality and sustained it by an invitation to go to Church.

When anything serious is being said, the congregation dozes and squirms. But if the ranter—I mean the reverend—begins some old wives' tale, as often happens, everyone wakes up and strains to hear. You will also see more devotion paid to such fabulous and poetic saints as George, Christopher, or Barbara than to Peter or Paul or even to Christ Himself.[1]

He likewise gave the inside story of theologians, monks, popes, priests, and laymen. The names "religious" or "monks" are complete misnomers, he declared, "since most of them stay as far away from religion as possible, and no people are seen more often in public."[2] He would be overwhelmed, Folly continued, "if the Supreme Pontiffs, who are the vicars of Christ, tried to imitate His life, His poverty, labors, teaching, His cross, and contempt for life."[3] So also the ordinary priests. They fight for their tithes like soldiers and think they have done their job if they mutter a few prayers, "which I always wonder if any God hears or understands." They slough off responsibility, tossing it back and forth like a ball and leaving all concern about piety to the common people. But the latter react just like the clergy. They pass off religious responsibility to the "ecclesiastics," "as if they themselves had nothing to do with the church and were not bound at all by their baptismal vows." So the wheel turns.

The priests who call themselves "secular," as if initiated to the world rather than to Christ, push it off onto the regulars; the regulars onto the monks; the monks, who have more liberty, onto those who are stricter; both together onto the mendicants; the mendicants onto the Carthusians, among whom alone piety lies hidden, and so lies that it can hardly be seen. Similarly, the popes, who are most diligent when it comes to making money, delegate their surplus apostolic duties to the bishops, the bishops to the pastors, the pastors to the vicars, the vicars to the mendicant friars, and they return the care to those who shear the wool from the sheep.[4]

Ideas like this gradually filtered down to the rank and file. Meanwhile, they helped to crystallize some of the pious discontent latent in the minds of the latter. When Luther posted his *Ninety-five Theses*, the smoldering faggots underneath burst into flame. In this respect, at least, Renaissance humanism enhanced personal piety. In feeding oxygen to warm coals it fanned the desire to find a deeper level of piety. The actual realization of this may never have occurred, but from the resurgent doubt and skepticism came some of the greatest classics of Christian devotion, spawned particularly by German and Dutch mystics.

German and Dutch Mysticism

German and Dutch mysticism adopted the basic objective of all mystics, namely, union with God, but differed markedly in its practical, this-worldly orientation. This helped it to avert in part the deadly peril of individualism, which all mysticism faces. In contrast to the mystical theology of Bernard, Hugo and Richard of St. Victor, Bonaventure, and others, the German-Dutch brand appealed to laymen as well as to the "religious" or clerics. It emphasized instruction and preaching rather than ascetic exercises in order to achieve the vision of God, used the New Testament rather than the Old, and the words of Christ rather than the Canticles in interpreting the mind of Christ. Putting Christ in place of the Church as the mediator of salvation, German-Dutch theology declared that salvation was in the reach of all and demanded a pure life as a necessary companion of the higher religious experience and humility as an exemplification of the gospel. The end product was a fresh way of interpreting religion upon which the Protestant Reformers could build.

The noted exponents, all of whose writings deserve careful reading in a study of the Renaissance classics, included Meister Eckhart (1260-1327), John Tauler of Strassburg (c. 1300-1381), Henry Suso (1295?-1366), John of Ruysbroeck (1293-1381), Gerard de Groote (1340-1384), Thomas á Kempis (1380-1471), and two "schools"—"the Friends of God" and "the Brothers of the Common Life."

Eckhart, Tauler, and Suso were Dominicans. Eckhart, whom Hegel tagged "father of German philosophy," was the most philosophical. His tendency toward pantheism aroused the suspicion of Church officials and John XXII declared some of his statements heretical in 1329. However, his emphasis upon "total self-detachment" (*Abgeschiedenheit*) from created things wielded a potent influence on subsequent mystics. Tauler, a disciple of Eckhart, was an extremely popular preacher. His emphasis upon the agency of the Holy Spirit in conversion and the need for simple faith understandably evoked Luther's praise. His prescriptions for an abiding experience of union with God, interwoven into the fiber of each sermon, were simple: Deny and detach yourself from the world and the things in it; put aside sin; follow in the footsteps of Christ, imitating his humility and love. Suso, who had practiced an extreme form of asceticism until he experienced a "conversion" at age forty, adopted Tauler's views and proclaimed them with little change.

The term "Friends of God" was applied in the fourteenth century to coteries of pietists scattered along the Rhine River, laymen and priests whose spiritual longings the customary church services failed to satisfy. Though not an organized sect, they shared a concern for the study of Scriptures, close personal fellowship with God, holiness, and godliness. Leaders included Rulman Merswin (1307-1382), whom many have thought to be the often quoted "great Friend of God from the Oberland." It was from this circle of pietists that the *German Theology,* textbook of German and Dutch mysticism, came into existence.

John of Ruysbroeck, a Flemish monk, seems to have formed the bridge between "the Friends of God" and "the Brethren of the Common Life." His enthusiastic preaching earned for him the title, "the ecstatic doctor." While laying some emphasis upon ascetic exercises, he made love the hub of his theology. In his famous treatise *Adornment of the Spiritual Marriage,* he prescribed three things by which a few might attain the vision of God: (1) live virtuously, (2) love God constantly, and (3) lose themselves in the darkness of contemplation, no longer conscious of creaturely methods. He did not advocate the contemplative life for all.

De Groote, a co-founder along with Florentius Radewyn (1350-1400) of "the Brothers of the Common Life," was a pupil of Ruysbroeck, but rejected his mysticism. Instead, he and the "Brothers" concentrated upon a form of apostolic life which, it was hoped, would improve Church life in their day.* Their

---

*Groote's methods of instruction and discipline were *small group* methods. These groups were incubators of considerable spiritual vitality. One wishes for more information about the nature of their *disciplined* fellowship. Disciplined churches, such as the Mennonites, the Quakers, etc. as we know them today were themselves established on the principle of face-to-face confrontation of each other. The Mennonites used the occasion of the Lord's Supper to put everything in order according to ethical relationships between the brethren. Today there is a flourishing emphasis, both in psychology and in many churches, upon "renewal through small groups." The educational methodology and communal principles of Gerhard Groote points to the dynamics of a disciplined and openhearted fellowship.

This raises an issue for the modern worshiper: "To what extent are the small groups in which I participate able to worship freely and openly together?" Such a question moves the devotional life off a purely personal onto an intimately social level. Groups may be therapeutic or they may be destructive. As L. C. Marsh, one of the founders of the group therapy movement in contemporary psychotherapy said, "By the crowd have they been broken, and by the crowd shall they be healed."

schools, scattered all along the Rhine valley in the Netherlands and Germany, sought to educate youths both intellectually and morally.

A distinguished product of their school at Deventer was Erasmus, greatest of the humanists. Following the death of Gerard de Groote in 1384, the Brothers' movement became more formal. In accordance with the desire of de Groote, Radewyn established an order called the Order of Canons Regular with the first monastery located on Mount St. Agnes, where Thomas á Kempis was to spend much of his life. The major concerns of the Order included work and voluntary contributions as a means of support, sharing of all possessions, commitment to a simple, voluntary rule, the primacy of Scriptures and translation of them into the vernacular, mutual confession to one another daily, careful study of the person and life of Christ, stress on inward moral purity rather than rites and rituals, and a deep interest in the education of the young. Most of these concerns received brilliant exposition in *The Imitation of Christ*.

The English Mystics

The fourteenth century English mystics also reflected the impact of new theological currents on the continent, particularly in their practical orientation and use of the vernacular. However, the otherworldly, medieval cast of their writings is more pronounced than in German and Dutch mysticism, so that, despite the popularity of some writings among monks and clergy, they failed to attain widespread usage. With the exception of the remarkable Margery Kempe, the authors were recluses.

Richard Rolle (d. 1349), the first to translate the Psalms into English, started the stream. Strongly affected by the life of Francis of Assisi, he remained aloof from religious orders and affirmed vigorously the freedom of conscience. In his *The Fire of Love* he described a "mystical feeling" which possessed him about twenty years after his conversion as "an unwonted and pleasant fire." Like both Bernard and Francis he judged renunciation of the world the prerequisite and love the medium for the encounter with God.

A man must be truly turned to him and in his innermost mind turned away from all visible things before he can experience the sweetness of divine love, even a little . . . for all love that is not devoted to God is evil, and renders evil those who have it . . . those who love worldly excellence with an evil love are inflamed with an evil passion and are further distant from the fire of divine love than is the distance between the highest heaven and the lowest place in the earth. They are indeed made like to their beloved, for they give way to worldly desire and holding fast to the old man take pleasure in the emptiness of visible life instead of truly happy love. . . . And indeed, as it is written, nothing is more evil than to love money, for while the love of any temporal thing fills the heart, it suffers him to have no inward devotion.[5]

Along similar lines and dependent in varying degrees on Richard Rolle were an anonymous work entitled *The Cloud of Unknowing* and the writings of Walter Hilton and Julian of Norwich. *The Cloud of Unknowing,* composed between the years 1345 and 1386, drew heavily from the *Mystical Theology* of Pseudo-Dionysius. Addressed to someone seeking to enter upon and pursue the life of solitude and contemplation, it elaborated the Dionysian theory of progression from light to darkness ("the cloud of unknowing"). If ever one "sees" God, "it must always be in this cloud and in this darkness." The cloud can be pierced only by "a sharp dart of longing love."

Walter Hilton (d. 1396), an Augustinian canon, employed the same schema as the *Cloud* in his *Scale of Perfection.* But his tone was more pastoral, and he displayed more psychological insight than either Rolle or the author of the *Cloud.* Like Augustine, he based the spiritual life upon the pillars of meekness and love. By gradual education in these, he maintained, man ascends the ladder of perfection to union with God.

Julian or Juliana of Norwich (1343-1396), the most philosophical of the early English mystics, bequeathed to posterity only one book, *Revelations of Divine Love.* The latter consisted of

visions Dame Julian experienced at age thirty, when during a
serious illness she came to a deeper understanding of Christ's
passion, an event for which she had prayed. Julian's recurrent
prescription for sin is childlike repentance. For her, the saint was
not one who had done no wrong, but one who had transcended
it by God's grace.

Margery Kempe (c. 1373-1450?) stands in a category by
herself. Unlike all other medieval mystics, she lived an active life,
having married at age 20 and borne a number of childen. The
Book of Margery Kempe, rediscovered in 1934, has exceptional
importance for the history of the English language and offers a
rich mine of data about late fourteenth and early fifteenth century
England. A candid spiritual autobiography, written with the
help of a priest, it portrays vividly the dramatic struggle of
Margery Kempe with sin and records a host of visions which
occurred during her earthly pilgrimage. Although naive in comparison with the writings discussed above, the book has a genuine
ring about it, akin to the *Journal* of George Fox.

The German Theology

This brief survey of English and Dutch-German mysticism
demonstrates that the Renaissance was an age of spiritual classics.
The two writings which stood head and shoulders above all the
others and epitomized the most worthy pietism of their day were
The German Theology and *The Imitation of Christ.*

The Author. The little book entitled *The German Theology* is
an obscure work of the late fourteenth century. We possess no
personal information about its author other than that stated in
the preface. He was "a friend of God," formerly "a Teutonic
Knight, a priest, and a warden in the House of the Teutonic
Knights at Frankfurt." From the book itself one can tell that he
knew the teaching of Augustine, Pseudo-Dionysius, Gregory the
Great, Bernard, the Victorines, Francis of Assisi, and John Tauler.
Several times he expressed his distaste for the "Brethren of the

Free Spirit," a German pantheistic sect of the thirteenth and fourteenth centuries. From certain references to the sacraments and to the institutional Church, he let it be known that he was a dedicated churchman and aware of the dangers of individualistic mystical theology. His pastoral concerns shine throughout. He wanted disciplined discipleship, but he knew well the weakness of the flesh.

The Book. The substructure for *The German Theology* is Neoplatonism. Woven into its warp and woof are Augustine's doctrine of grace, Bernard's theory of love, Francis' call to poverty and obedience, and Tauler's challenges to discipleship (*Nachfolge*).

God is the One Eternal Good, from which flows all that is. Man consists of body and soul. As a creature of God, he is good, and by virtue of his participation in *the* Good, he can be deified. Even while in the body, he may have a foretaste of eternal bliss. The whole purpose of man is God Himself. Man's desire and will, therefore, should be focused entirely upon Him, never upon himself or upon the creation. Sin is to do whatever is contrary to God's will, to turn away from the unchangeable Good, and to partake of the changeable; it is self-love and denial of God.

All men sin like Adam did by putting themselves in the place of the One Eternal Good. But He, knowing their helplessness, rectified the situation by assuming human nature. Man cannot amend himself without God. Amended and enlightened by Him, however, he can direct his desire and will to the Eternal Good. The ascent to God involves three stages (as per all mysticism): purgation of sin, illumination, and union.

Christ's life is the perfect life, for it involved perfect obedience to God. In order to achieve our goal of union with God, we must follow after Him, renouncing our selves and all things. Following Christ will entail suffering, for the life of pleasure stands in antithesis to discipleship. The Devil entices us to pleasure and to a false freedom. The answer to him is obedience to God and to all creatures. True freedom derives from such obedience and not from following our own will or desire. Union with God means nothing but this:

That we should in truth be purely, simply, and wholly at one with the One Eternal Will of God, that we should be without will and that the created will should have flowed into the Eternal Will, and be dissolved and destroyed therein, so that the Eternal Will alone should will what is done or left undone.[6]

United thus with God, one may not be tossed to and fro. As God is Light, so also the follower of Christ shares the light. In him Love is pure and unsullied; he desires to love all Creatures and to do the best for them.

The author closes with a warning to beware lest anyone think he has arrived at his goal. Continually must one deny and renounce self, forsake all things, die to self-will, and live to God alone and to His Will. For this God's grace alone suffices.

Not surprisingly, the *German Theology* received ready approval by later pietists. Luther published an edition of it in 1516 and praised it highly in a letter to Georg Spalatin as "a pure and thorough theology," thinking it an epitome of Tauler's sermons. Later, however, under pressure to work out some satisfactory institutional form for the Lutheran movement, he lowered the temperature of his commendations a bit. Calvin repudiated it entirely as "a bag of tricks produced by Satan's cunning to confound the whole simplicity of the gospel." Yet, despite such censure, humanists and pietists still used it as a major textbook. The pietistic movement of Spener and Francke thrived on it, and through them it has been bequeathed to the modern era as a classic of devotion.

The Imitation of Christ

The Author. For several centuries debate about the authorship of the *Imitation* has waxed hot. With thirty-five or more claimants, the historian has to weigh a mass of evidence, both internal and external, and choose which seems the *probable* author. Despite a fairly strong English manuscript tradition in favor of Walter Hilton, Thomas á Kempis usually gets the nod on the basis of (1) an explicit statement by an á Kempis student, John Busch, in his *Chronicon Windesemense*, composed seven years before á Kempis' death, that the latter wrote the *Imitation*; (2) thirteen manuscripts dating from before 1500 which bear his name; and (3) agreement in style and content with his *Meditation on Christ's Incarnation*. A manuscript discovered at Lübeck, Germany, in 1921 has led some scholars to support Gerard de Groote as the author. Joseph Malaise, S. J., has proposed more specifically on the basis of this discovery that the *Imitation* was de Groote's spiritual diary, which Thomas á Kempis edited for the Brothers of the Common Life about 1441. The latter is, therefore, merely to be credited as a popularizer and not as the author of the book. Due to the structure of the book, it may be accurate to call Thomas á Kempis its "editor," as Thomas Kepler has. The weight of evidence still favors his authorship, however, and the book is best understood with that supposition in mind.

Thomas was born in Kempen, Holland in 1379 or 1380, the son of John and Gertrude Haemmerlein or Hemerken. His father, an artisan and farmer, and mother both contributed to his early training in religion. He received a formal education in the village school at Kempen and in the Brothers' school at Deventer. His brother John, fifteen years his senior, had also been trained in the latter and became one of the first of six canons admitted to the newly formed Order of Canons Regular at Windesheim.

Florentius Radewyn, co-founder of the Brothers, took the young Thomas in charge for a time and provided money for his education. Strictly disciplined by his teacher, John Boehme, he became an excellent copyist, Latin scholar, and student of the Scriptures.

While at Deventer, á Kempis contracted a serious illness, which plagued him for many years. During this siege, he wrote his spiritual biography, called *Soliloquy of the Soul*, a work which resembles Augustine's *Confessions*. The illness produced a crisis in his religious pilgrimage. After much struggle of soul, he finally resolved his problem in what was apparently a mystical encounter, recorded in the *Soliloquy*.

In 1406, after a six year novitiate, á Kempis was admitted formally into the Order of Canons Regular. Eight years later he was ordained to the priesthood. Those who accept the traditional theory of authorship believe that he began the *Imitation of Christ* shortly thereafter, completing it at least by 1425.

The years at Windesheim were hard ones. A disastrous plague hit Deventer, Zwolle, and Campen in 1421, taking a heavy toll. Like others in his Order, á Kempis labored tirelessly, caring for the sick and seeing after the needs of others. From 1425 until 1440 he spent hour after tedious hour preparing a copy of the Latin Bible, later employed in the monastery. In 1425 he was chosen subprior, an office which entailed the charge and training of novices. He suffered considerable reproach from his fellow monks by virtue of his ecstatic nature. Frequently, he would slip away from a group and without explanation or apology seek the privacy of communion with God.

In 1427 the monastery was caught up in the struggle of the See of Utrecht. Thomas and his fellow monks had to flee to Lunenkerc in order to avoid the wrath of certain nobles, who attacked them for obeying the orders of the Bishop of Utrecht to cease all worship services. Four years later his elder brother, John, fell ill. In keeping with his sensitive, thoughtful spirit Thomas resigned the subpriorship and stayed at his brother's side for fourteen months, until the latter died in 1432. Another plague struck in 1441.

In the interim Thomas had returned to Mount St. Agnes. The subpriorship having been filled, he was appointed procurator or bursar, an office which ill suited his retiring personality. He was again appointed subprior in 1447, but retained the position only a short time apparently. His last years were spent in ill health; he succumbed to dropsy on July 26, 1471.

The humdrum character of the monastery notwithstanding, Thomas á Kempis' biography depicts in a vital manner some of the Christian traits which made the *Imitation* one of the world's best-loved devotional writings. Woven into the fabric of his soul were the qualities he received from following the Master: love, humility, self-denial, gentleness and tenderness, and self-discipline. Surely one can forgive him for minor faults, for example, his overcredulousness. This merely underlines his humanity, his limitation by space and time. But in his other qualities he proved himself bound by the Eternal, who had come in Jesus Christ, and to that extent he transcended easily his four score years and ten.

The Book. The keynote of the *Imitation of Christ* is an unyielding demand for self-denial in following the pattern of Christ as the *sine qua non* for union with God. The little book is replete with quotations from classical and Christian writers; it is, in fact, a virtual mosaic of quotations. Most of these were taken from the Scriptures—the Psalms, words of Jesus, and Paul's letters appearing most often. But the writing manifests also a heavy dependence upon Augustine, Bernard of Clairvaux, and the German mystics—Eckhart, Tauler, Suso, and Ruysbroeck. J. E. G. de Montmorency has advanced the plausible theory that á Kempis borrowed the groundplan of the work from Henry Suso. Quite clearly, the writer had at hand a wide range of sources and used them freely.

But he was by no means a plagiarist. What he used, he digested and made his own. Indeed, he did not fail to criticize those he admired when the occasion demanded it, and he tailored his quotations carefully to fit the master plan. The truth of this can be seen readily in his repudiation of the learning of the schoolmen, which, he believed, engendered pride and hindered self-denial. "In fact," he avowed frankly, "a poor peasant that serves God is better than a proud philosopher who neglects himself and ponders the course of the stars."[7] On the other hand, the *new* learning of Renaissance humanism seems to have exercised a negligible influence, too; in his estimation it had the same fault as scholasticism.

What really matters, insofar as Thomas could see, is one's relationship to God.* God is the Sovereign Good, the Source and Substance of all things. If man is to partake of the Good, he must concentrate wholly upon Him and seek to do His will only. He can do so only by absolute self-denial and acknowledgment of his utter insufficiency. Any human desire is alloyed with self-interest, so only *total* self-denial will suffice to bring one into acquiescence with the divine will. This self-denial, in turn, demands rejection of things and of the world. No one can hold on to God and the world at the same time.

The conquering of self is a gift of God. Man's nature, á Kempis insisted in Augustinian fashion, has been corrupted by the fall of the first man. "The little strength which it retains is like a spark hidden in ashes."[8] God's grace alone is adequate to bring it again into line with the divine will. In Christ He came down from

---

*Whereas Thomas was apathetic to what the *new* learning was to be, his point of view that what really matters is man's relationship to God tends to produce what might be called a *Christian* humanism. This has been espoused more recently in our own times by Stephen McNeil in his book *A Genuinely Human Existence*. His contention is that in Jesus Christ we see humanity *genuinely* restored without facade, counterfeit, or distortion caused by the subhuman behavior of man as a sinner. As one person in a counseling session said, "I do not expect them to be perfect, but I do expect them to be human!" My own contention in my book, *Christ and Selfhood,* is that we discover our *real* selves in confrontation with Christ. The devotional life is the continuation of that discovery as we take the humanity of Jesus seriously as being impossible had He not also been divine. We have in Him the genuinely human existence without sin, and through Him we can bring our sinful selves to God in time of need and find help through His intercession. He was tempted in all points like we are. He was both completely human and without the distortions of sin.

heaven for our salvation, taking upon Himself our miseries out of love, in order that we might learn patience and follow His example. The whole summation of the religious life is contained in His admonition to do as He did: "Forsake all, and you shall find all; relinquish base desire, and you shall find rest."[9]

Forsaking all things and following Christ's example of self-denial will bring true peace, viz., the kind of peace that Christ gives. The more fully one strips himself of self-will and resigns himself to the will of God the greater will be his reward. Then only can he master himself and become a free man. "Man draws the nearer to God, the further he withdraws himself from all earthly solace. So much the higher also does he ascend to God, the lower he descends into himself, and the viler he becomes in his own estimation."

This repeated demand for utter self-denial is perhaps overly stern. Before dismissing it as too harsh, however, one must remember that Thomas á Kempis was a monk and, for many years, teacher of novices. He was writing a book of directions for monks, especially novices. He expected the highest level of performance from those who had ostensibly renounced all in order to follow Christ. Yet, even for them, he tempered his demands with a realization of our common human frailties. We cannot always pursue only the highest virtues, he conceded, no matter how pure our aspirations; sometimes we must fall back into menial performance. If we fall, we must not be too dejected. "Although you often find yourself afflicted or grievously tempted, all is not lost. You are a man and not a god; you are flesh and not an angel."[10]

The *Imitation of Christ,* as popular as it has been with the millions of faithful, has received scathing criticism for its intense concentration on the salvation of the individual. H. H. Milman, Dean of St. Paul's Cathedral, London, labeled the title a misnomer, charging that it reflects nothing of Christ's concern for feeding the hungry, clothing the naked, visiting the prisoner. The Spanish philosopher Miguel de Unamuno called it the most unChristian book ever written. To some extent such criticisms are

fair. The author obviously wrote with the individual in mind.
Quite often, in fact, he warned against worrying about the salvation of anyone else. His recurrent advice is, Look to yourself;
let God care for others. "The truly inward man puts the care
of himself before all other cares; and he that looks diligently to
himself finds it easy to be silent about others."[11] When such observations are made, however, one must not fail to remember
the monastic context in which á Kempis wrote. The monastic
life generated a temptation to compare and find fault with what
others were doing. Such comparisons are wrong-headed, á Kempis knew. To avoid them, the monk had to put a fence around
his area of scrutiny and worry first about the *divine* measuring
rod. In line with this, á Kempis made plain occasionally that he
had not forgotten the Christian's obligation to serve and help
others. The man who pays attention first to his own religious
development, he pointed out, will be prepared to act on behalf
of others. "Therefore, be zealous first of all regarding yourself,
and then may you justly exercise zeal towards your neighbour
also."[12]

Furthermore, one of the four sections of the *Imitation* is a
discourse on the Eucharist as a means of union with Christ. Had
the author been purely individualistic, he would never had included this section. Finally, if á Kempis were the author, his
biography should suffice to dispel any doubt. He who ministered
to the sick and dying in time of plague and even left his position
as sub-prior of the monastery in order to spend fourteen arduous
months ministering to a dying brother hardly deserves criticism
for self-centeredness. To whatever extent he failed to interpret
correctly Christ's call to discipleship, perhaps he could be for-
given with the same graciousness that he was ready to forgive
others on the basis of their humanity. He believed, with other
devout men of his time, that the whole end of man is to worship
and serve God. Whatever else man would do, he must do as a
by-product of this, not separate from it. When we criticize this
premise, we criticize not Thomas á Kempis alone, but those

pious generations of men and women who had not yet reached the stage where humanism added its intense concern for man as a counter-weight. But the time was not far off. Within less than a century the new premise came forth clearly in the Protestant Reformation: The whole end of man is both to worship God and, in so doing, to serve his fellow man.

Selected Bibliography

The Renaissance and Personal Piety

Burckhardt, Jacob. *The Civilization of the Renaissance in Italy.*
2 vols. (New York: Harper & Bros., 1929.)

Schaff, Philip. *History of the Christian Church,* Vol. VI. (New
York: Chas. Scribner's Sons, 1910.)

German and Dutch Mysticism

Clark, James Midgley. *The Great German Mystics: Eckhart,
Tauler and Suso.* (Oxford: Basil Blackwell, 1949.)

Jones, Rufus M. *The Flowering of Mysticism.* (New York: Macmillan Co., 1939.)

Meister Eckhart

Works. Translated by Raymond B. Blakney. Harper Torchbooks.
(New York: Harper & Bros., 1941.)

Henry Suso

Little Book of Eternal Wisdom and Little Book of Truth. Translated with an introduction and notes by James M. Clark.
(London: Faber & Faber, 1953.)

The Life of the Servant. Translated by James M. Clark. (London: James Clarke & Co., Ltd., c. 1952.)

John Tauler

*The History and Life of the Reverend Doctor John Tauler of
Strasbourg; with Twenty-five of His Sermons.* Translated
with notes by Susanna Winkworth. (London: H. R. Allen-
son, 1905.)

John Ruysbroeck

*The Adornment of Spiritual Marriage, the Sparkling Stone, the
Book of Supreme Truth.* Translated by C. A. Wynschenk.
Edited with an introduction and notes by E. Underhill.
(London: J. M. Dent & Sons, Ltd., 1916.)

The Chastening of God's Children, and the Treatise of Perfection of the Sons of God. Edited by Joyce Bazire and Eric Colledge. (Oxford: Basil Blackwell, 1957.)

The Seven Steps of the Ladder of Spiritual Love. Translated by F. Sherwood Taylor. (London: Westminster Dacre Press, 1944.)

Petry, Ray C. *Late Medieval Mysticism,* pp. 285-91.

Underhill, Evelyn. *Ruysbroeck.* (London: J. M. Dent & Sons, Ltd., 1916.)

Gerard de Groote

The Following of Christ. Translated with an introduction by Joseph Malaise, S. J. (New York: America Press, 1937.) This editor maintains that De Groote wrote the *Imitation of Christ;* á Kempis merely edited it. He interprets the writing as De Groote's spiritual diary.

English Mysticism

The Cloud of Unknowing

The Cloud of Unknowing. 6th ed. With a commentary by Father Augustine Baker, O.S.B. Edited by Abbot Justin McCann. (London: Burns Oates, 1952.)

Richard Rolle

Selected Writings. Translated and arranged by John G. Harrell. (London: S.P.C.K., 1963.)

Walter Hilton

The Scale of Perfection. Translated with an introduction and notes by Dom Gerard Sitwell, O.S.B. (London: Burns Oates, 1953.)

Julian of Norwich

A Shewing of God's Love. Edited by A. M. Reynolds. (London & New York: Longmans, Green & Co., 1958.)

Margery Kempe
The Book of Margery Kempe, 1436. Modernized by W. Butler-
    Bowdon. (London: Jonathan Cape, 1936.)

The German Theology

The German Theology. Translated by Susanna Winkworth. In-
    troduction and notes by J. Bernhart. (New York: Pantheon,
    1949.)
Petry, Ray. *Late Medieval Mysticism,* pp. 321-6.

The Imitation of Christ

Of the Imitation of Christ. Translated by Abbot Justin McCann.
    (New York: Mentor, 1957.)
Kettlewell, S. *Thomas á Kempis.* 2 vols. (New York: Putnam,
    1882).
Montmorency, J. E. G. de. *Thomas á Kempis, His Age and
    Book.* (London: Methuen & Co., 1906.)
The Imitation of Christ. Edited by Thomas S. Kepler. (New
    York: The World Publishing Co., 1952.)

THE CLASSICS OF THE AGE
OF REFORMATION

Reformation and Catholic Personal Piety
Spanish Mysticism
Reformation and Protestant Personal Piety
Protestant Literature of Devotion
Selected Bibliography

V

The Classics of The Age of Reformation

The Protestant Reformation was a complex historical occurrence which resulted from a multiplicity of contributing factors. But in its central thrust it was a religious movement. Insofar as it betokened a radical reappraisal of long cherished ideas and institutions and their replacement by others, it created a demand for new types of devotional literature, which would express the new theology and religious life. Whereas Catholic devotional writings could still follow the patterns of monastic piety, Protestant writings could not, for in Protestant circles monasticism came to an abrupt end with the revolt of Martin Luther. Hence, the latter would no longer address the pious man who had retreated *from* the world; now it had to address him *in* the world.

This new situation *vis-a-vis* Christian devotion had been just barely touched upon by Renaissance mystics and humanists. The humanists, on the one hand, stated the layman's dissatisfaction with the Church and blazed away fiercely at its faults. The mystics, on the other hand, still firmly tied to the hierarchy, were trying to bridge the yawning gulf they saw fixed between the layman and the Church. Consequently, they made some proposals for piety which the layman, as well as the recluse, could use to satiate his desire for knowledge of God. Neither humanists nor mystics, unfortunately, appreciated fully the religious importance of what the other was trying to do. It took a major upheaval and the sundering of the Church to wed the two in the piety of Protestantism.

The Reformation of the sixteenth century was both the cul-

111

mination and the beginning of a battle for the emancipation of
the human spirit. In a sense it was a D-day before V-day. For
in that century the decisive blow was struck against forces which
had held man captive for centuries—ignorance, feudalism, and
moral decadence in the Church. The fight against all three still
continues, of course, but never again, may we hope, will they
incarcerate the human spirit in the western world in the same
vise-grip they possessed in the Middle Ages.

Only accidentally, or perhaps providentially, did Martin Luther touch off the powder keg on which all Europe sat in 1517.
Had he not applied the match, someone else undoubtedly would
have. At the outset this humble monk had no other desire than
to discuss some abuses which burdened the ecclesiastical structures of his day. Hundreds of others had made the same criticisms he made, many with greater vehemence. But somehow his
manifesto, *The Ninety-Five Theses,* managed to light a fuse
which others had missed.

Almost simultaneous with the explosion in Germany came one
in Switzerland, ignited first by the young Zurich pastor, Hul-
dreich Zwingli, and sparked further by John Calvin. Not many
years afterwards, the growing revolt brought the discontent of
the pious in England to a head. When Henry VIII waxed bold
enough to declare the nation and Church of England severed
from Rome, in 1534, the Reformation got under way. However,
in England it assumed a less radical form than in Germany or
Switzerland and, with the cautious sponsorship of the brilliant
virgin queen Elizabeth I, gained the support of a larger segment
of the population.

From these nations the Protestant flame spread to other countries. From Germany it spread quickly to the Scandinavian countries, where it gained an almost complete victory by 1527. From
Switzerland it spread to France, the Netherlands, and Scotland.
In Scotland, led by "the thundering Scot," John Knox, Calvin's
brand of Protestantism triumphed completely over resurgent elements of Catholicism. In the Netherlands, however, Protestants

fought for their lives and achieved a grudging tolerance only through a disastrous war which split the low countries into Holland and Belgium in 1581. In France Calvinists managed to stay alive and, after more than thirty dreadful years of civil war, to get a guarantee of tolerance in the Edict of Nantes, 1598, only to see it revoked by Louis XIV in 1685.

In addition to these three reform groups—Lutheran, Reformed, and Anglican—there was also a fourth, more radical, wing of the Reformation. Having closer ties with the disaffected masses of peasants, they were treated with contempt and hatred by both Catholic and Protestant leaders. The latter dubbed a large segment of them Anabaptists, "re-baptizers," thus bringing them under the ban of the Empire. Their connection with the peasant uprising of 1523-1525 in Germany and then later with a millenarian rebellion at Münster, under the leadership of John Bockelson and Jan Matthys, assured their expulsion from most European lands and England. The remnant that remained regrouped in the Netherlands under the leadership of a converted priest named Menno Simons, from whom comes their present name, Mennonites.

The tragic feature of the Reformation, no matter how one might laud its positive contributions to religion, was that it set brother against brother and father against son. Except where one denomination or another triumphed completely—Presbyterians in Scotland; Catholics in Spain or Italy; Lutherans in Sweden, Denmark, and Norway; Anglicans in England—the revolt sundered nations into many fragments. Just like France, Switzerland and Germany also suffered from disabling civil wars. Switzerland, perhaps more fortunate than others, called a halt to the fighting in 1531, and the country was partitioned into Catholic and Protestant areas. In Germany the battle went on and on. The so-called "Peace of Augsburg," a compromise treaty signed by the warring sides in 1555, merely multiplied the problems. Its provision that the religion of an area would be decided according to the religion of its ruler invited social, political, and economic chaos, for when a ruler changed, religion also might change. That this could not work became clear when the Thirty Years' War erupted in 1618. After the latter costly and indecisive struggle between Catholics and Protestants, the Peace of Westphalia instituted a more stable formula, letting things stand as they were in the year 1624.

Whether the Reformation was worth all of the heartache it entailed depends in large measure upon its contribution to Christian piety, both personal and corporate. In embracing humanism as well as the traditional types of piety and modifying both, Protestants unleashed a tiger which they have since often found hard to tame. The scientific approach of humanism has frequently spelled trouble for the accepted modes of doing things, and even for religion itself. So often has this been true, in fact, that we must ask with complete candor whether we have kept adequately in control this useful and yet wild creature. Was it right to try to wed humanism and pietism? Stated in another way, should religion be used in order to enhance human values, or is man's only purpose to worship God and serve Him?*

A study of both Catholic and Protestant classics of Christian devotion which have appeared since the Reformation supplies at least a partial answer to these questions. From this point on, one

---

*This question is an ever-recurring one in Protestantism. We face it in the ministry to the sick, in marriage counseling, in issues of social reform, particularly in the ministry to the poor. The question can be answered institutionally or devotionally, and the answer one gets depends upon which route he takes in answering the question. We can "use" religion to motivate people to give money *in order that* an institution that is only secondarily concerned with religion may foster its *human* values. For example, a hospital is begun by a denomination and specific religious appeals are made. However, the whole presupposition of the medical staff by necessity makes the healing of the patient primary and his religious concern, his relationship to God, even, secondary to this.

On the other hand, if we attempt to answer Dr. Hinson's question

cannot fail to detect a change in tone which humanism has injected into devotional writings. Protestant compositions are this-worldly, Catholic other-worldly; Protestant individualistic, Catholic Church-centered; Protestant secular, Catholic monastic; Protestant lay-orientated, Catholic clergy-orientated. The ancient Christian tradition naturally shines through both, but more strongly in Catholic literature. Those things in which Protestants parted ways with Catholics definitely give a different flavor to their writings. In the classics of the age of Reformation the different roads were charted unmistakably.

Reformation and Catholic Personal Piety

The Renaissance had set in motion a wave of concern about personal piety throughout the nations of Europe, so it is with some accuracy that Catholic scholars have contended that the Reformation interrupted movements of reform already under way within the Church. On the eve of the Reformation, for example, groups of pious laymen and clergy in Italy met, somewhat as "the Friends of God" had met along the Rhine valley a century before, to study the Scriptures, to pray, and to discuss the state of the Church. Six clergymen from one such group, called the Oratory of Divine Love, took part in a commission appointed

---

devotionally, we would say that God is to be loved for His own sake first and foremost; then all the human values are put into their right perspective and place. For example, the home that prays *just* to keep from coming apart is operating at the survival level of prayer, i.e., the husband and wife are expecting of religion and prayer a way "around" the demands of the human institution of marriage. However, if the conservation of the human values of the home is accepted as a discipline of prayer itself, then the two may be focused into a clear perspective.

Seen this way, the hard work of a student in his studies *is* a form of prayer if done "before God" consciously. Here the daily work and way becomes a form of prayer. As the motto of the Monks of Cluny said: *"Laborare est orare:* To labor is to pray."

by Pope Paul III in 1536 to study the state of the Church and set forth a program of reform. Luther could not have delivered a more scathing indictment than did this commission.

Similar groups of concerned persons met in France. With the scholarly backing of the humanist Jacques le Fevre d'Etaples and ecclesiastical sanction of William Briconnet, Bishop of Meaux, they sought ways to correct the faults of the Church. The sister of King Francis I, Marguerite d'Angoulême, read Luther's and Calvin's publications with interest in her quest for an improvement in public morality. She wrote a collection of scandalous tales designed to teach moral truths, the *Heptameron,* patterned after Boccaccio's *Decameron.* Le Fevre d'Etaples prepared translations and commentaries of Scriptures, read avidly by concerned laymen and clergy.

The direction eventually taken by Catholics after discussions of reunion with Protestants failed was supplied by Spanish reformers. Cardinal Ximenes, a Franciscan monk, father-confessor to Queen Isabella and Archbishop of Toledo, drew up the master plan, which consisted mainly of three things: purification of the morals of the clergy, the establishment of new schools for training them, and the improvement of church life by a revival of the Inquisition. In other words, he suggested revival along medieval lines rather than reform along Protestant lines. The piety of the average Catholic, therefore, continued as it was in the Middle Ages except for the excitement of greater fervor. Not surprisingly, it was from Spain that Catholic personal piety came to its best expression in the wake of Catholic reaction to Protestantism.

Spanish Catholicism produced two types of piety. One was the stern, military, disciplined type of Ignatius Loyola and the Jesuits, which combined the best in medieval monasticism with mysticism. The other was the more world-rejecting type of mysticism, which, in its extreme form, produced quietism.

Spanish Mysticism

Ignatius Loyola_ and the Spiritual Exercises. Loyola (1491-1556), a well-educated son of a noble Spanish family and once a page at the Court of Ferdinand and Isabella, aspired to pursue a military career. But while serving in the garrison at Pampeluna, he suffered a leg wound which thwarted his hopes. After long and anguished reflection, he resolved to pursue the life of a hermit, and with that in mind he entered a Dominican convent at Manresa. His spiritual crisis during ten months there, 1522-3, paralleled in many respects Luther's struggle in the monastery at Erfurt. Neither confession, penitence, prayer, nor fasting gave him comfort. Finally, in the depths of despair he cried out, "Show me, O Lord, where I can find Thee; I will follow like a dog, if I can only learn the way of salvation." Having contemplated suicide even, he cast himself upon the mercy of God. Peace came at last. The one great contrast with Luther's experience was, as T. M. Lindsay has pointed out, that whereas Luther quietly continued to discharge his daily chores, Loyola, always a soldier at heart, sought to storm the kingdom by force.

Out of Loyola's spiritual struggle at Manresa came the famous *Spiritual Exercises*, the soul of the Counter-Reformation and one of the great manuals of Catholic piety.* The final form appeared

---

*Ignatius developed a "pattern for the spiritual life" in these exercises. The group process is again evident. Renewal comes through small groups again. However, there is more to this than just group discipline and retreat. We see about us today the "use" of both psychology and religion to bring a patterning in the lives of people. The work of Norman Vincent Peale is a form of thought conditioning. The disciplines of the Unity, Theosophy, Christian Science, and other groups are "uses" of both religion and psychology to promote health, wealth, wisdom, and success. Hence, these movements have been enormously popular because of their tangible methodology and their overtly expressed purpose to accomplish earthly ends for the devout person. There is no preoccupation with purgatory, the hereafter, or abstractions. The immediate, pragmatic need of the person is uppermost.

in 1540, the year the Society of Jesus received official papal endorsement, but in 1522 Loyola published his first draft. He designed the little treatise as a manual to assist persons making a retreat. Accordingly, it addressed both directors of the retreat, which Loyola believed essential, and retreatants. In its main substance, the *Exercises* is divided into four parts, each part to be used for one week of a four-week retreat (presently retreats usually are confined to a briefer period).

First Week. Meditation upon the end of man and its consequences and upon sin and its consequences. The aim of this meditation is to lead to conviction of sin and unworthiness and to repentance.

Second Week. Meditation upon the Kingdom of Christ and Christ as Savior and consideration of one's service to Him.

Third Week. Meditation upon the passion of Christ. The aim of the meditations of the second and third weeks is to engender a desire to devote oneself fully to Christ, the heart of Jesuit piety.

Fourth Week. Contemplation of the risen and glorified Christ, concluding with a "Contemplation for obtaining divine love."

Note that the general outline follows the typical mystic "way" to union with God—purgation (first week), illumination (second and third weeks), and union (fourth week). Yet, in one respect the *Spiritual Exercises* surpassed medieval directives,

---

One can moralize about this and say that it is not good; it is a productive half-truth. The larger truth, however, is that these movements tend to appeal to people who are past the age of thirty-five. They have put away the easy comforting thoughts of their "old time religion" in some respectable denomination. They have nothing to replace it. They hit what Viktor Frankl calls an "existential vacuum," a complete encounter with meaninglessness. These forms of religion provide them with a tangible ritual and a way of personal security in the "here-and-now."

The meaning of prayer here, then, is to establish specific rituals of one's own with other people of one's own age group. Thus prayer can come alive. The manual of discipline of Ignatius will give you some beginnings for your life as a group. Modify it all you please. But read it together.

namely, in its emphasis upon service to man. Love, Loyola insisted, "ought to be manifested in deeds rather than words."

In addition to directions for four weeks of retreat, the treatise also contains four appendixes: (1) rules concerning the distinction between good and evil spirits which confront the retreatant, (2) rules concerning distribution of alms, (3) notes concerning the difference between serious faults and "scruples," and (4) "Rules for Thinking with the Church." The last was added by Loyola in reaction to the Protestant Reformation. Its main thrust is summed up in Rule 13: "If we wish to be sure that we are right in all things, we should always be ready to accept this principle: I will believe that the white that I see is black, if the hierarchical Church so defines it."[1]

Such slavish obedience to the institutional Church, the very sum and substance of Roman Catholic piety since the Reformation and the charter of the Society of Jesus, both puzzles and rankles Protestants. It clashes head on with the Protestant principle that no institution in which we as men have a part can ever speak with such finality. The human spirit and conscience must be free to question the decisions made even by the Church. And insofar as slavish obedience has an integral connection with the spirituality of Ignatius Loyola, it limits the usefulness of the *Spiritual Exercises* for the Protestant faithful. Despite the fact that he grasped the essential meaning of love as concerned action, Loyola failed to comprehend the *breadth* of divine love, which acts impartially toward the just and the unjust. Unfortunately he understood "fellow-men" to mean "fellow-Catholics," not all mankind.

The enduring value of the *Spiritual Exercises* lies in the program it outlines for training in piety. Borrowing from the *Imitation of Christ* and other traditional works on Christian piety, and uniting their thoughts with his own mystical experiences at Manresa, Loyola set forth a pattern for retreats which both Catholics and Protestants have found useful. Wisely, he built in some instruments for adapting retreats to varied circumstances and needs. Protestants who have an increasing interest in the retreat would do well to go back to this original source and construct their own retreat manual along similar lines.

Teresa of Avila and John of the Cross. Catholic mystical theology reached a new peak in the life and writings of Teresa of Avila (1515-1582) and John of the Cross (1542-1591), co-founders of the Discalced Carmelites, an order which practiced the strictest kind of poverty, self-denial, and prayer life. Living in an era when the Church turned every stone to ferret out the smallest vestige of heresy (Protestantism), both sought to align their extraordinary experiences of visions, raptures, ecstasies, auditories, and the rest with traditional stereotypes. As a result of this, Teresa's three major writings—the *Life,* the *Interior Castle,* and the *Way of Perfection*—offered the best summary to date of the whole Latin mystical tradition. Her descriptions and prescriptions concerning Christian devotion and union with Christ reflect the austerity and fear of demons of the desert fathers, Augustine's emphasis on grace and his theory of recollection, the Dionysian theme of progression from light to darkness (knowing to unknowing), the purgatorial theology of Gregory the Great, Bernard's twin themes of love and humility, Hugo of St. Victor's concept of progressive stages in prayer, Francis of Assisi's love of poverty, the self-denial and call to discipleship of the *Imitation of Christ,* and the directions of Ignatius Loyola concerning retreats. She took special pains in her autobiography, composed about 1562-1565 at the insistence of her Dominican Confessor, Fray Garcia of Toledo, to show how her experience corresponded faithfully with recorded mystical experiences of previous centuries.

Father Garcia's command, of course, responded to the severe criticism Teresa and her supporters had aroused in founding a reformed house of Carmelite nuns. The harassment she recorded in her *Life* was, however, only a prelude to something more severe, the brunt of which was borne by her contemporary John of the Cross. The latter entered the Order of Carmelites in 1563. Five years later, after meeting Teresa, he became active in the reform movement initiated by her and helped to found several new monasteries. He crossed paths with her regularly when appointed chaplain and confessor to the hundred and thirty nuns of the convent of the Incarnation at Avila, where she was prioress.

The opposition to the austere reformers reached such an intensity that on the night of December 3, 1577, opponents seized and imprisoned* John and his companion, Germano de Santo Maria, charging them with disobedience to the Master-General and to the chapter at Piacenza. John was thrust into a cell six feet wide and ten feet long with one tiny window, fed only bread and water, scourged by the friars, and deprived of Mass and

---

*No Christian *wants* to be put in jail, but some of the most effective men and women of prayer have discovered the depths of their contribution to our spiritual devotions in periods of time spent in jails. Some of Paul's writings come to us from his days of imprisonment. Here, St. John of the Cross was thrown into prison. Later, Bunyan's *Pilgrim's Progress* came from the Bedford jail. These times of forced isolation and confinement reduced the degree of concourse with other people. The sensory deprivation was extensive. Dr. Hinson says that only one tiny beam of light was available. He was "an hungered," as was our Lord in the wilderness. Here was a *natural* condition for the expansion of consciousness, the dilation of the spirit as opposed to the "quickie" efforts of LSD enthusiasts today.

The point I want to make is that we can *voluntarily* construct conditions where we are out of the hub-bub of life, when sensory stimulation is lowered and even deprived, when food is simple and minimal for the body's needs. Couple this with solitude, and the conditions of revelation are set. Not many of us think of the ways a businessman can spend a quiet day in a hotel to himself alone in meditation; a student can spend a day on the campus during holiday seasons, etc. On these occasions, quite without making ourselves conspicuous, we can discipline ourselves. One more thought: take St. John of the Cross' *Dark Night of the Soul* with you! It can be bought inexpensively for it is in paperback edition.

the Sacraments. During this period he seems to have had his first mystical experience, alluded to later in his four major writings—*The Ascent of Mount Carmel* (1578), *The Spiritual Canticle, The Flame of Living Love* (1582-1589), and *The Dark Night of the Soul* (c. 1579).

John escaped in 1578 and was hidden for a while by sympathetic Carmelite nuns. For the next ten years he labored tirelessly at the reform of monasteries, but he lost his various posts when the General Chapter met in Madrid in June, 1588. Refused permission to go to Mexico, he fell ill of a fever on September 12. Thus disgraced and humiliated, he chose to spend the last years of his life in the monastery at Ubeda, where he died December 14, 1591.

The element of persecution and the sensitive religious atmosphere involved in the spiritual life of both saints naturally raises some provocative questions about their recorded experiences. To what extent did stereotypes shape both the experiences and the record of them? To what extent did persecution and harassment of various kinds induce visions, raptures, etc.? Both questions have considerable bearing upon the proposals each writer makes concerning the devotional disciplines, such as prayer, by which one strives to achieve the goal of union with God. If the experiences are genuine and the reports accurate, we might be wise to engage in the rigorous exercises employed by them. If the contrary is true, then we can dismiss their observations and make another approach to Christian piety.

Both Teresa and John reflect the type of religion William James called "the sick soul" or "twice-born." They maximized their personal evil and unworthiness, suffered periods of intense depression or melancholia, and tended toward a form of monism. In John's case the foreboding, gloomy countenance seldom lifted, although Teresa occasionally managed a wan smile in her writings. John's mystical experience, which he associated with suffering, seems to have been shaped especially by the dark cell in which he lay a prisoner for several months, the gloom broken only by a tiny ray of light. Teresa's fluctuations from the valley of depression to the mountain top of exhilaration, a frequent occurrence, may have resulted from the physical illness she suffered at various periods in her life as well as from her sensitivity to persecution.

When one has subjected the records to searching criticism, however, he still has to concede that both John and Teresa had some remarkable spiritual experiences. These they managed to weave skillfully into the fabric of traditional piety so as to escape the inquisitors, something many less astute persons failed to do.

John's distinctive contribution lay in his talent for depicting his experience in poetic imagery. His thought is summed up pretty well in three famous images he employed as parallels to the traditional "way" of purgation, illumination, and union. First occurs the "dark night," "the inflowing of God into the soul." Unaccustomed as it is to the pure Light, the soul loses control of all its faculties. It is as though one were to look at the sun with the naked eye, and the eye, due to its weakness, were to recoil, blinded and in pain. Next comes the "betrothal," wherein the purified will responds without pain to the impressing of the divine will upon it. As described in the Canticles, "the Spouse grants the soul great favors and visits it most lovingly and frequently." Purification continues, but in place of pain comes joy, the joy of communion with the spouse, i.e. the Trinity. Last, the goal of the mystic, is the "spiritual marriage." At this stage the soul experiences the indwelling of God. This experience differs from God's indwelling in all men in that the soul "feels this intimate embrace within it." It is comparable to the beatific vision in heaven, except in its transiency. How does one go about ascending the mountain? By emptying self.

In order to arrive at having pleasure in everything, Desire to have pleasure in nothing.
In order to arrive at possessing everything, Desire to possess nothing.
In order to arrive at being everything, Desire to be nothing.

In order to arrive at knowing everything, Desire to know nothing.

In order to arrive at that wherein thou hast no pleasure, Thou must go by a way wherein thou hast no pleasure.

In order to arrive at that which thou knowest not, Thou must go by a way that thou knowest not.

In order to arrive at that which thou possessest not, Thou must go by a way that thou possessest not.

In order to arrive at that which thou art not, Thou must go through that which thou art not.

When thy mind dwells upon anything, Thou art ceasing to cast thyself upon the All.

For, in order to pass from the all to the All, Thou hast to deny thyself wholly in all.

And, when thou comest to possess it wholly, Thou must possess it without desiring anything.

For, if thou wilt have anything in having all, Thou hast not thy treasure purely in God.*[2]

Whereas John attracted attention by virtue of his descriptive powers, Teresa of Avila found avid readers and disciples of her method of prayer. Employing the traditional steps of the mystical

---

*The wisdom of St. John of the Cross is reminiscent of Viktor Frankl's principle of "paradoxical intention." The healing of the soul comes from the willing of the opposite of one's fear, ambition, or intention. The person who intentionally sets out for pleasure in sexual relationships, for example, and tries with every effort he or she can exert is often self-defeated. A medical student of Frankl's had a terrible fear of one of his professors. He trembled in his presence. He decided, after hearing Frankl lecture, to say to himself when the professor entered the room: "Oh, here is the instructor! Now I will show him what a good trembler I am—I'll really show him how to tremble! But whenever I deliberately tried to tremble, I was unable to do so!" (Viktor Frankl, *Psychotherapy and Existentialism*. New York: Washington Square Press, 1967, p. 167.)

Also, St. John of the Cross catches the spirit of some of the Oriental religions. Take, for example, the Taoist proverb: "By not doing, all things are accomplished." The person whose devotional life directs him to God in the resolution of things over which he himself actually has no control will find what St. John of the Cross means here.

scale, like Hugo of St. Victor, she envisioned three (in the *Life* four) corresponding steps of prayer: (1) Prayer of recollection or meditation. At this level the devout soul must meditate upon the life of Christ in an active way, as it were, drawing up water from the well.[3] (2) "Prayer of quiet." This prayer originates in God and ends in a sense of "the greatest peace and quietness and sweetness within ourselves." All faculties are quiet except the will, which "allows itself to be imprisoned by God, as one who well knows itself to be the captive of Him Whom it loves."[4] This prayer advances naturally to "a sleep of the faculties," which Teresa called the third degree of prayer in her autobiography but apparently combined with the prayer of quiet in other writings. (3) "Prayer of union." In this highest step the soul is united, though momentarily, with God. In such an experience "there is no feeling, but only rejoicing, unaccompanied by any understanding of the thing in which the soul is rejoicing. It realizes that it is rejoicing in some good thing, in which are comprised all good things at once, but it cannot comprehend this good thing."[5] It almost withdraws from the body in order to be with the Lord.[6]

In considering the overall contributions of Teresa and John of the Cross to the tradition of Christian piety, we today would have to observe in their thought the same weaknesses medieval monasticism and mysticism suffered from. By being overly concerned with devotion as the whole purpose of man, they failed to see clearly man's obligation to man as a creature of God. Along this line, for example, both frequently decried the "active" life, inasmuch as it restricted the life of prayer and devotion. Moreover, their own disciplines were too austere even for many of their fellow Carmelites. And, like so many others who counted otherworldliness everything and this-worldliness nothing, they burned with zeal to snatch souls from the fires of purgatory, but did little to alleviate their miseries in this life. Somehow the divine love they talked about so intensely failed to spread its arms wide enough to encompass the whole of human life, whether past, present, or future.

Reformation and Protestant Personal Piety

While the Reformation forced Catholics to intensify the mystical and monastic devotion of the Middle Ages, it compelled Protestants to create new forms of devotion in response to a new understanding of salvation. Essentially four changes occurred. (1) A deeply personal experience of communion with God was looked upon as within the range of every man, not merely the "religious." (2) Both public and private forms of worship were stripped to bare essentials in order to accommodate the masses. (3) The minister replaced the monk or priest as the leader of devotion. (4) Worship became more man-centered and less God-centered. Let us consider these more carefully.

The Reformation doctrine of salvation by grace through faith made the concept of salvation intensely personal. Whereas medieval man had looked to the Church for assurance regarding his salvation, now he had to accept ultimate responsibility himself. Neither Church, nor sacraments, nor pope, nor works, nor any other institution could guarantee spiritual safety. Christ alone, coming in word and sacrament, has power to save. Therefore, only by entrusting one's life to Him and receiving the gift of His Spirit can one feel confident about the ultimate things in life. This kind of experience of God lies within the grasp of everyone, for everyone can have faith through God's grace. Hence, there is no difference between the layman and the priest or the layman and the monk; all are equal, except in function.

The confidence that all men can have a personal encounter with God in Christ naturally required a change in the forms of piety. If Christ comes in response to faith alone, then elaborate rites and rigid disciplines have no place in the Christian's regimen. In accordance with this, the mass, statues, images of the saints, rosary, hours and stations of prayer, signing with the cross, and a host of other props designed to aid worship and stimulate piety were amputated. The substitute for these was, in most cases, a disciplined kind of piety based on reading of the Scriptures and

prayer. The Protestant faithful attended a church whose ornamentation was reduced to a minimum and participated in a
service of worship of which the reading of the Scriptures and a
sermon formed the main part. In his home he read the Bible
before meals and at other times and prayed extemporaneous
prayers. Mary, the saints, and relics played no part in his liberated
mind. His aim was communion with Christ alone.

When the evangelical had particular problems, he brought
them to the parish minister and sought counsel from one who
shared his foibles and weaknesses and lived in the world with
him. In replacing the priest and the monk, the minister had an
awesome task. He had to minister to the sick and dying, comfort
the bereaved and despondent, instruct the perplexed, uplift the
fainthearted, look after the persecuted and imprisoned, champion
the cause of the poor and needy, counsel those in distress and
trouble—in a word, do whatever had to be done.

Although in general scope this ministry did not differ from
that of his counterparts in the Catholic fold, it did differ decided-
ly *in tone*. The focus of concern rested on the living; the ministry
was, therefore, *this*-worldly in its basic orientation. Accordingly,
Protestants did not offer prayers for the dead or administer
extreme unction to the dead and dying. The Protestant principle
allowed no room for purgatorial prayers such as one finds throughout the writings of Teresa or John of the Cross. In this orientation
Protestantism embraced within its basic theology the Renaissance
concern for man and his wholeness. At the same time it rejected
the medieval tendency to make a definite dichotomy between soul
and body and to express concern primarily for the soul as the
eternal and therefore important side of man.

As we glance backwards to retrospect, we cannot help but
reconsider the high cost of adopting a radically new attitude toward Christian worship as expressed in these four changes. The
emphasis upon personal experience, for instance, led to excesses.
Radical "spiritualists" repudiated Christian community entirely.
The most radical of them, the socalled "Zwickau prophets,"

initiated an iconoclastic campaign which would have destroyed all semblance of order had Luther not intervened to prevent it. Through this experience, Luther and other leaders came to detect some of the dangers in their proposals and thereafter proceeded with greater caution. To try to accommodate all, they realized, may mean that none will be accommodated. When deism and the rationalism of the Enlightenment hit in the next two centuries, Protestants began to concede the need for some forms, even if simple ones, in order to lift the level of the masses. This admission led to a return to certain traditional modes of worship abandoned in the first spurt of reformation. The result was a type of piety which stood midway between spiritualist and Catholic.

The humanistic interests of Protestant piety also generated some problems that required redress in the next century. The theological principle behind this change was sound, that is, that man has an obligation both to worship God and to serve man, even while he lives. And in order that the Christian might be charged with his full duty, preaching rightly regained a major role in Protestant worship and the Eucharist assumed a lesser role. But, on the negative side, in directing attention manward as well as Godward, devotion to God sometimes trailed behind concern for man, even to the point that He was regarded simply as man's servant. Sermons spoke more about God's help for man than about man's duty to God. Hymns had more "I's" than "Thous." Prayers of praise gave way to prayers of petition.

Protestant Literature of Devotion

The basic weaknesses of Protestant personal piety are attested undeniably in a failure to produce any true classics of devotion. Other classics—theological and ethical—yes; devotional classics, no. Luther, Calvin, and others were barely able to cope with the broad theological and institutional crises and problems generated by the Reformation; nor in the institutional reorganization of the churches was there monastic leisure for meditation and the development of disciplined prayer life.

This should not be taken to imply that the Reformers had a shallow piety. Luther was a deeply religious person and, notwithstanding serious personal faults such as a violent temper, frequently demonstrated in sermon, letter, or treatise the depth of his spiritual experience. His religious sensitivities, as Erik H. Erikson has tried to point out in his *Young Man Luther,* were shaped by his pious but stern Saxon parents, Hans and Margareta. His father's harsh, demanding discipline especially, Erikson thinks, fashioned Luther's image of God as a stern, disapproving Judge and generated his inner uncertainties which finally led to his discovery of the principle of justification by faith through grace. Luther also inherited the superstitious bent of his parents and their typically medieval fear of demons, as the story of his decision to enter a monastery illustrates.

After elementary education at Mansfeld, Magdeburg, and Eisenach, Luther entered the University of Erfurt to prepare for a career in law according to his father's wishes. Although he did excellent work in school, thoughts about a religious vocation never left him. The death of a friend about the time he received the M.A. from Erfurt in 1505 may have intensified the latter. Then, as he took refuge under a tree one day during a violent thunderstorm, lightning struck the ground beside him. Terror stricken, he cried out, "Help me, St. Anne! I want to become a monk." Two weeks later he entered the Augustinian convent in Erfurt.

Luther pursued the monastic career with intense vigor. What he discovered there, and later made the criterion for the development of Protestant worship, was that no amount of self-castigation, ascetic disciplines, or pious activities will bring assurance of salvation. That, God alone can grant—freely and without any falderal.* Although Luther maintained devotional exercises after

---

*In other works, Erikson systematically sets forth certain principles that are especially applicable to both Luther and the reader of *Table Talks*. One of these principles is that of the set of neurotic symptoms known as a "work paralysis." From ceaseless effort the

his break with Rome, he made them quite uncomplicated, contrasting strongly with his previous monkishness. For a time, he could continue to employ theological and devotional treatises like the *German Theology*, but eventually even it had to be cast aside. The one book which took the place of all others was the Bible, *the* classic of Christian devotion.

Calvin, possessing quite a different background and personality than Luther, did not have any earth-shattering spiritual experiences. Without fanfare, in 1532 he quietly slipped away from the Roman fold and identified himself with the reform movement then underway in France. As a leader of the Reformation in Switzerland after the publication of his *Institutes of the Christian Religion* in 1536, he centered the ecclesiastical reform of Geneva around religious education in theology and personal piety. After an initial rocky period as a result of which he and his associate in reform, William Farel, were expelled from Geneva, Calvin led Genevans in building a model Christian community. Personal faith, self-denial, prayer, meditation, good works, and perseverance became the key words in the vocabulary of the faithful. Public and private worship alike assumed the simple forms.

----

person becomes paralyzed in his motivation for any form of work. He falls exhausted, as did Luther. In connection with this, Erikson sets forth another principle of the "psychological moratorium" from the drive to achieve. This is a time of wandering, symbolized by the questing of Jesus in the Wilderness, the silent years of Paul in Arabia, and necessary as a time of respite from the imperial demands of an acquisitive society such as the one in which we live. The conception of justification by faith and not by works underlies these principles of Erikson. Nothing is required of us except trust, basic trust. God receives us, "just as we are."

The harrassed college student, the over-ambitious professional school student, the fretful and unhappy married couple—these need a time of respite from the imperial demands around them. This can be a time of prayer and meditation. This should be its core reason. As such, it can be a time of re-discovery of oneself, one's direction, and one's God.

Both Calvin and Luther, although by training academicians, were good pastors. It was in this pastoral role that they came nearest to producing devotional classics. Luther's *Table Talks,* letters, and sermons, for example, frequently opened a window and laid bare his soul. The *Table Talks,* discussions of various matters in the presence of friends and recorded by his students, circulated widely, satisfying the need of the Protestant faithful for spiritual guidance. Unfortunately the *Table Talks* were addressed to too many occasional matters to become classics. Today they have to be sifted, along with Luther's other writings and speeches, for the gems set among less precious stones.

Even before Luther's death in 1546 a kind of scholasticism, cast aside at the start of the reform movement in favor of a fresher approach to theology, began to revive. Preoccupation with theological preciseness dampened the spirit of Luther's pietism. By the end of the sixteenth century, caught up in constant religious wars as well, Lutheranism began to go downhill. In the seventeenth century, however, a revival of pietism occurred, fostered by the mystic Jacob Boehme. Subsequently all Protestant groups, reacting to the challenge of deism and the Enlightenment, reassessed the situation. From this reassessment came the most prolific flow of devotional classics in any comparable period of Christian history.

Selected Bibliography

Ignatius Loyola

The Spiritual Exercises. Translated by Anthony Mottola. (New York: Image Books, 1964.)

Rahner, Hugo, S. J. *The Spirituality of St. Ignatius Loyola.* Translated by Francis John Smith, S. J. (Westminster, Maryland: The Newman Press, 1953.)

Teresa of Avila

The Complete Works. Translated and edited by E. Allison Peers. 3 vols. (London and New York: Sheed and Ward, 1946.)

The Life of St. Teresa of Avila. Translated by David Lewis with an introduction by David Knowles. (London: Burns & Oates, 1962.)

John of the Cross

The Complete Works. Translated and edited by E. Allison Peers. 3 vols. (Westminster, Maryland: Newman Press, 1964.)

Frost, Bede. *Saint John of the Cross, 1542-1591: Doctor of Divine Love.* (London: Hodder & Stoughton, 1937.)

Reformation and Protestant Personal Piety

Luther, Martin. *Letters of Spiritual Counsel.* Vol. XVIII of *The Library of Christian Classics.* Edited and translated by Theodore G. Tappert. (Philadelphia: The Westminster Press, 1965.)

Bainton, Roland H. *Here I Stand: A Life of Martin Luther.* (New York & Nashville: Abingdon Press, 1950.)

―――. *The Reformation of the Sixteenth Century.* (Boston: Beacon Press, 1962.)

Bornkamm, Heinrich. *The Heart of Reformation Faith.* Translated with an introduction by John W. Doberstein. (New York, Evanston & London: Harper & Row, 1963.)

Herrmann, Wilhelm. *The Communion of the Christian with God.* Translated by J. S. Sandys Stanyon. 4th German ed. (London: Williams & Norgate, Ltd., 1930.)

THE CLASSICS OF THE AGE OF DEISM AND THE ENLIGHTENMENT

PART I: ROMAN CATHOLIC CLASSICS

Roman Catholic Personal Piety

Quietism and Jansenism

Francis de Sales' Introduction to the Devout Life

Pascal's Pensées

Brother Lawrence's The Practice of the Presence of God

VI

The Classics of The Age of Deism and The Enlightenment

Part I: Roman Catholic Classics

The two centuries bounded by the rise to power in England of the Stuart King James I (1603) and the beginning of the French Revolution (1789) gave birth to a veritable deluge of devotional classics. From the pens of Catholic faithful came such favorites as Francis de Sales' *Introduction to the Devout Life,* Brother Lawrence's *Practice of the Presence of God,* and Pascal's *Pensées;* from those of Protestants, Lancelot Andrewes' *Private Devotions,* Jeremy Taylor's *Holy Living* and *Holy Dying,* John Bunyan's *Grace Abounding* and *Pilgrim's Progress,* George Fox's *Journal,* Jakob Spener's *Pia Desideria,* William Law's *A Serious Call,* and John Woolman's *Journal*—all superb in depth of insight and unequaled in sheer numbers.

Behind this remarkable outpouring of religious literature lay an equally remarkable era of shifting and change in the foundation of European civilization and culture, less heralded but not surpassed in importance by the age of the Renaissance. Actually, this era saw the maturation of certain values which the Middle Ages and the Renaissance had spawned: In politics, the coming of age of nationalism; in economics, the death of feudalism and the birth of capitalism; in society, the rise to power of the middle classes; in science, the fuller application of rational-critical methodology; and in religion, the development of deism. Few sensitive

135

souls, whether within or outside of the Church, could have seen it as other than a disruptive and disquieting time. Fortunately for us, however, their agony produced some of the prize pearls of Christian devotional literature.

By the time of the Protestant Reformation the map of Europe had begun to undergo a dramatic redrawing. The Holy Roman Empire existed in name only. Out of the rubble rose two powerful new states as contenders for the mastery of Europe: Prussia under the rule of Frederick William I (1713-40) and Frederick the Great (1740-86) and Austria under the Hapsburgs. Russia loomed large on the eastern horizon as Ivan the Terrible (1533-84) welded the people into a rough but unitary mass, and then Peter the Great (1682-1725) and Catherine the Great (1762-96) turned their gaze westward. Portugal, once a leader in exploration, succumbed to the hegemony of Spain. Soon afterwards Spain, the majestic queen of the seas during the late fifteenth and early sixteenth centuries, saw her sun of glory sinking over the horizon as her powerful Armada suffered a crushing blow in 1588. The Dutch ascended for a time and took Spain's place as mistress of the seas, but their mastery proved shortlived. England, relishing the taste of power displayed in her victory over the Spanish fleet, put a crimp in the Dutch control of sea trade and finance. Through the use of economic sanctions against Dutch shipping, she enriched and emboldened her own fleet; through the use of her battle arm, she sealed her bid for mastery of the seas.

The remaining contender of great influence was France. Her star rocketed skyward under the brilliant but enigmatic chief minister of state under Louis XIII, Cardinal Richelieu (d. 1642). By playing one side against another during the Thirty Years' War (1618-48), he pushed France into the forefront of European politics. Louis XIV (1643-1715), in effect, built his gigantic edifice on the sturdy foundation laid by the Cardinal.

Apart from religious wars, the main bone of contention fought over by the great powers was their colonial holdings. Spain and

Portugal had placed their mark on South America early and then let their influence decline. France, England, and for a time Holland, struggled to be first to plant flags on other continents— Asia, Africa, and North America. Her powerful fleet gave England the edge eventually, so that she added most of North America and India to an already opulent treasury. She lost her richest prize, the American colonies, in the late eighteenth century, largely as a result of monarchical mismanagement; but even up to World War II, her holdings kept her at the top of great world powers.

While the major powers carried on their programs of imperialist expansion, they began to discover the *cost* in terms of economic and social revolution within. The social structure in these nations had not changed much since the Middle Ages, although feudalism had rotted away gradually for centuries. Society in general now consisted of two major classes—agrarian and mercantile. Marked contrasts existed within the framework of each. On the eve of the French Revolution, for example, French society consisted of the nobility on one extreme, the peasants and poor artisans on the other. The clergy formed a class of their own and identified first with one end of the spectrum, then with the other. But what was important for the Revolution was the growth of a new middle class, who took an intense interest in the maturation of their countries. Well educated, they refused to declare allegiance to king or church, except insofar as the performance and ideas of these served the national interest. They could forecast intuitively the disaster that lay ahead in continued oppression of the lower classes and in the inequality of the French monarchy. The geniuses among them—Rousseau, Voltaire, Diderot, D'Alembert—propounded a philosophy which would accord with the dignity of man. Under their tutorship the Renaissance and Reformation made a stride forward.

Intellectually, this movement is known as the Enlightenment. Sickened by constant conflict, oppression, inhumanity, poverty, and a multitude of other problems, its formulators appealed for

a reasonable or enlightened approach to all matters of life—
whether politics, economics, society, or religion. In human affairs,
for instance, reason would dictate doing what is best for the majority of the people. Accordingly, Rousseau drafted his brilliant
plan for a democratic society which insisted that all "are endowed
by their Creator with certain inalienable rights," among which
are "life, liberty, and the pursuit of happiness." In economics,
capitalism dominated, and the framers of the enlightened approach failed to provide adequately for regulation of economics
according to need and not simply by the law of tooth and claw.
A century later, economists sought to bring economic theory more
in line with the elsewhere rational approach of the Enlightenment.

In religion, the Enlightenment engendered deism. Deism, to
summarize briefly, substituted natural religion for revealed and
appealed to reason instead of the Scriptures as the basis for
doctrine or behavior. God, it was believed, has created a world
which operates according to certain natural laws, like a clock.
If man wishes to be happy, he must cooperate with these laws.
Reason, also a natural gift of God, helps us to discover the import
of natural law and to regulate our lives accordingly. In personal
behavior, therefore, I must let reason dictate my habits of eating,
sleeping, drinking, and so on. In social matters, I must do what
is best for the society of which I am a part. The rightness of any
act must be judged by its correspondence to reason rather than
by certain prejudices toward the literature of religion.*

----

*The psychologists of the era, such as John Locke, thought of the
human mind as being a depthless surface, like a sheet of white paper.
The senses—seeing, hearing, smelling, touching, and tasting—in-
scribed impressions upon the passive mind of man. Deeper levels
below the surface or higher levels above the surface of man's mind
were relegated to the trivial, the irrational, or the "animal" nature
of man. In other words, anything that was not rational was considered subhuman. This mood has prevailed in Western Christianity.
It affects our prayers. We assume that our less rational desires are

Such thinking had a profound impact on religion and church in the seventeenth and eighteenth centuries. An optimistic, this-worldly attitude, based on confidence in the upward evolution of man, undercut the role of the Church. In the Catholic countries the Jesuits, who had done a remarkable job of restoring the Church to power following the first wave of reform, met with criticism and then open resistance from the new intellectuals. The anti-religion wave caught them with full force. First Portugal (in 1759), then France (in 1762-64), then Spain (1767), and finally the kingdom of Naples (in 1768) demanded their with-drawal. So intense became the hostility to their activities that Pope Clement XIV issued a decree which authorized the sup-pression of the Society of Jesus in July, 1773; the order was not reinstated until the close of the French Revolution. The centuries of deism and the Enlightenment signaled the onset of an uncom-fortable time for religion.

Roman Catholic Personal Piety

In this difficult era Roman Catholic personal piety continued to follow traditional lines. The Council of Trent (1545-63) had laid these out with as much clarity as possible. Formulating a plan for more adequate instruction of the clergy, it charged the bishops to set in motion the program of revival discussed in Chapter V. The laity were to be obedient in all things to the Church, com-plying with the decisions and decrees reaffirmed or instituted at Trent. They were to observe faithfully prescriptions concern-ing foods, fasting, religious festivals, worship, and so on. "Heret-

---

beyond the reach of God's care. Yet, these very desires are given to us by God. He "satisfies our desires with good things," says the Psalmist. This note needs to be made at this juncture of the book by Dr. Hinson. The reader needs to ask himself in what ways the outlook of the Enlightenment is in deed and fact our own. For example, the deistic God is "far away" and the need for intimacy is a hunger and thirst of the person who prays. That person has an awareness of the need to feel that God is "with" him.

ical" books were taken out of their hands by placing them on an index of prohibited books.

The average Catholic thus followed a regimen very like that of his medieval counterpart. The Jesuits, burning with zeal to put the pope's house back in order, recorded noteworthy successes in France, Germany, and Spain, until the Enlightenment halted their efforts and brought a setback to the Church. Conducting retreats for the parish clergy and devout laymen, they set an example which bishops such as Francis de Sales of Geneva imitated with profit.

In the humanistic, this-worldly setting of the Enlightenment, the strategy of perceptive Catholic leaders was to deepen personal piety among the laity. Bishop de Sales' *Introduction to the Devout Life* had exactly that aim. Pious women responded readily to the guidance of the clergy. But men seem to have balked, some regarding the practice of personal devotion suited only to women or the effeminate. They attended public mass in a perfunctory fashion, with no enthusiasm for what they felt constrained to do. When nationalistic pressures toppled the Jesuits in 1773, Catholic piety reached an all time low. New orders, for example, the Order of the Sacred Heart, the Passionists, and the Redemptorists, sprang up and sought to pump new life into a dying Church. All three orders were devoted to the mission of restoring the faithful to the fervor of an earlier era. Try as they might, however, they could do little to repair the damage inflicted by the assault of liberalism. The monastic orders shrank, universities disappeared, and the papacy lost its temporal power. Catholicism was on the wane.

Quietism and Jansenism

Meanwhile, two leftist religious movements, which the Church felt obliged to squelch, arose. One of these was an outgrowth of Spanish mystical piety called "Quietism." The originator was a Spanish priest named Michael Molinos (1640?-1697), who helped to initiate a revival of religion in Spain and received numerous honors from Pope Innocent XI. In his major book, *The Spiritual Guide,* Molinos called for concentration on prayer, disregard of external images and acts, and the abandonment of extreme asceticism. His proposals soon aroused the opposition of the Jesuits. Through the influence of Louis XIV of France, they managed to haul him before the Inquisition and to have him condemned as the propagator of a heresy. Unlike Teresa and John of the Cross, whose views he advanced, Molinos refused to bow to the ceremonialism and external machinery of the Church and these crushed him.

The theology and methods of Teresa and John of the Cross found their way into France via the Carmelites. There, too, it bore fruit in the quietism of Madame Guyon (1648-1717), who also borrowed heavily from Molinos. A woman of noble birth; an unhappy marriage increased the religious sensitivities of Madame Guyon. Through the practice of rigid asceticism, she discovered "the prayer of interior silence." Judging this to be the substance of the religious life, she inculcated a worship of passivity and self-abandonment, akin to Quaker worship, which incurred censure by Church officials and earned her a stay in an ecclesiastical prison.* Among forty volumes which she wrote, the most famous is *A Short and Easy Method of Prayer.* It was her good fortune to be defended by Francis Fénelon, tutor of Louis XIV's grandson and the Archbishop of Cambrai. He, too, wrote works on Christian piety, notably *Christian Perfection,* but propounded a moderate type of mystical theology.

The other trend in mystical theology, occurring simultaneously with the first, harked back to Augustinian theology. Its first exponent was a professor of Scripture at the University of Louvain,

---

*Here again we see the role of the imprisonment of people on the development of a "prayer life of interior silence." The days of political prisoners, prisoners of belief, are not over yet. Could it be that out of this is being generated right now the kind of spirit of worship with which all the bound spirits of mankind can feel akin?

Michael Baius, whose neo-Augustinianism the Church condemned in 1567 and 1579. Subsequently, the same theology received fuller exposition in a book titled *Augustinus,* the work of Cornelius Jansen, Professor of Scripture at Louvain and Bishop of Ypres (1635-38), published posthumously in 1639. Stressing the role of grace in salvation in Protestant fashion, Jansen attacked with fervor the Society of Jesus, the practice of frequent communion, and the sacrament of penance without emphasis on contrition. Despite condemnation of the *Augustinus* in 1641 and 1642, the influence of Jansenism spread widely, supported even by leading French clergy, notwithstanding further denunciation by Pope Clement XI in 1705. The center for its propagation was the famous convent at Port Royal, where Blaise Pascal took sides against the Jesuits and became the leading proponent of the Augustinian approach.

From both orthodox and unorthodox sources came some religious classics. Francis de Sales' *Introduction to the Devout Life* represented the orthodox approach to the problems jointly posed by Protestantism and the Enlightenment, Pascal's *Pensées,* the Augustinian approach of an intellectual, and Brother Lawrence's *Practice of the Presence of God,* a red-tape-cutting approach devised by a simple but devout lay monk. Although other books have nourished the Catholic faithful and could be considered classics, these three together embrace the main shades of devotional thought in the age of deism and the Enlightenment.

Francis de Sales'
Introduction to the Devout Life

Author. Francis de Sales heads the list of Catholic bishops in whom, as Philip Hughes has said, "the French renaissance is baptized and humanism becomes devout."[1] Born at Thoren in the duchy of Savoy on August 21, 1567 of aristocratic parents, he studied rhetoric, philosophy, the classics, and Hebrew at Clermont College, Paris, under the Jesuits (1583-88). A special interest in theology possessed him, however, and, while a student in Paris, he experienced an extended period of depression regarding the question of predestination.* This experience led to a vow of chastity and consecration to the Virgin Mary. He continued his studies in civil and canon law at Padua under the Jesuit Father Antoine Possevin, where he obtained the doctorate in 1591. The next year he was appointed Provost of the Chapter of Geneva.

In 1594 the new provost began the evangelization of the predominantly Protestant area near Geneva, Le Chablais. He had modest success among the peasants and nobility and even attempted, but without avail, to convert Theodore Beza, Calvin's successor as patriarch of Geneva. This moderate first effort led him to advocate forcible conversion of Protestants in Le Chablais in 1597. His abilities as a Catholic apologist procured an appointment as coadjutor to Claude de Granier, Bishop of Geneva. Two years later and upon the death of de Granier in 1602, he was consecrated Bishop of Geneva.

He immediately set in motion a general religious reform, patterned perhaps on the Calvinistic reform of the previous

---

*Occasionally a psychiatrist will mention that certain kinds of depression are "the religious man's emotional disorder." Out of the depths of depression have come some of the new bursts of the Spirit in the life of contemporary religious leaders. H. Wheeler Robinson wrote the magnificent book, *The Christian Experience of the Holy Spirit,* upon having fallen into a period of great discouragement and debilitating despair. E. Stanley Jones speaks of having come to the end of his resources and, jaded in spirit, discovered the power of the Living Christ. Out of this came such books as *Christ of the Indian Road,* etc. Harry Emerson Fosdick rediscovered the depths of prayer after a breakdown of his emotional resources. Out of it came his handbook of prayer. The injunction of Ecclesiastes 11:8 is a guide for the person who takes prayer seriously: ". . . if a man lives many years, let him rejoice in them all; but let him remember that the days of darkness will be many." The dark night of the soul is, apparently, the time when the God of both the darkness and the light appears most vividly.

century, which involved the catechetical instruction of all the faithful. Together with Jane Frances de Chantal, he founded in 1607 the Institute of the Visitation of the Blessed Virgin for young girls and widows who had a religious calling. An excellent preacher, he made a profound impact on the Church in France and elsewhere. He died December 27, 1622, shortly after moving to Lyons with the Court of Savoy. Pope Alexander VII canonized him in 1665; Pius IX declared him a Doctor of the Universal Church in 1887, an honor reserved to a very few.

The Book. Bishop de Sales' *Introduction to the Devout Life,* first published in 1609, represents a superlative example of the deliberate application of the Jesuit method, the Ignatian spirituality, to the cultivation of Christian devotion for someone living "in the world."[2] De Sales himself made clear in the preface that he wrote for those who led "an ordinary life" and even considered undertaking a devout life impossible.* "I will show them," he vowed in his characteristically picturesque style, "that a strong and resolute person may live in the world without being tainted by it, find spiritual springs amid its salt waters and fly through the flames of temptation without burning the wings on which they soar to God."[3] Having composed his spiritual directions at the request of a certain Madame de Charmoisy, whose husband, ambassador of the Duke of Savoy, was a relative, he submitted them to a publisher at the urging of another spiritual director, Father Jean Fourier. The latter's belief that they might help others far exceeded anyone's expectations, for the *Introduction* immediately became a favorite of Catholics and remained so in succeeding centuries.

----

*Ministers today who have been educated thoroughly in the principles of dynamic psychology are expressing the same need DeSales felt: a guide for the prayers of "ordinary life" kinds of people. Malcolm Boyd's little book, *Are You Running With Me Jesus?* is an example of this.

The book's success was due in large measure to de Sales' simple, lucid, yet vivid style, capped off by a remarkable ability to employ rich and illuminating illustrations or quotations at exactly the right spot. There is nothing startling or out of the way in his proposals for attaining the devout life. On the contrary, the Bishop confesses repeatedly his dependence on Ignatius Loyola, Bernard of Clairvaux, Augustine, and a host of other saints. The book is shot through with allusions to the massive tradition of Christian devotion from Jesus to Loyola.

The Introduction's five major sections offer advice concerning the embracing of the devout life, prayer and the sacraments, the practice of virtue, overcoming temptations, and the renewal and preservation of devotion. The heartbeat of the whole work is the firm conviction that every man can live a life of devotion, if he wills to do so with zeal; in fact, de Sales believed, whoever truly loves God *will* do so. Wisely, however, he distinguished between the life of devotion demanded of the "religious" (monks or nuns) and clerics and that demanded of those living in the world. God, he notes, evaluates our devotion in terms of our vows. No one should be discouraged if he cannot practice the same virtues as a monk or cleric; God expects of him what he *can* perform.

The life of devotion begins with the severing of ties (purgation) with mortal and venial sin, with useless and dangerous things, and with evil inclinations by means of a series of meditations, confession, and resolution. This accomplished, the heart is ready for communion with God through prayer and meditation. The Bishop recommends with particular emphasis the practice of mental prayer, "a lost art in our age." This prayer requires one to place himself first in God's presence and ask His help. Moreover, one must perform his spiritual acts and resolutions with zest, not thwarted by dryness in prayer, a problem all sometimes face. Besides prayer, offered with regularity and enthusiasm, true devotion is stirred by taking communion frequently, attending

Church, invoking the saints, reading the Scriptures or classics of devotion, and doing other acts which show one's zeal.

De Sales' advice regarding the practice of virtue shows much common sense. "Virtues differ according to our state of life," he comments repeatedly. One's station will obviously affect the authenticity of his actions, therefore. One ought never to deal too severely with himself. "One of the best exercises of gentleness is to be patient with ourselves and our imperfections," he insists.* Perfection in virtue lies beyond the reach of all, although all may aspire to it. The best advice is to act reasonably, for "we are human beings because we have reason." Temptations will naturally occur, but they can be resisted by concentrating on the cultivation of positive virtues. "An act of the love of God," de Sales observes, "is the surest weapon against temptations great and small; for the love of God contains to an eminent degree the perfection of all the virtues and is the most perfect remedy for vice."[4] As surely as a clock must be rewound, so the true believer needs periodically to take stock of himself and and renew his

---

*One of the first books in pastoral counseling in the present day definition of that word was by Rollo May, entitled *The Art of Counseling*. He addressed himself to the topic of having "the courage of imperfection." He resonates well with de Sales' spiritual instruction of his readers here. The Apostle Paul undergirds the whole idea in Galatians 6 when he urges us to be patient with those who are overtaken in any fault and to look to ourselves, "lest we also be tempted." Gerald Heard once said that the secret of patience with others is a sense of humor about ourselves. The subtle psychology of this wisdom points to a basic perceptual problem. The accurate perception of reality requires that we maintain perspective, clear and clean. Doing this is a form of prayer. The request for *perspective* that comes from God is the heartiest prayer of all. This we can do in the spirit of I John 3:19: "By this we shall know that we are of the truth, and reassure our hearts before him; for God is greater than our hearts, and he knows everything." If we had God's knowledge, our perspective would be complete and the divine joy would be ours, a laughter of love and not a laughter of cynicism.

resolution. He must scrutinize his behavior towards God, self, and fellow man, then renew his devotion by considering the excellence of his soul, the excellence of the virtues, the example of the saints, Christ's love for us, and God's eternal love for us. In this way he will continue in the life of devotion.

With old insights and truths about the Christian's devotional life stated with such freshness and clarity, it is small wonder the book became a classic. The Bishop had created the kind of manual of piety which would stimulate any Christian to a firmer resolve in prayer. His impact can be seen stamped not only on Catholic devotion, but just as ineradicably on William Law's *A Serious Call to a Devout and Holy Life* and, through him, on John Wesley and the vast throng of us who owe a debt to the latter's zeal for gospel holiness.

Pascal's Pensées

The author. Only a year separated de Sales and Pascal, but their approaches to Christian devotion stood centuries and worlds apart. Perhaps this was due in part to Pascal's family heritage. His paternal grandfather, Martin, for example, had tried Protestantism briefly, but abjured this view after the massacre of St. Bartholomew's Day in 1572. His father, too, an aristocrat of aristocrats, had an independent turn of mind. Thoroughly imbued with humanism, he was both anti-monastic and ardently nationalistic (Gallican). Not inaccurately, Jean Mesnard charged that "Étienne Pascal did not do much to incline them (his children) towards piety, but that his own bent of mind prepared them to sympathize with some of the tendencies of the Jansenist movement."[5]

In the case of a genius of Pascal's rank, however, one must not give too much credit to any single formative factor. Pascal was an extremely complex man. The third of four children born to Étienne Pascal and Antoinette Bégon, he suffered ill health from the start. His mother died when he was three, leaving the unenviable task of rearing three children (the first child died in infancy) to her husband. In 1631, Blaise's eighth year, the Pascal's moved from Clermont, his birthplace, to Paris. The youth obtained his education at the hands of his brilliant mathematician father, who did not wish to risk sending him to public schools.* As a tutor, the latter followed the plan of teaching Blaise a certain subject after he had passed the age when such instruction normally would begin. This, he thought, would keep him always straining at the leash, so to speak. But the prodigious child second-guessed his father in this. When Étienne refused to teach him geometry until age 15 or 16, Blaise taught himself at age 12. At sixteen he wrote an advanced *Treatise on Conics*.

This genius, of course, was enhanced by rubbing shoulders with the intellectual elite of France during these years. The Pascal children saw the great come and go from their home with regularity. The influence of their father reached a peak when, after a year's hiding as a result of his ardent opposition to Cardinal Richelieu's policies regarding finance, Richelieu forgave him

---

*The instruction of highly creative personalities by their own fathers is an event in Pascal's life as was true in the lives of other men, some of whom also did not consider the schools around them adequate to meet their children's real needs for individual attention. The father of Soren Kierkegaard, as well as William James' father, had a heavy hand in the formal education of their sons. Similarly, John Stuart Mill had this experience. The farmer, for example, can teach his son his own work in a way that the traveling businessman cannot. Pascal's rebellion appears in *showing* his father that he could learn geometry without him! This was a very different kind of rebellion from that of Luther, Francis of Assisi, and others.

The father who takes the devotional life seriously wonders how to communicate this to his sons and daughters. A day to day concern with their school work that is not restricted to their report cards is one way of expressing a consecrated interest. Exploration with them of things *not ordinarily included in the school curriculum* is another. Prayer has its wellsprings in fellowship. What better place for this to take place than between father and son?

and appointed him finance minister of Normandy in 1639. This appointment inspired Blaise, with his father's encouragement, to design and produce a calculating machine, which would alleviate the burden of the tax man.

Blaise Pascal's religious pilgrimage hardly got started during these years. When it did, it proceeded via a route laid out by Cornelius Jansen. The reading of Jansen's *Disquisition on the Reformation of the Inner Man,* in fact, precipitated Pascal's so-called "first conversion." Together with his whole family, he entered into a period of religious unrest and self-scrutiny. For about three years, 1643-46, he concentrated on the reading of the Bible, Augustine, Bernard of Clairvaux, and others. A three month period of recuperation for Étienne in 1645 gave occasion for the brilliant family to trouble the waters even more.

Blaise resumed his scientific studies in 1646. Experiments concerning the problem of vacuum consumed much of his time during the next four years. In the meantime, several incidents intervened to assure that religious questions never vanished entirely from his thinking. One was the publication by a Capuchin monk named Jacques Forton of a work on *The Conduct of Natural Judgment,* which asserted the complete concord of faith and reason; Pascal disagreed violently. At about the same time Blaise's health declined. He suffered migraine headaches, stomach pains, and paralysis of the legs—symptoms perhaps of the beginning of a cancer or intestinal tuberculosis.[6] He sought solace and direction by going to hear sermons by the Abbot of Port Royal, M. Singlin. Meanwhile, his brilliant younger sister, Jacqueline, had decided to enter the convent at Port Royal, but could not gain her father's consent. Then, to cap off a series of disturbing events, on September 24, 1651, Étienne Pascal died.

At this stage Pascal must have stood on the brink of despair, lonely and uncertain. His religious ardor cooled a bit. He and Jacqueline, who had entered Port Royal after her father's death, had a tiff over their inheritance, the latter wishing her portion as a dowry to be given to the convent, Blaise wishing it for himself. Actually, in the midst of these confusing circumstances, Blaise entered into the "worldly" period of his life, which explains why he needed the money from Jacqueline's inheritance. Striking up an acquaintance with Antoine Gombaud, a friend of Balzac, he obtained a quick lesson in self-understanding. Gombaud introduced him to Montaigne, rationalist and critic of religion. Pascal may even have had some ·sort of love affair, though this is questionable.*[7]

Despite his wavering, however, the young genius held on with a tenuous faith—perhaps himself the *automaton* driven along by custom until he could gain assurance. On the night of November 23, 1654, the assurance came in that unparalleled experience which he so carefully recorded in the *Memorial*. Through the fire of self-purgation Pascal came to the fire of love. He knew for a certainty the God of Abraham, Isaac, Jacob . . . the God of Jesus Christ. Now, he who had found his inquiring mind previously so untameable, always asking why, found himself submitting at last. The untameable was tamed by the discovery that "He is not found except by the means taught in the Gospel," and that "He is kept only by the means taught in the Gospel." What means? "Total and sweet renunciation. Total submission to Jesus

---

*The loss of his father and the alienation from his sister thrust Pascal back upon resources that could not be shaken. Bereavement will teach us that dependence upon other human beings is at best a *proximate* and not an ultimate dependence. We cannot genuinely become interdependent upon others without first becoming independent of them. Yet, this calls for a shaking of the idolatries that hold us in order that the hold of the real God may be evident. One of the advantages of the school system which Pascal's father decried is that it breaks the parental hold gradually and not all of a sudden as does death. One of the advantages of organized religion is just here, also. Yet, for Pascal, it came in one blow.

The important truth we can learn here is that bereavements are times of germination of the new need for God. Here one learns to "call no man father" but only God and to rely, not even on one's grief, but upon the grace of God.

Christ and to my director." To what end? "Eternally in joy in return for a day's striving on earth."*

The last years of Pascal's life were controversial ones. He nearly exhausted himself in debate with the Jesuits regarding the doctrine of grace. From the point of view of his Augustinian bias they were Pelagians, though he was himself careful to avoid the pitfall of Calvinism. In his famous *Provincial Letters,* composed with the encouragement and assistance of his Port Royal friends between the years 1656 and 1658, he attacked the Jesuits with rapier thrusts at their moral casuistry and with a defense of Jansenism against charges of Calvinism and the calumny of the Jesuits. Invigorated by his success in this regard, in 1658 he began to jot down brief notes in preparation of an apology for Christianity, the *Pensées,* occasionally finishing parts to be read to friends. He also wrote during this period his letters of spiritual counsel to Mademoiselle de Roannez, with whom some have linked him romantically, his *Écrits sur la Grâce,* and educational and scientific treatises.

---

*Pascal is spoken of as an existential contemplative. He is directly related to the existential movement in contemporary psychology and philosophy. Probably one of the most significant ways in which he is related is in his enablement of the worshiper to recognize that sin is not always a conscious thought or act, but lies in the depths of the unconscious of man. As David Roberts says, "Men are attracted to it (sin) in ways which often lie outside consciousness and reflection. . . . Pascal was a forerunner of existentialism because he begins with the human situation as viewed within. . . . Moreover Pascal was a forerunner of *Christian* existentialism, because he believes that man's confidence in his own self-sufficiency must be shattered and a sense of need awakened before the Christian message of forgiveness can be presented meaningfully." (David Roberts, *Existentialism and Religious Belief.* New York: Oxford University Press, 1957, p. 35.)

The reader will find the mood of Pascal and the modern psychologist in what has been called the "mood of insufficiency" found in Psalm 139. As O. T. Binkley has said, the person who feels perfectly adequate as a Christian has not found what being a Christian is, yet.

Late in 1658 or early in 1659 the frail genius fell seriously ill. His health improved momentarily in 1660, but he still felt weak. Retiring from active controversy after a serious split with his Port Royal friends, who had signed a document condemning Jansenism, he applied himself increasingly to care of the poor. He secured money for their needs, visited in their homes, and even took one child into his own home. He adopted an austere personal regimen. Though friends came to visit, he avoided "attachment" and "frivolity." During his illness Pascal composed his "Prayer Asking God for Good Use of His Illness." This *Prayer,* unparalleled for its insight, exposed the very heart of Pascal:

. . . Illness no more than health,
neither discourses nor books,
neither your Sacred Scriptures, nor your Gospel,
neither your holiest mysteries,
neither alms nor fasts,
neither mortifications nor miracles,
neither the use of the Sacraments nor the sacrifice of your Body,
can do anything at all to bring about my conversion,
unless you accompany all those things
with the wholly extraordinary help of your grace.[8]

Pascal died August 19, 1662 at Paris, thirty-nine years of age. He died as he had learned to live, wholly dependent upon the God of Grace.

The book. As indicated above, the *Pensées* consists only of notes jotted down by Pascal in preparation for a defense of Christianity to atheists and agnostics. Unfortunately, Pascal did not live to complete it. Rather, he left behind a pile of "thoughts," some of which are clear, but many of which could be interpreted with certainty only if one knew the complete pattern of Pascal's complex thinking. Later generations of scholars have made numerous suggestions regarding their author's intended plan and have arranged and rearranged the notes in a multitude of different ways.

Despite this, nevertheless, the general trend of the work seems unmistakable. And, notwithstanding our inability to fathom the *plan* of the book in detail, the main substance still speaks clearly and powerfully to those to whom Pascal intended to direct his apology.[9]

Certain reflections in the notes seem to indicate that Pascal planned first to undermine the stance of the agnostic or atheistic critic of Christianity and then to offer "proofs" of the Christian religion. The first part could be titled, therefore, "Disturbing Man's Complacency," the second part, "Leading the Disturbed Man to God."* Accordingly, a large number of fragments point up the wretchedness of man without the knowledge of God brought to him in Christianity. Christian faith teaches two things, Pascal affirms repeatedly, which sets it apart from all other religions: "that there is a God whom men are capable of knowing, and that there is an element of corruption in themselves which renders them unworthy of Him." Both must be held together. To know God we must understand ourselves and to understand self we must know God.[10] Though we, as men, can "recognize God

---

*The *disturbed* person is the concern of the contemporary pastoral counselor. The pioneer of these pastoral counselors is Anton Boisen, a minister who learned to respect the disturbed person from having been deeply disturbed to the point of open psychotic episodes. In his book, *The Exploration of the Inner World,* he distinguishes the disturbed persons from each other by saying that some of them are *malignantly* disturbed in that they have adopted their disturbance as a way of life. Others, he says, are suffering from benign disturbances in that their disturbance is an attempt to discover a solution of the dilemma of their existence before God. These persons, he said, are struggling with matters of life and death in a feverish attempt to find the divine revealing of their redemption. They are characterized by concern, humility, and hunger for wholeness. He wrote the whole story of his life in a modern classic of devotion, *Out of the Depths.* He would agree with Pascal wholeheartedly in the statement that we cannot know Jesus Christ without knowing both God and our own wretchedness.

clearly without recognizing our own wretchedness, and vice versa," we "cannot know Jesus Christ without knowing both God and our own wretchedness."[11]

Nature can tell us only that God hides Himself. We can escape from the darkness through Jesus Christ, however. If man would find himself, therefore, he must submit in humble obedience to the God of Abraham, Isaac, Jacob—yes, the God of Jesus Christ. So long as he looks for the God of the philosophers and scholars, he will have no light. Pascal, of course, knew very well how hard it was for the intellectual to bend the knees of his mind on this point. Had he himself not experienced the same arduous struggle? In answer to this problem, he set forth his famous "Wager Argument." Christians, he concedes, cannot prove the existence of the God they believe exists. By reason, we cannot defend either the proposition that God exists or that He does not exist. Thus, we must gamble. Whoever bets that God is, Pascal reasons, takes the least risk. For if we bet that God exists and it turns out that He does not exist, we have lost nothing. But if we bet that He does not exist and it turns out that He does, we have lost everything in terms of happiness, the end of life.[12]

The Christian journey, then, begins with submission. Reason follows. Doubt, submission, and reason are all necessary to life. But each has its proper place and time. "We must be able to doubt when necessary, to be certain when necessary, submitting ourselves when necessary," contends Pascal.[13] Once a man has made the initial act of submission, however, certain "proofs" regarding the Christian religion will assume importance for him. For Pascal the stoutest of these consist in the gospel's accurate assessment of man's nature and in the fulfillment of prophecy. "No other [religion]," he argues, "has recognized that man is the most excellent of creatures." And while some realize man's baseness, they have neglected his greatness.[14] Christianity alone among the world's religions, therefore, has been able to see man as he really is and thence to cure his ills. By the "simplicity of the Gospel" it cures at once reason's pride and nature's corruption.

For it teaches the righteous, whom it raises even to the point of sharing in divinity, that in this sublime condition they still carry about with them the source of all corruption, which makes them subject throughout their lives to error, misery, death and sin; while it proclaims to the most ungodly that they are capable of their Redeemer's grace. Thus the Christian religion, causing those whom it justifies to tremble, and consoling those whom it condemns, so justly tempers fear with hope, through the twofold capacity for grace and sin which is common to all, that it humbles men infinitely more than reason alone can do, but without causing them to despair, and it exalts them infinitely more than natural pride, but without puffing them up.*[15]

Fulfillment of prophecy also sustains the claims of the Church. The Christian Scriptures alone are reliable and suited to all men because of their teachings. In accordance with his discovery that God is found and kept only by the means taught in the gospel, Pascal devoted endless hours to study of the Bible. His superb intellect enabled him to do this critically, though far in advance of modern critical studies. At a rather sophisticated level, he apparently planned a massive case for Christianity based upon the Scriptures in which he saw fulfillment of prophecy as the key.

---

*A perceptive psychiatrist, Andras Angyal, in his book, *Neurosis and Treatment,* sets forth a principle which is remarkably expressed in Pascal's words quoted above. He calls this the principle of Universal Ambiguity. We are never completely well or completely sick, but in varying states of health-unhealth at all times. Put in Paul's terms, one who thinks he stands must take heed lest he fall. The person who thinks he is totally lost, must take heed lest he be on the verge of his redemption. Pascal's terms put this much more clearly than do Angyal's, but the two men's thoughts are highly compatible. The words of the gospel song put it well:

> 'Twas grace that taught my heart to fear;
> 'Twas grace my fears relieved.

Therefore, we fall upon the element of paradox in life. We find ourselves praying for a *simple,* non-ambiguous life. But, as Paul Tillich says, the *un*ambiguous life can only be approximated and never realized except in Ultimate participation in the Spirit. We pray, prophesy, and speak in part.

Through Jesus Christ alone can one know God and self. Through the Scriptures one can know Jesus Christ.

Pascal's great insight coincides in the final analysis with Augustine's in more than externals. How very like Augustine's "O eternal God, let me know myself. Let me know you,"[16] is Pascal's "recovery of man's wholeness," as Albert N. Wells has phrased it. These intellectual giants knew well man's baseness and his greatness. They, in fact, framed a healthy Christian humanism, which may offer a potent word to the modern humanist and rationalist. Their ever-recurrent challenge is: If you would find the meaning of life, you must look to Jesus Christ, the clue both to the meaning of personal existence and to the meaning of reality. None has phrased it better than Pascal himself:

Not only do we know God through Jesus Christ alone, but we do not even know ourselves except through Jesus Christ. We understand life and death only through Jesus Christ. Apart from Jesus Christ we know not what is our life, or our death, or God, or what we ourselves are.*[17]

Brother Lawrence's The Practice of the Presence of God

The author. It is a refreshing experience to turn from the complex, often puzzling writings of Pascal or the ornate, polished style of Bishop de Sales to the straightforward, avowedly simple conversations and letters of Nicholas Hermann, Brother Lawrence. Unfortunately, we know all too little abut this humble lay

---

*The pastoral counselor is called upon for "the answers" to people's problems. A few of the simpler ones can be so given. But the really great questions would require that he "play God" to try to answer them. Each time he tries, his answers are not enough. He must try harder. Then he fails. Then he is rejected as being of no help, if indeed he has let himself move out of the position of being a "man of like passions with all other men." Thus, people fail in their attempts to turn him into a phony "Christ." In the process of his confession, they are prompted to face themselves as weak and

brother in the Order of Carmelites. His thoughts, preserved by his friend Monsieur Beaufort, Cardinal de Noailles and Grand Vicar to Monsieur de Chalons, provide only fragmentary biographical data. Apparently, he was of humble parentage, and before entering the Carmelite convent in Paris in 1666, he served as a footman. Crippled and a self-confessed "great awkward fellow who broke everything," he was converted at age 18, when

> . . . in the winter, seeing a tree stripped of its leaves, and considering that within a little time the leaves would be renewed, and after that the flowers and fruit appear, he received a high view of the providence and power of God, which has never since been effaced from his soul.[18]

This vision, he went on to say, "set him loose from the world, and kindled in him such a love for God that he could not tell whether it had increased during the more than forty years he had lived since."[19]

Brother Lawrence became a cook in his convent. His serenity in the midst of often irksome activities earned him the admiration of his fellow monks, and his fame stretched far beyond the Parisian kitchen. Friends near and far sought his counsel concerning their religious problems. Such contacts probably helped to temper a bit the drudgery of his daily chores. But they meant far less than the profound discovery Brother Lawrence had made about life in general, namely, the practice of the presence of God. This discovery turned pain and suffering into joy and tedium into a blessing. Eighty years of life, despite an admixture of

---

sinful men. Their unreal need for him to be God in human form introduces them to their real need for the real Christ, who is in deed and fact God become man. In Him we meet our true humanity and discover God revealed.

From this point of view, the person who uses this book as a guide for his prayers can ask to what extent is he or she looking to some religious authority to take the place of Christ in their lives? In Christ we can come to understand ourselves and to know God.

miseries, held an abundance of pleasure in the knowledge that
God shares fully the agony of human life.*

The book. Brother Lawrence relates in one letter how he made
his remarkable discovery. After entering the monastery at the age
of forty, he says, he had tried the traditional methods of seeking
God, but these had not worked. For ten years he suffered anxiety
and apprehension about his devotion. His spirit rose and fell. He
doubted whether he might be saved. But suddenly in an experience surprisingly like that of Luther, he experienced a change.
"I found myself changed all at once"; he confesses, "and my

---

*As I read this paragraph, I was caused to think of the use of the
hands in relation to the focus of attention upon the reality of God.
The menial tasks of life can be learned with the same kind of
automatic precision that *touch*-typing is learned. The eyes are freed
while the fingers "see" the keys for the eyes. The higher function of
reading is set free as the lower function of the fingers become disciplined. The brain *seems* to be stimulated to higher activity and to
more precision by the exercise of *manual* skills. This is why at Kirk-
ridge Retreat at Stroudsburg, Pennsylvania, the people who go there
for spiritual renewal are expected to work *with their hands* as a part
of spiritual discipline. The Iona Community practices the same discipline, as do the Trappist monks.

Brother Lawrence, in his *Practice of the Presence of God,* sets his
prayers to the music of the pots and pans. The housewife will find
this an aid to prayer. The kitchen prayers—from those of the devout
housewife to those of the irate soldier on K.P. duty—are consecrated
in the wisdom of Brother Lawrence.

As a minister-teacher, I have times of unproductive doldrums of
spirit as I search for some new revealing of the Spirit. I have found
that to clean a basement room, to paint a door, to fix a bothersome
piece of tile in the kitchen releases many unaccustomed sources of
thought and revelation. Why let the world of abstraction drive us to
distraction and then be sent to someone's occupational therapy de-
partment in somebody's hospital? The hands . . . the brain . . . the
prayer . . . they must be connected some way or other. I think so.

soul, which till that time was in trouble, felt a profound inward peace, as if she were in her center and place of rest."[20] What he discovered in essence was what John Tauler and Henry Suso had preached—the primacy of "simple faith." He resigned himself wholly to God's will. His anxieties and tensions vanished "because I have no will but that of God, which I endeavor to accomplish in all things, and to which I am so resigned that I would not take up a straw from the ground against His order, or from any other motive than purely that of love to Him."[21]

The key to Brother Lawrence's philosophy, then, is God-centeredness. His only "method" was to remain attentive to the presence of God, as his conversations and letters affirm again and again. God, he believed, could be experienced as readily in the kitchen, among the pots and pans, as in the Church while taking the Eucharist. He writes:

I have quitted all forms of devotion and set prayers but those to which my state obliges me. And I make it my business only to persevere in His holy presence, wherein I keep myself by a simple attention, and a general fond regard to God, which I may call an *actual presence* of God; or, to speak better, an habitual, silent, and secret conversation of the soul with God, which often causes me joys and raptures inwardly, and sometimes also outwardly, so great that I am forced to use means to moderate them and prevent their appearance to others.[22]

All prayer, therefore, should involve attention to God's presence; this, as utterly uncomplicated as it is, is all that is necessary. Over and over again, Brother Lawrence restates the point: We must recognize that God is intimately present with us, address Him every moment, and beg His assistance in everything that we do. Stung by charges of passivism, delusion, and self-love, the monk admitted the first but vehemently denied the other two. The soul which is attractive to God cannot love itself, and that which enjoys God cannot be deluded because it desires nothing but Him. "If this be delusion in me," he adds, "it belongs to God to remedy it."[23]

The Practice of the Presence of God sounds amazingly evangelical. "God has many ways of drawing us to Himself," Brother Lawrence points out. "He sometimes hides Himself from us; but *faith* alone, which will not fail us in time of need, ought to be our support, and the foundation of our confidence, which must be all in God."[24] When one trusts God with his whole heart, suffering will not cast him down; rather, it "will become full of unction and consolation." To arrive at this state is difficult, for it requires an act of pure faith. "But though it is difficult, we know also that we can do all things with the grace of God, which He never refuses to them who ask it earnestly."[25]

In Pascal and Brother Lawrence the Catholic wheel turned full circle toward the Protestant concept of piety. In their Protestant contemporaries the Protestant wheel also made the full cycle toward Catholicism. In both instances the time was ripe for the revolution.

Selected Bibliography

Quietism

Bigelow, John. *Molinos the Quietist.* (New York: Chas. Scribner's Sons, 1882.)

Upham, T. *The Life of Madame Guyon.*

Fénelon, Francois. *Christian Perfection.* Edited by Charles F. Whiston. Translated by M. W. Stillman. (New York and London: Harper & Bros., 1947.)

Sanders, E. K. *Fénelon, His Friends and His Enemies,* 1651-1715. (London, New York, and Bombay: Longmans, Green & Co., 1901.)

Jansenism

Abercrombie, Nigel. *The Origins of Jansenism.* (Oxford: The Clarendon Press, 1936.)

Piéclin, Edmond, and E. Jarry. *Les luttes politiques et doctrinales aux XVIIᵉ et XVIIIᵉ siécles. (Paris: Bloud & Gay,* 1956.)

Francis de Sales

Introduction to the Devout Life. Translated by Michael Day, Cong. Orat. (London: J. M. Dent & Sons, Ltd.; New York: E. P. Dutton & Co., Inc., 1961.)

On the Love of God. Translated with an introduction and notes by John K. Ryan. 2 vols. (Garden City, New York: Image Books, 1963.)

Charmot, Francois. *Ignatius Loyola and Francis de Sales: Two Masters, One Spirituality.* Translated by Sister M. Nenell. (St. Louis: B. Herder, 1966.)

Henry-Coüannier, Maurice. *Francis de Sales and His Friends.* Translated by Veronica Morrow. (Staten Island, New York: Alba House, 1964.)

Kleinman, Ruth. *Saint Francois de Sales and the Protestants.* (Geneva: E. Droz, 1962.)

Trouncer, Margaret. *The Gentleman Saint: St. Francois de Sales and His Times,* 1567-1622. (London: Hutchinson of London, 1963.)

Blaise Pascal

Pensées: Notes on Religion and Other Subjects. Edited with an introduction and notes by Louis Lafuma. Translated by John Warrington. (London: J. M. Dent & Sons, Ltd.; New York: E. P. Dutton & Co., Inc., 1960.)

The Provincial Letters. Translated by Thomas McCrie. (New York: Robert Carter & Bros., 1850.)

Oeuvres de Blaise Pascal. 14 vols. Publiées suivant l'ordre chronologique, avec documents complementaires, introductions et notes, par Léon Brunschvicq et Pierre Boutroux. (Paris: Hachette et Cie, 1904-14.)

Cailliet, Emile. *Pascal: The Emergence of Genius.* Second edition. (New York: Harper Torchbooks, 1945, 1961.)

Mesnard, Jean. *Pascal, His Life and Works.* Translated by G. S. Fraser. (London: Harvill Press, 1952.)

Mortimer, Ernest. *Blaise Pascal: The Life and Work of a Realist.* (New York: Harper & Bros., 1959.)

Patrick, Denzil G. M. *Pascal and Kierkegaard: A Study in the Strategy of Evangelism.* 2 vols. (London & Redhill: Lutterworth Press, 1947.)

Périer, Madame Gilberte. *Vie de B. Pascal.* In *Moralistes Francais.* (Paris: Firmin Didot, 1741.)

Steinmann, Jean. *Pascal.* Second edition. Translated by Martin Turnell. (London: Burns & Oates, 1962.)

Wells, Albert N. *Pascal's Recovery of Man's Wholeness.* (Richmond, Virginia: John Knox Press, 1965.)

Brother Lawrence

The Practice of the Presence of God. (Westwood, N. J.: Fleming H. Revell Co., 1958.)

THE CLASSICS OF THE AGE OF DEISM AND THE ENLIGHTENMENT

PART II: PROTESTANT CLASSICS

The Development of German Pietism

England and Puritanism

Lancelot Andrewes' Private Devotions

Jeremy Taylor's Holy Living and Holy Dying

*John Bunyan's Pilgrim's Progress
   and Grace Abounding*

William Law's A Serious Call

The Journals of Fox and Woolman

Selected Bibliography

VII

The Classics of The Age of Deism and The Enlightenment

Part II: Protestant Classics

A combination of things prompted Protestants to take a second look at devotional practices cast aside in the initial flurry of reform. Internal dissension and turmoil, the Thirty Years' War (1618-1648), scientific progress, and a host of other happenings had combined to put Protestant faith to a stern test. The happy outcome on the continent and especially in England was the production of a spate of devotional books designed to recall the faithful to the deepest level of commitment.

On the continent, from Luther's twilight years onward, both Lutherans and Reformed (Calvinists) began to bog down in a type of Protestant scholasticism. In consequence, whereas both movements had once laid aside the medieval confessions and textbooks and sought to let the Bible speak plainly and without encumbrance to the faithful, they now began to create their own library of confessions and textbooks. To the minds of many second generation Protestants, what Luther or Calvin or other Reformers had written or said took precedence over what the Scriptures themselves said. Theological quarrels tortured the whole Protestant communion. After many years of endless debate over grace and predestination, the Lord's Supper, and other matters, Lutherans finally managed to secure an uneasy truce in the Formula of Concord, signed by most Lutheran princes and ecclesiastical leaders in 1580.

The ink had hardly dried on the latter document, however, when the disastrous Thirty Years' War erupted. The result of a maze of political, social, economic, and religious factors, the long conflict centered around Protestant-Catholic tensions left unresolved in the so-called Peace of Augsburg in 1555. Save for France, everyone came out a loser in the war, for it merely demonstrated that both Catholicism and Protestantism were here to stay and that neither side would vanquish the other. When Lutherans counted up losses and gains at Westphalia in 1648, they found that they had paid a heavy toll in numbers and even more significantly in spirit. The Protestant tide had ebbed.

The Development of German Pietism

It was in the sequel to this setting that German Pietism was born. Though formally associated almost exclusively as a self-conscious movement with Philip Jacob Spener and August Herman Francke, Pietism possessed a distinguished genealogy which included early Christian mystics such as Augustine and Pseudo-Dionysius); medieval mystics like Francis and Bernard; German and Dutch mystics like Eckhart, Tauler, Suso, Ruysbroeck, "the Friends of God" and "Brothers of the Common Life"; the early Luther; Jacob Arndt; and, more immediately, the theosophist Jacob Boehme. Boehme, by trade a cobbler without formal schooling, developed a brilliant, though enigmatic type of mystical philosophy from which Spener and later pietists borrowed freely, even if cautiously. Writing in a time of intense preoccupation with orthodoxy (1612-24), Boehme ran afoul of the watchdogs against heresy. Yet his intuitive genius did not go unnoticed and many of the learned of his day eagerly gobbled up his fresh, creative approach to a reconciliation between Christian faith and knowledge of nature. In advance of René Descartes (1596-1650) and Sir Isaac Newton (1642-1727) he effected an uncomfortable union between these two by way of a theory of evolutionary process in God and nature. What bothered his less creative contemporaries was that all of this did not fit precisely into the neat theological formulas of Protestant tradition. So Boehme, like the Protestant spiritualists a generation earlier, was hardly tolerated, often persecuted.

Philip Jacob Spener (1635-1705). Still, Boehme's mysticism helped some. Spener, a concerned and reflective pastor, found it a useful counteragent to the typical "Pharisaic orthodoxy" of his day. Given a devout education by his parents and an even deeper religious instruction at the hands of his godmother's chaplain, one would have expected Spener to react as he did. As a pastor in Strassburg, where he had received both the M.A. and the Ph.D. degrees, he began his attack on the deadening of Church life by preoccupation with theological correctness. In 1670 he initiated in his own home the small devotional groups, called *collegia pietatis,* which formed the basis of his proposals for reform. Five years later he published the famous *Pia desideria,* setting forth his program: (1) earnest Bible study, (2) lay participation in Church government, (3) practical rather than theoretical knowledge of Christianity as revealed in charity, forgiveness, and devotion, (4) sympathetic treatment of unbelievers rather than denunciation of their errors, (5) reorganization of theological training with more emphasis on devotion, and (6) more practical and less rhetorical preaching.

Opposition naturally reared its head and it plagued Spener for the rest of his life. After departing Strassburg he served briefly as chaplain to the Elector of Saxony, with whom he soon found himself at odds for criticizing the latter's licentious court. When he got to Berlin in 1691, he set aflame the smoldering faggot ignited in Strassburg. As provost of the Nikolaikirche, Spener exerted a powerful influence over the newly founded University of Halle. Lutherans split their loyalties, some opposing and some favoring the new movement. Unfortunately, Pietism got linked onto certain chiliastic or millenarian tendencies, which eventually spelled its doom. Though a stout controversialist, in 1698 Spener deemed further debate useless and retired from leadership of the movement until his death in 1705.

August Hermann Francke (1663-1727). August Hermann Francke, Professor of Greek and Oriental languages at the University of Halle and pastor in the Parish of Glaucha in Berlin, gathered up the reins laid down by Spener. The son of a prominent lawyer who received considerable prodding in the home toward the study of theology, Francke experienced a conversion during a period of intensive Bible study at Lüneberg (1687-89). Returning subsequently to his alma mater, the University of Leipzig, to teach, he inaugurated a pietistic movement among the students. Opposition forced him to move first to Erfurt and finally to Berlin. In connection with his pastoral charge there, Francke made the lasting contribution to Pietism for which later generations have remembered his name. With the support of a growing and vigorous congregation, he set up charitable institutions for the care of orphans. Into these he injected his intense interest in foreign missions. To his credit and to that of Pietism, three of the pioneers of modern missions—Ziegenbald, Plutschau, and C. F. Schwarz—were trained in Francke's schools.

The Moravians. Even though Pietism as a movement withered and died following the death of Francke in 1727, its influence lived on, leaving its mark on Christianity in Germany and elsewhere around the world. Its most telling impact fell upon the Moravians, spiritual descendants of the reformer John Huss of Bohemia, whom the Council of Constance had burned as a heretic in 1415. Persecution, of course, had nearly eliminated Huss's most ardent followers during the 16th and 17th centuries. The small band of refugees which survived had fled Bohemia for Moravia, Poland, and other more tolerant countries. They found permanent refuge in 1722, when Count Nicholas von Zinzendorf (1700-1760) opened his spacious estate at Herrnhut in Saxony to a company of them.

The "Unity of the Brethren," as the Moravians called themselves, grew rapidly. Ten years after they came to Herrnhut, they dispatched two missionaries to preach the gospel among the Negroes in St. Thomas islands. Soon thereafter others went to Greenland, South and North America, South Africa, Persia, Ceylon, Egypt, Algiers, and the West Indies. Their pietistic influence touched people in all walks of life. Invitations to send missionaries to other countries flooded Zinzendorf and his community. Among the most momentous of these official visits was the one to England in 1735, for in 1738 a Moravian meeting in Aldersgate Street became the setting for the dramatic "conversion" of John Wesley. Through him Pietism gained an opening into world Christianity.

England and Puritanism

Behind John Wesley's story, however, lies a movement of equal or even greater moment than Pietism for the fashioning of Protestant devotional literature, that is, Puritanism. Puritanism harked back to the Calvinistic wing of Protestantism and represented the stricter English Calvinists' dissatisfaction with the Settlement under Elizabeth I. The Elizabethan program of reform involved an adoption of Calvinistic theology but not of the Calvinistic attitude toward the modification of religious practice. Whereas, in the Genevan reform, Calvin had pursued the principle of bringing both theology and practice into line with those of *most* primitive Christianity, i.e. with those found in the New Testament, Anglican leaders did this principally in theology. Practice, in the minds of more ardent Calvinists, remained essentially Roman. Consequently, they demanded the stripping away of Romanist vestiges —clerical vestments, liturgical observances, ornamentation of churches, and the rest.

But the Puritans were not to have their way. Elizabeth, and then James I and Charles I, proceeded cautiously in accordance with the advice of eminent churchmen. Various "Acts of Uniformity" enforced conformity to the Settlement. Puritans every-

where voiced dissatisfaction with the snail's pace in reform.
Though a lot of them contented and reassured themselves in the
hope that the powers that be would eventually purify the Church,
many lost patience entirely with the establishment. So long as the
Church remained wedded to the state and to episcopacy, they
reasoned, it would never undergo reform. We must have reform
now, as Robert Browne, the father of Separatism put it, "without tarrying for any."

The brilliant Queen Elizabeth managed to escape the develop-
ing storm. James (1603-1625) and Charles (1625-1644) were
neither so fortunate nor so wise as she, however. Not only did
they not attempt to conciliate the Puritan dissenters, they turned
a deaf ear to their pleas, such as the Millenary Petition of 1603,
and staked the future of their monarchies upon the complete
triumph of episcopacy. "No bishop, no king!" declared James,
and sought to impose episcopacy even on Presbyterian Scotland.
With the encouragement of certain of the clergy, he openly defied
Puritan resentment against desecration of the sabbath with games
by issuing his Book of Sports (1618), which even encouraged
Sunday gaming. Though England seethed and fumed when
James died in 1625, Charles continued the anti-Puritan program
of his father, as a result of which thousands fled the country. The
price of this program was a costly civil war, 1637-44, and the
loss of his own life.

The Puritan sun finally rose in the Commonwealth era (1648-
60). Oliver Cromwell, himself a Puritan and Independent, gave
signs of concern and encouragement, but his reign was plagued
with too many other maladies to allow a Puritan triumph. Instead, the Puritans had to remain content with tolerance of their
views and scattered successes in implementation of them. That
even toleration was no small matter became evident when the
monarchy was restored in 1660. Under Charles II the composi-
tion of the Parliament changed instantly and episcopacy was
restored. A series of acts clamped down once more on dissenters
—forbidding unlicensed preaching, meetings for worship, and

other practices which did not fall in line with the Book of Common Prayer. Puritan leaders like John Bunyan suffered harassment, imprisonment, and even death for their refusal to conform. Fortunately for English dissenters, though, Charles and his son, James II, made a serious mistake. Covertly sympathetic to Catholicism, Charles issued in 1672 a Declaration of Indulgence which granted freedom to all dissenters. Parliament revoked it, and the next year passed another restrictive act to counter it. James, two years after succeeding his father on the throne, issued a like Declaration. This time, Parliament reacted by inviting William of Orange and Mary, James' daughter, to wear the crown. Shortly after their accession, William issued the famous Act of Toleration (1689), which in effect granted liberty to all dissenters except Roman Catholics and unitarians.

This turbulent era was followed by a decline in religious fervor. The fire which dissent and conflict had fanned into a bright flame lost its glow in the early 18th century. The establishment of the Anglican Church and the predestinarian bent of Calvinism closed the damper on evangelism and missions. Deism, springing up in the 17th century, made all and sundry critical of a faith so often rent by strife. As the flame appeared about to go out, however, the Wesleyan revivals began to take hold. Churches once dead sprang to life again. A new era of Christian devotion had dawned.

Lancelot Andrewes' Private Devotions

In these turbulent two centuries both Anglicans and dissenters turned out some superlative devotional literature. Lancelot Andrewes' *Private Devotions* stands at the head of the stream of Anglican classics.

The author. A gifted scholar, Andrewes (1555-1626) topped the list of distinguished Anglican clergymen who gradually formulated a distinctively Anglican theology, i.e., independent both

of Rome and Geneva. Though educated in a Puritan strong-
hold, Cambridge, he manifested independence of mind from the
first. Paul Welsby has shown in his recent biography, in fact,
that Andrewes never held the Calvinistic view of scriptural authority, thus being "less Puritan than the Church of England
itself" and "less Calvinistic than the tone of some of the Thirty-
Nine Articles of Religion."[1] As he assumed increasingly consequential appointments within the Church, his bias against Puritanism grew ever more pronounced. His militant criticism of
presbyterianism and support of episcopacy naturally endeared
him to James I. Andrewes knew at least fifteen languages and
was selected by James to serve on the translation committee for
the Authorized Version, published in 1611. A stylistic preacher,
he frequently addressed the court on significant occasions during
James' reign and sat on many important commissions as Bishop
of Chichester, Ely, and Winchester.

Oddly enough, Andrewes' greatest gain may have caused his
greatest failing. In later years, he seems to have become a pawn
of the king, moved here and there in order to implement the
latter's policies and decisions. Along with others, he perhaps deserves to be blamed for the disastrous outcome of James' theory
of the divine right of kings in the reign of Charles. Had he and
other intimates of the king advised caution, they might have
directed James away from the fatal course which he and his son
pursued so recklessly.

Andrewes' weakness is all the more surprising when one con-
siders his independence in other areas. He did not feel compelled
to take the Puritan line in Puritan Cambridge, for example.
Moreover, he carried on a brilliant debate with the Roman
Catholic apologist Robert Bellarmine regarding the authority of
the Anglican Church and refused to identify with Arminians,
even though stoutly opposed to some Calvinist tenets. The only
explanation for the lapse must be that he was sincerely and
irrevocably committed to kingship as a divinely ordained form
of government to which even the Church must submit.

The book. Whatever faults he might have had in this regard, they cannot detract from his lasting contribution to personal devotion in the English Church. His *Private Devotions* became the most widely read of all Anglican classics, wielding an obviously profound influence on later devotional writings.

The *Preces Privatae*, literally "private prayers," were exactly what the name implies, for they were not published until several years after Andrewes' death. Apart from a prefatory note concerning preparation for prayer with reference to times, places, and circumstances, the small volume consists entirely of prayers to be employed in daily devotion. The first and largest group of these supply an order of prayers for the week with an established pattern of introduction, confession, prayer of grace, profession of faith, intercession, and praise. The remaining prayers apparently served in the main as alternates for those given in the initial section, for they are listed under similar categories, but they include also special prayers for morning and evening and for the communion service.*

Contentwise, the prayers depend heavily upon biblical phrasing, although they also echo the Church Fathers, medieval authors, classical writers, traditional liturgies, and some reformers.[2] One striking feature betrays the Puritan influence on Andrewes, that is, the excessive emphasis upon repentance and confession of

---

*As I read the foregoing pages of this chapter, and as I have heard recounted many times the intrigue of the period of history about which we are concerned here, I have been impressed afresh with the ways in which these persons kept their distance from each other, engaged in political games with each other, and sought to get the best of each other. Little wonder is it that Lancelot Andrewes' book was of *private* devotions, published *after* his death. He really went into his closet and shut the door. Then he prayed. This is the tone as well of the present day John Baillie's *Diary of Private Prayer*. Similarly, Dag Hammarskjöld's *Markings* reveal an intense inner life of a man who spent his whole life as an adult in the swirl of international and national subterfuge and intrigue. The roles men play before each other obscure their inmost selves and

sin. Apart from this, the prayers reveal a deeply pious Christian, who searched the Scriptures with diligence in order to keep himself in proper perspective in relationship to God. Andrewes, obviously, was feeling his way toward a disciplined prayer life which fell somewhere in between medieval monastic piety and the complete absence of such forms among some Protestants.

Jeremy Taylor's Holy Living and Holy Dying

The author. Jeremy Taylor carried further what Andrewes and others had begun in establishing an independent type of Anglican theology and personal devotion. Professor Trevor Hughes has classified both men as representatives of the sacerdotal as opposed to the evangelical (Bunyan) and mystical (Fox) types of piety. Sacerdotal piety, as described by R. H. Coats in *Types of English Piety,* had a special concern for religion in its institutional expression.

Its strength lies in its historic appeal, its attraction for the sensuous imagination and its skill in enlisting all the arts in worship. It has, as its crowning act of worship, the Holy Eucharist. Its weakness lies in its tendency to pride, exclusiveness and rigidity; it may become the champion of the reactionary and of effete authority, and the foe of spiritual progress, civil and religious freedom and political

---

parch their thirst for openness with each other.

The analysis of this role-playing today is called "transactional therapy," or the therapy of the pastimes, games, and scripts of the drama of human life. No one psychotherapist has made this clearer than Eric Berne, in his book, *Transactional Analysis in Psychotherapy,* and his more popular presentation of the same ideas in the book, *Games People Play.* But as Anne Morrow Lindbergh says in her meditative book, *Gift From the Sea,* there is nothing more tiresome than wearing a mask. Yet the real desire in prayer is to call the "games off" and to be as we are in relation to God. For, as Jacob Boehme is quoted as having said, "We cannot by failing to confess our sins, act as if God has no knowledge of them thereby."

reform. Christ's yoke may be made difficult and his burden heavy. . . . To express it in another way, religion may become something a man carries instead of something that carries him.[3]

In at least one respect, Taylor did not fit this stereotype. Though a supporter of episcopacy and monarchy, he was a strong advocate of religious toleration; his *The Liberty of Prophesying,* published in 1647, being "far ahead of the general thought of his own day."[4] This observation surprises one a bit, especially in light of Taylor's career.

Hardly anyone experienced more variable fortunes than Taylor. Born in 1613, the son of a churchwarden in Cambridge, he entered Cambridge University at age 13 and took the M.A. degree in 1633. A brilliant sermon in St. Paul's Cathedral, London, preached as a substitute for a friend, brought him to the attention of Archbishop Laud. Laud secured his appointment to a Fellowship at All Souls College, Oxford, in 1636, then as Rector of Uppingham, and finally as Chaplain to King Charles I, in 1638. He married in 1638 also.

A few years later, his time of trials began. An infant son died in 1642. His benefactor, Archbishop Laud, was impeached, imprisoned, and later executed. Taylor himself was captured while serving as chaplain in the royal army and imprisoned in January, 1645. His happiest days came after his release and appointment as chaplain to Lord Carbery at Golden Grove in Wales. He wrote extensively during these years, producing both *Holy Living* (1650) and *Holy Dying* (1651), the latter at the request of Lady Carbery, who died after a long illness even before he finished it. His own wife died about the same time. He remarried later.

Taylor, of course, had the misfortune of being a royalist in the day of the Commonwealth and an Arminian in the heyday of Calvinism. This meant frequent attack from both outside and inside the Anglican Church. He suffered two other imprisonments and finally ended the Commonwealth years, 1658-60, as chaplain to the Conway household at Portmore, Ireland. When the monarchy was restored, he was nominated by Charles II as

Bishop of Down and Connor, Ireland, and Vice-Chancellor of the University of Dublin. In both positions he faced hostility and harassment. Appointment to the Irish Privy Council and as administrator of the diocese of Dromore in 1661 only heightened his problems. To this was added a disappointment because the King refused to honor his request for an English bishopric. A few days after the death of his only surviving son, Taylor himself fell ill and died on August 13, 1667.

Holy Living. Written at the ebb tide of an exceedingly trying ministry, *Holy Living* and *Holy Dying* offered to Taylor's contemporaries some rich insights regarding the manner in which one may cope with life in both prosperity and adversity. The immediate occasion for the first was the distress of Church and nation following the Civil War—moral and social chaos, the execution of Archbishop Laud and King Charles, prohibition of the Book of Common Prayer, proscription of bishops, and shattering of the Church's orderly life. Taylor's answer to these problems was, C. J. Stranks has stated, "an ordered life of devotion, in which the vision of God, and the grace of God, lead us into the fullest service of our fellow men."[5]

In several respects, *Holy Living* evinces a lot of similarity to Francis de Sales' *Introduction to the Devout Life,* written about forty years earlier. Both works, for example, underline the necessity of a sincere intention to pursue the goal of Christian perfection and set forth rules by which the devout Christian may follow up his intention. Both also take a realistic look at the obvious difficulties involved in living devoutly in a secular setting. In discussing problems of prayer, in fact, Taylor may have borrowed from de Sales, for he too offers remedies for wandering thoughts and tediousness of Spirit ("dryness" in de Sales).

Nevertheless, if Taylor did borrow from de Sales, he was not a slavish imitator. The strong Puritan concern for gospel holiness in his day everywhere pervades *Holy Living* and *Holy Dying.* Apart from his commitment to the monarchy and the episcopate, certainly, he reflects the Puritan spirit. He prefaces *The Rule and Exercise of Holy Living* with three general rules about serving the holy life—care of one's time, purity of intention, and the practice of the presence of God. The last rule calls to mind Brother Lawrence's little work published several years later.

The main body of *Holy Living,* comprised of one treatise on "Christian Sobriety," another on "Christian Justice," and another on "Christian Religion," manifests a combination of influences from the whole panorama of Christian history, with special flavoring by the early Christian Fathers and Puritanism. Under "Christian Sobriety," Taylor lists virtues which all men should strive for—sobriety or self-control in general, temperance in eating and drinking, chastity, humility, and modesty. He divides "Christian Religion" into three types of acts—internal, external, and a combination of these two. *Internal* acts should evoke the chief Christian triad of spiritual fruits—faith, hope, and love. *External* acts consist of reading or hearing the word of God (in Scripture and sermon), fasting, and observance of Christian holy days. Prayer and giving of alms belong partly to internal and partly to external religious acts. The theme consistently woven through the fiber of the discussion is that holiness requires self-discipline. Though God's grace in the Incarnation and through the gift of the Holy Spirit aids in its attainment, the faihful Christian must strive mightily to measure up to God's expectations.

Holy Dying. The Rule and Exercises of Holy Dying, published the year after *Holy Living,* and from the first appended to it as a companion volume, contains the same basic thrust. Just as Christian living requires discipline, so also does Christian dying. Part one reminds the sick person of the vanity, brevity, and miseries of man's life and turns his attention to the glories of heaven. Part two sets forth rules and exercises of preparing for a holy death. Taylor insists that one's whole life must be a preparation for death. To this end, he advises daily examination of one's actions and continuous attention to the practice of charity, for

"Charity is the life of Religion; . . ."[6] Part three discusses the major temptations faced by the sick—impatience and fear of death—and expounds the practices of prayer and repentance by which they may overcome the temptations. Part four gives advice to the clergy who must minister to the dying.*

What Taylor counseled regarding Christian holiness in either life or death doubtless had much relevance to his contemporaries. We who live in an age of scientific triumph over disease would find both works a bit gloomy. His pronounced Arminianism forbade too much confidence in God's mercy toward sinners certainly, and one cannot help but feel that the scholarly bishop placed a sort of pharisaical burden on the shoulders of his parishioners. Yet, like Francis de Sales, he did give valuable insights

---

*This is the first author of those whom we have considered to come to grips with the effects of the fact of death upon the devotional life of a person. One of the modern psychotherapists, Otto Rank, likens death to the birth experience in that both the prenatal experience and the postnatal experience of mankind have an *end* set to them, one by birth and the other by death. The Greek word *eschaton* means "end." The feelings of anxiety we experience as we face death cause us to live life with an eschatological sense of urgency. Rank chose to use this concept in his discipline of persons whom he treated. Together they agreed upon a certain amount of *time* they would use. As they approached this set end of their therapy, they became more and more anxious and more and more responsible. They made decisions more seriously and did not act as if this earthly life provided them with unlimited amounts of time. The therapy amounted to a "new" birth, traumatic, for all that, but a birth!

In the crucible of life's testing situations, we have a way of saying: "Life is too short for that!" Then we make a clear, decisive move on the basis of the shortness of time. This is the kind of prayerful decisions the Early Church made because they as a community felt that the whole of time was imminently awaiting the consummation of the ages. One of their prayers was, "Maranatha," meaning "Come, Lord!" Holy living and holy dying are inseparable and prayer should be infused with this spirit.

into the strengthening of devotion, a few of which may have relevance even in our day, despite its avowed hostility to authoritarianism.

John Bunyan's Pilgrim's Progress and Grace Abounding

It is unlikely that Taylor heard the name of John Bunyan, tinker and Baptist minister, prisoner in Bedford jail, and blossoming author of religious tracts. Yet today Bunyan's fame surpasses Taylor's by far—the Bible and *The Imitation of Christ* alone vying with his *Pilgrim's Progress* for the top of the best seller list. The fact is, Bunyan knew better the heart and head of the common man; he lived and wrote at their level; he shared their religious pilgrimage. Thus, whereas Taylor wrote a tract for Lady Carbery, Bunyan wrote for Everyman. Bunyan's career tells why.

Grace Abounding. Born in November of 1628 at Elstow, about two miles from Bedford, he grew up in modest circumstances. Though his family tree could be dated back to 1199, and possibly to certain Buignons of Normandy who landed with William the Conqueror, the family property had dwindled to a tiny plot of land owned by John's father, Thomas, and mother, Margaret Bentley.

Not unexpectedly in the golden age of Puritanism, John developed a hyper-sensitive religious conscience.* "Even in my

---

*Contemporary psychologists are concerned with the way in which the conscience develops and the difference between an enlightened conscience and one that moves blindly, putting a person in bondage. Sigmund Freud said that the positive function of religion in the life of a person as he or she grows to maturity is threefold: It lowers the importance of the earthly parents, and wounds one has received from one's parents are not as lasting in their effects if the child has an effective religion to lower their importance. Religion, in the second place, "moors" the hostile and sexual urges of the person with a safe ethical anchor. And, in the third place, religion opens up the larger family of mankind to the growing child. Gordon Allport,

childhood," he confessed, God "did scare and affright me with fearful dreams, and did terrify me with dreadful visions. . . ."[7] He suffered frequent fits of depression at age nine or ten. Yet, not until he joined Cromwell's army at age sixteen, with some bitterness over his father's hasty remarriage, did he begin his earnest religious quest. His marriage after being released from military service in July, 1647 produced some further providential guidance in the right direction. Mrs. Bunyan's slim dowry, two devotional writings which had belonged to her father—*The Plain Man's Pathway to Heaven* and *The Practice of Piety*—inspired her husband "to go to church twice a day" and no doubt helped greatly to shape his later thought. *The Plain Man's Pathway,* in fact, as M. P. Willcocks has pointed out, "contains all the main trends of thought which lie below Bunyan's creative work: the misery of the natural man, and especially of himself; how to escape from this condition; and, finally, the corruption of the times, which was to drive him almost mad."[8]

In this period of earnest seeking a sermon by the parish parson on breaking the sabbath became a turning point in his life, for "at that time I felt what guilt was, though never before, that I can remember; . . ."[9] This momentous discovery incited him to lay aside his outward sins one by one. In the midst of this process of personal reformation, he chanced upon members of John Gifford's Bedford congregation talking about "a new birth, the work of God on their hearts."[10] He became a regular participant

---

in his book on *Pattern and Growth in Personality,* would say that self-esteem is something more than, other than, and different from pride and vanity. The self-esteem of the person may have been so wounded that ethical decisions are not made with clarity and accuracy. From a distinctly Christian point of view, we could say that "we have been bought with a price." We are persons for whom Christ died, made in the image of God. This realization is aimed, in the contemplation and reverie of a person each day, to avoid taking the arrows of those who reject one as "wounds" to infect our consciences daily.

in services there. Doubts about the possibility of his salvation assailed him savagely, and he searched the Scriptures intently. Gifford, a kindly pastor, aided him with personal counsel. But for some months Bunyan's frail conscience pitched to and fro like a tiny ship in a rolling sea. First, he doubted whether God could save him; next, he thought he had "sold" Christ like Esau had sold his birthright; then, he felt tempted to blaspheme God, the Church, the sacraments. His study of the Scriptures finally convinced him at long last that God's grace in Christ was greater than his sins, even the sins of the *chief* of sinners.*

About two years after his baptism (1653), Bunyan began privately to preach. Encouraged by his fellow Bedfordians, he "was more particularly called forth, and appointed to a more ordinary and public preaching the word, . . ."[11] At first, he tells us, he stressed divine judgment. Later, he emphasized Christ's "offices, relations, and benefits unto the world" and the "mystery of union with Christ." In his early preaching, Bunyan soon encountered the Ranters and the Quakers. Concern with Quakerism induced Bunyan to publish his first two treatises in debate with Edward Burroughs, then only twenty-three. He objected to

---

*Anton Boisen, of whom mention has been made before, felt great compatibility as a mental patient with the autobiography of Bunyan. He felt that he himself was struggling with the same feelings of guilt and condemnation with which Bunyan struggled. He saw both experiences as essentially constructive experiences, unpleasant like a fever in the body, but, similarly, a process of healing and protection from destruction.

In my book, *Religious Factors in Mental Illness,* I record case data of mental patients who felt that they had sinned beyond redemption, who were captured in the clutches of the despair which Bunyan describes so vividly in his works. The paralysis of the will of the person, leaving him helpless but aware of his plight, makes him feel the need of both the physician and the divine. Consequently, today, the care of a person like this is in the hands of both trained physicians and ministers working in cooperation with each other in numerable healing communities in this country.

the Quakers' replacing of Scriptures with the "inner light" and to the radicalism of the Ranters.

With the Restoration in 1660, Bunyan's unlicensed preaching resulted in a long imprisonment. The resumption of the monarchy gave royalists an opportunity to have their due against the overly zealous Puritans. Bunyan could have escaped his fate, of course, had it not been for this zeal. But he refused to stop preaching for one instant. Though he should have been freed after three months, he spent two six-year terms in jail, despite heroic pleas by his second wife, Elizabeth, to have him released.

By the end of his first six years the Bedford tinker had written nine books, including the first installment of his autobiography, *Grace Abounding*. He kept adding to this book throughout his lifetime. In the year of his death (1688), he published the sixth edition. During the second six-year term he wrote only two books—a testimony to the manner in which imprisonment sapped his spiritual and mental vigor. The hardest part of prison life must have been anxiety about his family, especially the blind child born by his first wife, who, he confides, "lay nearer my heart than all I had besides; . . ."[12]

Released in 1672, Bunyan received one of the first licenses to preach under Charles' Act of Toleration. Besides being pastor of Bedford church, which he had had some liberty to minister to from about 1668 on, he served as pastor-at-large to many churches and counseled a host of independent ministers. He continued to turn out books. In all, the brilliant but unlettered man wrote about eighty works. These represented an amazing assortment of literature—polemical, expository, allegorical, narrative, autobiographical, and poetical.

Bunyan experienced a six months term of prison in 1675, caught like other Puritans in the parliamentary reaction to Charles' Act of Toleration. Except for this brief episode, he ranged freely through the English countryside preaching the gospel he loved. In this ministry, death, which he had steeled himself many times to meet during his imprisonment, caught him. He contracted consumption while riding horseback in the rain from Bedford to Leicester, a distance of forty miles, and died on August 31, 1688.

The Pilgrim's Progress. Of his many works *The Pilgrim's Progress* has no rival for popularity. In a critical age such as ours, this acclaim may startle some a bit, for the book lacks the finesse and luster classics are made of. One modern wit has gone so far as to say, "No book, not even one with such pious claims to greatness, has the right to be as dull as this."[13] If this is true, writing style obviously did not make it a classic.

What captured the fancy of Bunyan's contemporaries and even later generations is rather the simple narration of a common religious experience, as the longer title puts it, "the pilgrim's progress from this world to that which is to come." The very ruggedness of the work gave it appeal to the masses who toiled to be Christian in a superficially Christian environment. They could identify with its homely language. Many of the places or names mentioned in the allegory must have struck a familiar chord. Who in that day, for example, could have missed the connection between the Sturbridge Fair at Cambridge and Vanity Fair? Bunyan did what many other great allegorists failed to do —he made his points of contact with reality obvious enough that his readers could always touch base. He made simple what others made a labyrinth.*

---

*Recently we have studied the characters in Bunyan's *Pilgrim's Progress* in relation to some of the personality disorders encountered today. Mr. Talkative, Mr. Pliable, and others like them remind us of the sociopathic and/or the "other-directed" people we meet today. Also, there are therapists, interpreters, and counselors such as Bunyan described in his Mr. Faithful, The House of the Interpreter and Mr. Good-Will. Jungian psychotherapist, Esther Harding, has taken the elaborate symbolic analysis of Carl G. Jung and applied it to *Pilgrim's Progress* imagery. She calls this *The Journey Into the Self.* Such imagery as Bunyan uses is a "forgotten language" much as is the imagery of dreams. Taking these symbols seriously, aided

As *The Pilgrim's Progress* has come to us, it consists of two separate tales, written at different times. The first, and most appealing, was probably penned during Bunyan's last imprisonment, in the year 1675, though not published until 1678.[14] The second did not appear until 1684. Both tales were set forth as guidebooks for Christian pilgrims. The pilgrimage had been a long time favorite in English literature, a convenient vehicle for conveying religious truth. Every Englishman of Bunyan's day had watched weary travelers making their way to Canterbury, shrine of St. Thomas Becket. He knew something about Chaucer's *Canterbury Tales*. So the Bedford tinker chose a happy medium of expression for conveying his conviction that one does not find the heavenly city in this world but in the next. His vision helped many tired souls keep their feet on the arduous and narrow path which led to the journey's goal. In Bunyan's words,

> This Book will make a Traveller of thee,
> If by its Counsel thou wilt ruled be;
> It will direct thee to the Holy Land,
> If thou wilt its directions understand:

by the reading of such a book as Harding has written, will develop the inner life, especially of the mature adult who has had enough experience to know the "feel" of an Iron Cage of Despair, a Slough of Despond, a Doubting Castle, or a Vanity Fair.

However, contemporary religious life has become considerably externalized and routinized, leaving out the labyrinthine ways of the inner self. Nathaniel Hawthorne, as recently as the 1850's saw how the difficult way to the Celestial City had become paved over and propagandized into a sort of "tourist attraction." He wrote his satire on it called *The Celestial Railroad*. Little wonder is it that these "smoothings" of the way have lost their challenge for many, and they seek "trips" through the use of drugs, exotic religions, and primitive rhythms to make up for the loss. The person who takes *Pilgrim's Progress* as a serious devotional book will find that the way is rough enough to make a person lay it aside for some more soothing reading or "dial-a-prayer" bit of comfort that comes without calling for change.

> Yea, it will make the slothful active be;
> The blind also delightful things to see.

The tale of Christian's wife makes the journey appear a bit easier and happier. Christiana, Bunyan's wife Elizabeth, had a far less arduous time of it than her husband. Since Bunyan was inclined in Puritan fashion to exaggerate his own unworthiness, this comes as no surprise. The story of Christian probably depicts accurately Bunyan's own oversized ups and downs throughout his Christian life. Both tales, however, come through clearly with the Puritan theme, i.e., that we are sojourners and pilgrims on our way to another land and that God will see us through.

William Law's A Serious Call

The streams of Pietism, Puritanism, and the new Anglican devotion were channeled again into the mainstream of Catholic devotion in the writings of William Law. A man of remarkable natural abilities, he produced an amazing synthesis of diverse currents. In the process he became a John the Baptist for the ministry of the Wesleys and George Whitefield.

The author. His background and education outfitted him well for the synthesizing task. Born at King's Cliffe, Northamptonshire, in 1686, the fourth in a family of eleven children belonging to a prosperous merchant, he entered Emmanuel College, Cambridge, as a sizar (poor student on scholarship) in 1705. His excellent scholastic record earned him a fellowship when he graduated in 1709. During his student days at Cambridge, Law reflected his Puritan bent, a hallmark of *A Serious Call*. In his eighteen rules for his future conduct, among other things, he vowed,

To avoid all concerns with the world, or the ways of it, but where religion and charity oblige me to act.

To remember frequently, and impress it upon my mind deeply, that no condition of this life is for enjoyment, but for trial; and that

every power, ability, or advantage we have, are all so many talents
to be accounted for, to the Judge of all the World.

To avoid all excess in eating and drinking.

To avoid all idleness.

To think humbly of myself, and with great charity of all others.

To forbear from evil speaking.[15]

In 1711 Law received ordination, but his non-juror views
brought his ecclesiastical career to a grinding halt within five
years. A speech in support of James II's right to the throne got
him into trouble with the crown during Anne's regency (1702-
1714); his refusal to swear allegiance to the House of Hanover
in 1716 cost him his fellowship at Cambridge and ended all hope
of ecclesiastical preferment. His Puritan sentiments would allow
no compromise.

In 1726 Law secured an appointment as a tutor to Edward
Gibbon, Jr., father of the famous historian, and accompanied
him to Emmanuel College, Cambridge. During this period he
gained fame through his writings. His Puritan leanings shone
through clearly in three treatises published in 1726—one an attack on the theater, another a critique of the insufficiency of
natural reason, and the third on *Christian Perfection*. The last
work prefigured *A Serious Call to a Devout and Holy Life*,
published in 1728. In all three Law gave his prescriptions for
the soul's salvation: read only godly and edifying books, shun
the theater, renounce the world, mortify the natural appetites,
and imitate Christ.

During this second stay at Cambridge, Law met John Byrom
(1692-1763), poet, hymnologist, and inventor of a shorthand
system. Together they undertook an intensive study of mystical
literature—Eckhart, Tauler, Boehme, Guyon, and the rest.
Though Law liked Tauler, Boehme took him captive. As early
as 1737, under the Boehmian spell his thinking underwent a
profound alteration. *An Appeal to All that Doubt*, dated 1740,
evinces a strong Neo-platonic flavor with its theory of the im-
mortality of ideas, of the will, and of the human soul. Subsequent-

ly, Law's writings reflected far less Puritan rigorism and legalism. His increasing mystical interest reached its finest expression in *The Way of Divine Love*. The "new" Law emphasized "love" as the key to the life with Christ. To him, love and goodness were identical.[16]

The matter of applied charity had concerned Law for a long time. In 1726, he had established a school for girls in his home town of King's Cliffe. Thereafter, he placed increasing weight on active Christian love. When the elder Gibbon died in 1739, he returned to King's Cliffe and spent the remainder of his life there in charitable pursuits. In 1744, two women—a Mrs. Hutcheson and Hester Gibbon, sister of his former pupil—moved into his home. The three companions followed a careful routine of work and devotion, centered around set hours of prayer. Pooling their resources, they established a school for boys like that for girls, a hospital for devout widows, and performed other benevolent deeds. They combined common sense devotion and Christian charity in a commendable way.

Law died on April 9, 1761. He lived long enough to see his example taking hold in the Wesleyan revivals. Even though John Wesley had repudiated him in later years on account of his mysticism, he could not deny that Law's concern for perfection in love had made its mark on him.* Both men made their indi-

---

*Whereas Wesley and William Law knew quite well what they meant when they used the word "perfection," the Pentecostal mood of "living without sin" has somewhat thrown the word into disrepute, even among Christians today. Among psychologists and psychotherapists perfectionism bears the marks of the obsessional neurosis, is called the "search for glory" (Karen Horney, *Neurosis and Human Growth*), and is a self-defeating way of life (Clara Thompson, "An Introduction to Minor Maiadjustments," *The American Handbook of Psychiatry*, Vol. IX, p. 241.) Yet, the earlier and authentic meaning of perfection still has merit as one of the goals of the contemplative life. But in order for this merit to be discovered, a more accurate translation of the goal must be made.

vidual contributions to this concern and "permanently enriched the Christian tradition alike by their life and character."[17]

A Serious Call. Law's best known work was written against the backdrop of religious indifference in eighteenth century England. People attend church, he complained, "but when the service of the Church is over, they are but like those that seldom or never come there." Such spiritual lethargy indicates that they "have no other devotion but that of occasional prayers." Their religion is mere pretext and sham. It has no correspondence to scriptural injunctions which call for self-denial and renunciation of the world. "If our common life is not a common course of humility, self-denial, renunciation of the world, poverty of spirit, and heavenly affection," insisted Law, "we do not live the lives of Christians.* A glance at Christians' behavior proves that we do not."[18]

---

*The plaintive appeal of Law validates the observations Hawthorne made about the routinizing and "programming" of the Christian life. He challenges their seriousness in all the motions through which they go.

Contemporary psychologists help us with this. Oskar Pfister, in his book *Christianity and Fear,* speaks as a Christian pastor who is also thoroughly equipped as a lay psychoanalyst. He says that the concept of maturity is the contemporary translation of the earlier thought of perfection. Maturity is brought about through the nourishment of love and acceptance; in the face of possible rejection, the contemporary person seeks to conform in order to get approval and affection. Therefore, what results in a neurosis is not maturity (or perfection) but conformity. The basic need is for love. Perfected love casts out the fear of rejection and punishment. This is true fidelity to the earlier meaning of Wesley and Law, although they were not exempt from the pressure of conformity either.

The Revised Standard Version speaks of love in a context of growth, and refers to what formerly was translated as "perfection" with the translation "maturity." (See I Cor. 2:6; Eph. 4:13; Hebrews 6:1.)

Why do Christians not live the gospel? Because they lack the
intention truly to please God. "It was this general intention that
made the primitive Christians such eminent instances of piety, and
made the goodly fellowship of the saints, and all the glorious
army of martyrs and confessors." Were this true intention common
among Christians, "it would change the whole face of the world."
This is not to minimize grace. Grace enables us to achieve perfection.[19] Whatever station one may occupy in life, he may pursue
a life of holiness, but only if he intends to please God. "It is therefore absolutely necessary for all Christians, whether men or
women, to consider themselves as persons that are devoted to
holiness, and so order their common ways of life, by such rules
of reason and piety, as may turn it into continual service unto
Almighty God."[20]

With great deft and compelling logic, undergirded by incisive
and provocative character sketches, Law drives home his thesis
that all Christians can and must strive for gospel holiness. His
appeal is to the reason. Great devotion, he contends, is the reasonable aim of every wise man, for "piety and goodness are the
laws of human nature."[21] Religion comes to man's aid, lifting him
from the world's absurdity to do what it is his nature to do.
With its rules, therefore, it does not *dull* life; it invigorates it; it
brings happiness! The whole world is a school of piety.

For the nurturing of devotion, Law prescribed regular hours
of prayer in which one would focus upon the cultivation of particular habits and attitudes. What he advised must have corresponded closely to his own household regimen at King's Cliffe.

Early (upon arising)—Prayer of praise and thanksgiving
  9:00 a.m.—Prayer for humility
12:00 noon—Prayer of universal love and intercession
  3:00 p.m.—Prayer of resignation to the divine will
  6:00 p.m.—Examination of sins, prayer of confession and repent-
                ance

In consonance with Anglican piety and theology he drew heavily
from the reservoir of early and medieval Christianity to refine

and defend his counsels. Much of his advice, indeed, has the ring of monastic devotion.* For example, he insisted upon beginning all prayers with the singing of Psalms.[22] His stress on the virtues of humility and love, resignation to the divine will, scrupulous examination of sins, confession, repentance, works of charity, and even manual labor, sound exactly like the Rule of Benedict. His insistence upon hostility to the world as "a greater and more dangerous enemy now" than in early Christian history,[23] and his warnings about education as a hindrance to humility,[24] emit the monastic ring.

Despite his assurances that a Christian in any vocation can pursue the life of devotion set forth in *A Serious Call*, Law

---

*The emphasis upon regular and specific times of prayer at the same time each day has its first appearance here. This order of life itself gives a holy context for the routine of life itself. One of the first evidences of illness in an emerging mental illness is a disruption of the routine of the life of a person. Today we have secular routines —breakfast, going to work, the coffee break, the lunch hour, the coffee break, the late afternoon rush, the evening news on television, and the evening meal. Then come the hours of home work, of which each member of the family has his own version. Yet, no predictable pattern seems to be reliable in the conditions of American city life. Rural life, where the family tends to remain a working unit as well as an affectionate unity, provides a bit more of this predictability. However, the spread of the pattern of the city to the rural areas through mass media makes this less and less so.

If we are really honest with ourselves, we must admit that the devotional life today, as in the days of Lancelot Andrewes, has become a very private experience of the individual. Even in theological seminaries this seems to be so. The common meal, the regular round of prayers and worship, and the *set* times for devotion, even privately, have tended to fade if not disappear.

However, this does not mean that the stream of devotional concern is dry. It may mean that the reader who finds reading a "way to worship" will find his own particular regimen of prayer and that Law's *Serious Call to a Devout and Holy Life* will be a guidebook for his doing so.

leaves one in doubt. To all intents and purposes, he and his companions, exempted from the burden of having to earn a living, followed a monastic or semi-monastic rule. As compelling as was his logic, therefore, only those with similar circumstances (and his character sketches would indicate that he wrote with such people in mind) could have fulfilled such a schedule faithfully. Law, unfortunately, did not really know those who, entangled inextricably in the mundane activities of life, find few hours to set aside for religious exercises. Like his Catholic counterpart, Francis de Sales, his exhortations were heeded by a privileged few, though greatly admired by all. His permanent legacy lies in his challenge to take our commitment seriously. Dr. Samuel Johnson's often quoted quip illustrates how compelling Law had made his "Call." "When at Oxford," he wrote, "I took up Law's *Serious Call to a Holy Life,* expecting to find it a dull book (as such books generally are), and perhaps to laugh at it. But I found Law quite an overmatch for me."

The Journals of Fox and Woolman

Fox's Journal. With his *Journal* John Bunyan's contemporary, George Fox, in part initiated a new line of devotional literature and in part revived an old one. The *Journal* rolled into a new mold a number of ancient devotional types—the diaries which recorded the pilgrimages of Christians to the Holy Land, e.g., the late fourth century *Pilgrimage of Etheria,* Augustine's *Confessions, The Book of Margery Kempe,* and the autobiographies or biographies of the saints. Its newness came from Fox's fresh and startling approach to religious experience. In a day of sham and hypocrisy, Fox sounded the call for honesty and simplicity in personal piety. Not forms but faith is what matters, he never tired of reminding people, either in word or by personal example.

Fox (1624-91) himself was a "nobody," judging by his origins. Possessing an extravagantly sensitive religious consciousness, he shocked his contemporaries by his straightforwardness and reli-

gious zeal. Despite his lack of formal education, soon after he began a public ministry in 1648 he had gained hundreds of followers, some of them well educated. William Penn and Robert Bar-
clay headed an impressive list of notables who saw in the Friends
movement of George Fox the spark of authenticity which Christianity in their day desperately needed. In his preface to the
Journal, Penn summed up pretty well what attracted others to
Fox. "For in all things he acquitted himself like a man, yea, a
strong man, a new and heavenly-minded man, a divine and a
naturalist, and all of God Almighty's making."[25]

This character shines through Fox's *Journal.* As it has come to
us, it represents not a log book of daily happenings and observations jotted down by "the man in leather breeches" but a com-
pilation of an autobiography dictated in 1675 to his stepson-in-
law, Thomas Lower, letters, pastoral epistles, and other papers.
Actually, the book is too long to be a popular devotional treatise
and, not surprisingly, it has not circulated as widely as a *Pilgrim's
Progress.* Nevertheless, it has made its mark in the cutting of a new
literary type, for in its track have run the notable journals of
John Wesley, pioneer of Methodism, and John Woolman,
distinguished American Quaker voice against slavery.

Woolman's Journal. Wesley's *Journal* is an actual diary, the
standard edition of which amounts to eight volumes, hardly
suitable for popular perusal. That of John Woolman, however,
written down over a much briefer period (1756-72), possesses
both the brevity and other requisite qualities which make it a
classic for later generations. The book stands out also because it
is one of few *American* spiritual writings with an international
reputation.

The author was one of thirteen children of Thomas Woolman,
farmer and weaver, of Burlington, New Jersey. Though born in
1720, a century and more before slavery became a critical and
divisive issue in America, his Quaker upbringing instilled in him
a deep sensitivity toward all of God's creatures. His travels

through some of the southern colonies, begun about 1746, aroused this inward love to the evils and inhumanity of slaveholding. Soon afterwards he felt a divine compulsion, like the call of Jeremiah, to articulate his concern. In order that he might let nothing interfere with this call, he restricted an unusually successful merchandising business, feeling "an increasing care to attend to that Holy Spirit which sets right bounds to our desires, and leads those who faithfully follow it to apply all the gifts of Divine Providence to the purposes for which they were intended."*[26] Urged on by this sense of divine call, he traveled thousands of miles, usually with a companion according to the Quaker custom, to express his concern to other Friends.

The same sensitivity to the plight of his fellow human beings impelled Woolman on several occasions to visit various Indian tribes, which he felt were unfairly treated. It forbade him to eat sugar imported from the West Indies, since oppression of slaves helped to produce it. It made him a pacifist and, as a consequence,

---

*The reader will note the beginning of a heavy emphasis of both Fox and Woolman on the work of the Holy Spirit. Remarkably enough, the devotional classics thus far have not singled out *one* person of the Trinity nearly so much as do these men. I have found by reason of my interest in psychology and psychotherapy that scientists in the field of personality sciences tend to understand and appreciate our exposition as Christians of our experience of the Holy Spirit if we are frank, candid, and relatively openminded about it. This prompted me to write the 1965 Norton Lectures at the Southern Baptist Theological Seminary on the subject of contemporary religious experience and the Holy Spirit. I would like to be presumptuous enough to suggest that the reader note the publication of these lectures under the popular title, *The Holy Spirit in Five Worlds,* (New York: Association Press, 1968).

In these lectures I am debtor also to the descendants of George Fox and John Woolman, the Society of Friends in Richmond, Indiana. These persons have revealed the power of silence, the sacrament of the common meal, the dignity of work with one's hands, and the source of social passion as seen through the cultivation of the presence and power of the Holy Spirit.

too scrupulous even to accept pay for quartering troops and horses. It caused him to raise a cry on behalf of the poor. It sent him to England to plead with his fellow Quakers to free their slaves. Having contracted smallpox on this last journey, he died in York, England, October 7, 1772.

The *Journal,* first published in 1774, reveals a gentle, sensitive spirit similar to that of the *Imitation of Christ,* which Woolman read and admired. Woolman's *credo* was as broad and all encompassing as his heart. He became convinced in his early years, he says,

> that true religion consisted in an inward life, wherein the heart doth love and reverence God the Creator, and learns to exercise true justice and goodness, not only toward all men, but also toward the brute creatures; that, as the mind was moved by an inward principle to love God as an invisible, incomprehensible Being, so, by the same principle, it was moved to love him in all his manifestations in the visible world; that, as by his breath the flame of life was kindled in all animal sensible creatures, to say we love God as unseen, and at the same time exercise cruelty toward the least creature moving by his life, or by life derived from him, was a contradiction in itself.[27]

In Woolman's life and creed we see Christian pietism and humanism perfectly wedded, which is as it should be. Christ's love impelled him to minister and, as he believed, it alone could guide him. "Christ puts forth his ministers and goeth before them; . . . Christ knoweth the state of the people, and in the pure feeling of the gospel ministry their states are opened to his servants."[28]

Selected Bibliography

German Pietism

Spener, Philip Jacob. *Pia Desideria.* Translated, edited and with an introduction by Theodore G. Tappert. (Philadelphia: Fortress Press, 1964.)

Drummond, Andrew L. *German Protestantism Since Luther.* (London: Epworth Press, 1951.)

Flew, Robert Newton. *The Idea of Perfection in Christian Theology.* (London: Oxford University, H. Milford, 1934.)

Stoeffler, F. Ernest. *The Rise of Evangelical Pietism.* (Leiden: E. J. Brill, 1965.)

Puritanism and English Piety

Bullett, Gerald. *The English Mystics.* (London: Michael Joseph, 1950.)

Davies, Horton. *The English Free Churches.* 2nd ed. (London, New York, Toronto: Oxford University Press, 1963.)

Stranks, C. J. *Anglican Devotion.* (London: SCM Press Ltd., 1961.) A helpful historical study of the development of Anglican devotion.

Lancelot Andrewes

The Private Devotions of Lancelot Andrewes. Edited and with an introduction by Thomas S. Kepler. (Cleveland and New York: World Publishing Co., 1956.)

Welsby, Paul. *Lancelot Andrewes,* 1555-1626. (London: S.P. C.K., 1958.)

Jeremy Taylor

The Rule and Exercises of Holy Dying. Edited and with an introduction by Thomas S. Kepler. (Cleveland and New York: World Publishing Co., 1952.)

The Rule and Exercises of Holy Living. Edited and with an introduction by Thomas S. Kepler. (Cleveland and New York: World Publishing Co., 1956.)

Works. 10 vols. Revised and corrected by C. P. Eden. (London: Longman, Brown, Green and Longmans, 1850-54.)

Hughes, H. Trevor. *The Piety of Jeremy Taylor*. (London: Macmillan & Co., Ltd.; New York: St. Martin's Press, 1960.)

John Bunyan

The Pilgrim's Progress. With an afterword by F. R. Leavis. (New York: The New American Library, Signet Classic, 1964.) A modernization.

The Pilgrim's Progress. Rev. ed. Introduction and notes by G. B. Harrison. (London: J. M. Dent & Sons, Ltd.; New York: E. P. Dutton & Co., Inc., 1954.)

Grace Abounding and The Life and Death of Mr. Badman. Introduction by G. B. Harrison. (London: Dent; New York: Dutton, 1928.)

The Complete Works. (Philadelphia *et al.*: Bradley, Garretson & Co., 1872.)

De Blois, Austen Kennedy. *John Bunyan the Man*. (Philadelphia: Judson Press, 1928.)

Brittain, Vera. *Valiant Pilgrim*. (New York: Macmillan Co., 1950.) A scholarly study of biographies of Bunyan.

Lindsay, Jack. *John Bunyan: Maker of Myths*. (London: Methuen & Co., 1937.)

Talon, Henri. *John Bunyan: The Man and His Works*. (London: Rockliff, 1951.) An excellent study of literature by Bunyan.

Willcocks, M. P. *Bunyan Calling*. (London: George Allen & Unwin, Ltd., 1943.)

William Law

A Serious Call to a Devout and Holy Life. Introduction by Norman Sykes. (London: J. M. Dent & Sons, Ltd.; New York: E. P. Dutton & Co., Inc., 1906.)

Works. 9 vols. (London: Printed for J. Richardson, 1762.)

Baker, Eric W. *A Herald of the Evangelical Revival: A Critical Inquiry of the Relation of William Law to John Wesley and the Beginnings of Methodism.* (London: Epworth Press, 1948.)

Green, John Brazier. *John Wesley and William Law.* (London: Epworth Press, 1945.)

Overton, J. H. *William Law, Non-juror and Mystic.* (London: Longmans, Green & Co., 1881.)

Whyte, Alexander. *Characters and Characteristics of William Law, Non-jurior and Mystic.* (London: Hodder & Stoughton, 1907.)

George Fox and the Quakers

The Journal of George Fox. Revised edition by John L. Nickalls. (Cambridge: University Press, 1952.)

Braithwaite, William C. *The Beginnings of Quakerism.* Revised by Henry J. Cadbury. (Cambridge: University Press, 1961.)

Brinton, Howard. *Friends for 300 Years: Beliefs and Practices of the Society of Friends since George Fox Started the Quaker Movement.* (London: George Allen and Unwin, Ltd., 1953.)

Jones, Rufus M. *George Fox, Seeker and Friend.* (New York and London: Harper & Bros., Publishers, 1930.)

Noble, Vernon. *The Man in Leather Breeches: The Life and Times of George Fox.* (London and New York: Elek, 1953.)

Trueblood, D. Elton. *The People Called Quakers.* (New York: Harper & Row, Publishers, 1966.)

John Woolman

The Journal of John Woolman and *A Plea for the Poor.* John Greenleaf Whittier edition text. Introduction by Frederick B. Telles. (New York: Corinth Books, 1961.)

The Journal and Essays of John Woolman. Edited by Amelia Mott Gummere. (New York: The Macmillan Co., 1922.)

Cady, Edwin Harrison. *John Woolman.* (New York: Washington Square Press, 1965.)

Steere, Douglas V. *Doors into Life.* (New York: Harper & Bros., Publishers, 1948.)

Whitney, Janet Payne. *John Woolman, American Quaker.* (Boston: Little, Brown & Co., 1942.)

THE CLASSICS OF THE AGE OF REVOLUTION

Personal Piety

Kierkegaard's Purity of Heart

Bonhoeffer's Letters and Papers

Alfred Delp's Prison Meditations

Teilhard's Letters from a Traveller

Selected Bibliography

VIII

The Classics of The Age of Revolution

The nineteenth and twentieth centuries have produced a revolution in devotional literature as in almost everything else. Gone is the otherworldly devotion of the High Middle Ages; faith has been drawn into a closer union with the things of *this* world.

This is hardly surprising. These two centuries have been revolutionary in more than religion. In the western world the major happenings have borne the name "revolution"—the American Revolution, the French Revolution, the Industrial Revolution, the Scientific Revolution, the Communist Revolution, and the rest.

Politically, this era has brought vast and dramatic shifts in the balance of power and in geography. England, for a long time mistress of the seas and of a far flung empire which stretched around the globe, has slipped gradually from the pedestal upon which her people's genius placed her. She has relinquished title to first one and then another of the colonies claimed in the centuries of colonial expansion—the American colonies and India heading the list. No longer can she control trade on the high seas as she once did. On the contrary, her leaders are faced today with the unenviable task of social and economic retrenchment, forced upon them by the shrinking of her borders.

For a while France dominated the European scene. The Revolution, 1789-1815, put an end to her monarchy, save for a brief return of the Bourbons, and injected into the French people a new pride and fighting spirit. Under Napoleon's skillful general-

ship the French army subdued almost all of the European heart-
land. Had it not been for Napoleon's extremely foolish error in
calculating the strength of Russia, France might have held sway
much longer. The French had their fling at colonialism, too. But
they lacked the fleet which gave England mastery of the seas
and the English genius for governing. So, though a great power
and skillful in diplomacy, France usually has had to take second
place behind England or other powers.

A few decades before World War II Germany stood near the
top. For centuries the German peoples had suffered from lack of
unity which even the so-called Holy Roman Empire failed to
secure. As a result, Napoleon had not found it difficult to deliver
a crushing blow which shattered this fiction. However, the
Napoleonic threat helped to crystalize the national pride of the
Germans. Under the leadership of the Prussian statesman Otto
von Bismarck (1815-18) they formed a powerful alliance against
the dominance of France and Russia. The industrial and financial
wizardry of the German people strengthened their hand.

Russia has had its ups and downs, not reaching the upper
plateaus until the last few decades. Located on the periphery
of Europe and boasting a predominantly Eastern culture, Russia's czars could never decide whether the great bear should face
east or west. Alexander I (Emperor, 1801-1825) had much to
do with the strengthening of Russia by internal reforms and in-
dustrialization. It was he who delivered Napoleon his awful defeat in 1812. Subsequently, Russia has been a power to reckon
with in European politics. World War I, the Communist Revolution in 1917, and World War II have spurred her to become
the industrial colossus of Europe and Asia.

In the meantime, as European nations have jockeyed for supremacy, new powers have sprung up around the world and,
thanks to improvement in communication and transportation,
politics have now become a world affair. The United States has
mounted the ladder to the top. A kind of half-awake giant with
endless reserves of power, she hardly took note of what went on

in other countries until 1917. Even then, long declaring her neutrality, she ambled reluctantly into World War I, still not sure it was a matter for her attention. Not until Pearl Harbor did she wake up to her international obligations. Since then, though, she has haltingly and unsurely led the western powers in a confrontation with avowedly communist states.

Since World War II other national powers, some great and some small, have begun to throw off the yoke of European dominance and to make their voices heard around the world. Latin America, Africa, and Asia have seethed with revolutions. The two power blocs, led by the Soviet Union and the United States, have fought an undeclared war for the allegiance of the rising powers. They have supplied their partisans with weapons of revolution, sometimes openly backing them with information, men and materiel. Who can predict what the ultimate outcome will be?

Bound up intimately with this political revolution has been a social and economic one. In one nation after another in these two centuries the mighty have fallen and the lowly been lifted up. The reform of the class structure stood at the heart of the French Revolution. In England this reform took place with less violence, guided skillfully along by brilliant statesmen such as Robert Peel and William Gladstone. In Russia it took the most violent possible form, costing millions of lives and resulting in a complete shift in the Russian way of life.

In the background of this social and economic upheaval lay the Industrial Revolution. Already, in the latter half of the eighteenth century, England began to witness dramatic new inventions which revolutionized industry and advanced her to the leadership position in production and trade. The designing of cheap means to produce steel, oil, and rubber made possible the development of all sorts of industrial machines previously unknown. Machinepower replaced manpower. Unfortunately this meant joblessness for thousands. The rich became richer and the poor became poorer. The doctrine of *laissez-faire* capitalism, like *laissez-faire* politics, proved unworkable. The jobless and the poorly paid workers channeled their opposition through trade unions, political agitation, and, in the last resort, insurrection.

In his *Communist Manifesto,* published in 1848, Karl Marx, a German Jewish Christian, having spent long years grappling tenaciously with the problem, put forth a theory which could guide insurrectionists. Nothing short of revolution would suffice, he argued. The proletariat (lowest class) must arise and destroy the bourgeoisie (capitalistic middle class). By careful economic management they can control the course of history.

Marx's theory has had both a positive and a negative impact in the shaping of modern history. On the one hand, it has served as the base for the entire Communist world movement. On the other, it has forced various nations to revise their commitment to capitalism. As population has mushroomed and crowded into large urban centers, more social and economic planning has been required. England, faced with economic chaos, deliberately adopted a form of socialism. Other nations have had to do the same. Even an affluent and expansive country like the United States has been forced, however reluctantly, to do more and more governmental planning.*

With such intense concern for human need, it is understand-

---

*Marx said that "the religious world is but a reflection of the real world" which would vanish finally if the practical relations of everyday life should offer to man nothing but "perfectly intelligible and reasonable relations with regard to his fellow-man and nature." Religion until this time of perfection in human relations remains "an opiate" or a drug of the people. (Karl Marx, *Capital: A Critique of Political Economy,* p. 91-92.) Yet, as we have an ascendant technology and increasing rationalism and humanism for a world and philosophy, *real* drugs—alcohol, LSD, marijuana, heroin, etc. —have come to mean more to people. In fact, real drugs seem to be a substitute for religion, whereby man may have either "absorption of the self into the All" or mystical ecstasy on demand and in the instant.

able that intellectual effort should be expended increasingly in the sciences with a practical orientation. Modern science barely got off the ground with Sir Isaac Newton (1642-1727). Its real strides forward came in the late eighteenth, nineteenth, and twentieth centuries as the great minds applied themselves to man's physical, intellectual, and social problems. Darwin's *Origin of the Species,* published in 1859, marked a new plateau in man's striving to understand himself. New sciences such as psychology and sociology widened the perspective. The scientific revolution was helping man "to come of age."*

The triumph of science generated a pragmatic approach to philosophy. The older theistic philosophies gave way to logical positivism, which concerned itself with the unification of the sciences by the analysis of the language of science and development of a vocabulary applicable to all sciences. Logical positivism naturally has tended to generate an optimistic view of man, an almost unbounded confidence in his abilities to solve his own problems. But two world wars in quick succession have

---

*The emergence of the psychological and sociological revolution marked a secularization of the ethic of the middle classes into such concepts as "adjustment," maturity, self-control, and personal serenity. I often think that the psychologists of today perform the same function in our world as did the Stoics of the Early Christian era: one can be a mystic, a believer in the Oversoul, a contemplative through the medium of the psychological without coming to grips with the personal reality of God. Yet, can he? If so, one needs to make careful note of how the most eminent of psychologists could not leave the problem of the personal reality of God alone: Marx's sociology had to deal with this Reality by negative exclusion. Freud was intensely preoccupied with the nature of personal religious faith, though he was an avowed atheist. Dewey came to equate God with experience. Jung elaborated a vast mystical system of symbolism and belief. Therefore, the person who takes the dark side of the moon of modern psychology seriously will discover the negative counterpart of the belief in and search for God in the meditations of modern psychologists.

helped to dampen such optimism and have created an opening for the development of a less pragmatic approach to things. Since World War II, consequently, existentialism has supplanted pragmatism. Man demands to know what life means and increasingly he has had to look at things in their wholeness.

The intellectual changes of these two centuries have not encouraged religion. In Europe and England the churches—Catholic, Protestant or Orthodox—have experienced only occasional instances of revival; the general trend has been downward. The nearly incredible discoveries of modern science have shaken the foundations of faith. Pragmatic concerns have relegated religion to the past for many, who consider it, as did Marx, "the opiate of the people." The established churches all too often upheld the status quo against social, economic, and political progress. So the oppressed and burdened who had once listened to the gospel of Jesus now listen to the gospel of Karl Marx, or of pragmatism, or of other "enlightened" philosophies.

In some contrast to this, the religious situation in America looks quite different. Church attendance is "in." Religion satisfies the social and cultural need of the middle classes. But, I suspect, a disaster is brewing. Many rightly accuse the churches of preserving the social imbalance—white and black, rich and poor, employed and unemployed—though they forget how much the churches have done to erase these. The lower classes are turning to other faiths for an answer. The most dreadful of these is the gospel of power.

The brightest ray of hope shining in the midst of darkness is the vast change of attitude among various Christian communions. Where fragmentation and division was once the trend, we can now see a striving for unity. Better relations have begun to grow among Catholics, Orthodox, and Protestants. A new look is being given even to other religious faiths. All religions have perceived a need to work together in whatever ways they can in order that mankind may survive.

In consonance with the universal concern about the future of man, the Christian churches have reconsidered their mission and purpose. They have cast aside their cloak of other-worldliness and put on a this-worldly one. Not since the Protestant Reformation has such a radical change occurred. The Churches' involvement in human affairs has reached the point of frenzy, and one wonders how far secularization will go. In time, surely, the pendulum will have to swing the other way.

Personal Piety

In an era dominated so completely by human concerns one is not surprised to see a considerable change in private and even public devotion. A dramatic shift has occurred in all Christian communions.

Catholic. To be sure, Roman Catholics have held to their mainstays. The Mass has retained its position in the center of Catholic devotion. In its battle against secularism, the Church has encouraged and exhorted its laymen to observe Mass with greater regularity. Priests have continued to observe the rite privately as well as publicly; its celebration being thought to aid both the living and the souls in purgatory. Monastic orders, both male and female, have continued to offer an example of devotion and to provide places of retreat for both clergy and laity. New orders have sprung up occasionally to fill a gap or to inject a new spirit into popular devotion.

During these two centuries, also, the Church has tended to cultivate the average layman's devotion to Mary. In 1854, countering the tides of liberalism, Pope Pius IX declared the Dogma of the Immaculate Conception. This dogma supposedly was confirmed miraculously four years later when a young shepherd girl named Bernadette Soubirous saw a vision of Mary and heard her say, "I am the Immaculate Conception." In 1950 Pope Pius XII promulgated the Dogma of the Corporeal Assumption of Mary. In 1954 he sought to heighten commitment to her further by declaring a Marian Year. John XXIII, however, slowed and perhaps reversed this trend. He called certain acts of devotion to Mary "perhaps excessive." Then, the bishops assembled at Vatican Council II refused to devote a separate schema to Mary, choosing instead to discuss her in relation to the doctrine of the Church. Only in strongly Catholic countries like Spain and Latin American nations has intensive pressure to increase Marian devotion continued.*

The Roman Church has produced some notable mystics who have helped to inspire personal devotion and evangelism—Francis Libermann (1802-52), Herman Cohen (1820-70), Isaac Thomas Hecker (1819-88), and Charles de Foucauld (1858-1916), among others. Libermann, a converted son of a Jewish rabbi, founded a missionary society which labored especially in Africa. Cohen, a brilliant musician who had studied under Franz Liszt, converted from Judaism after experiencing an unusual sensation when conducting the choir of a small Paris church,

---

*The Protestant has difficulty appreciating what the Virgin Mary means to the Catholic. Yet, we insist on the importance of the Virgin Birth to our faith, and rightly so. From a psychological point of view, the life of prayer is considerably influenced by that which we consider to be the "masculine" thing to do and the "feminine" thing to do. Whereas the Hebrew-Christian faith has resisted the fate of a division of the person of God into the masculine and feminine characters, nevertheless, the mystery of the nature of God is characterized in the mystery of the nature of marriage among His creatures as being "one flesh." In Christ, there is neither male nor female. Yet, the need for the recognition of the place of the pure woman in the mind and purpose of God is actualized in the person of Mary, the mother of Jesus. However, it does seem to the Protestant as he prays that the Virgin Mary demonstrates the participation of Christ in the completely human, and the necessity for deifying the Virgin Mary blurs this reality and completeness of the Incarnation. The unpretentious Catholic person at prayer probably finds in her a tie with the worshiper as human and a reaffirmation of the humanity of Christ. One wonders. Wonder itself is a form of prayer.

preached in both France and England and died ministering to POWs. Hecker, an American, founded the order of Paulists after the evangelistic order of Redemptorists criticized his progressive views and methods. Foucauld spent much of his active career among the Moslems in North Africa.[1]

One correctly detects in all of these practices the continuance of traditional modes of devotion. Nevertheless, the Roman Church has not weathered the age of revolution without change. Ever since the Reformation, a handful of progressives have pressed for updating; Pope John simply opened the gate when the time seemed to be auspicious. Vatican II allowed the liturgy to be translated into the vernacular so that the faithful might participate more fully. It laid aside some of the practices which offended the more critical. In all, it let in a breath of fresh air and revived many who gasped for breath in a room made stifling by ecclesiastical falderal.

Protestant. If Roman Catholic piety has suffered from the stranglehold of traditional modes, Protestantism has suffered from the opposite. Individuality has been the keynote of Protestant devotion; every man does what is right in his own eyes. As a result, one cannot put his finger on specific characteristics.

Certainly, attendance at public worship, the sermon, prayer, hymn singing, and acts of charity and good will have furnished the core of Protestant devotion. But the impact of secularization on the modern era has effected the most diverse reactions. Some have merely pitched in the towel to secular change and sought to live a life as nearly like that of contemporaries as they could. They have expressed dissatisfaction with "churchiness" and "religion." In extreme cases they have surrendered all affiliation with the Church and commitment to God and fashioned their own religious substitutes. Apart from the Church they have sought to meet the crises of life as "worldly" men.

On the opposite end of the spectrum, others have striven to revive traditional modes of Christian devotion. In England, monasticism, lopped off in 1538 by Henry VIII, was revived in 1841 by the Oxford Movement. Subsequently, it has flourished, though not on the scale of pre-Reformation monasticism. Other Protestant communions also have produced isolated monastic communities. In 1938 George MacLeod, a Scottish Presbyterian minister, started a Protestant community on the site of the ancient Iona monastery with membership open to both ministers and laymen. In 1940 a French Protestant inaugurated a similar project in Taizé, France. From 1944 on this community has contributed significantly to the ecumenical movement and to the general revival of religion on the continent. It has served as a model for similar communities all over Europe.

Such developments bear witness to a deficiency in Protestantism. The great Danish philosopher, Soren Kierkegaard, pinpointed the need in his *Journal* entry for November, 1847:

There is no doubt that the present time, and Protestantism always, needs the monastery again, or that it should exist. "The Monastery" is an essential dialectical fact in Christianity, and we need to have it there like a light-house, in order to gauge where we are—even though I myself should not exactly go into one. But if there is to be true Christianity in every generation there must be individuals with that need.*[2]

With its keen sense of calling to serve God in the world Protestantism has sometimes neglected the retreat. The result has been

------

*Kierkegaard reaffirms the importance of the single life as he speaks of the Monastery. He himself remained single. He did so "of himself" for the Kingdom of Heaven's sake. Protestants have, as a whole, left little or no room in the cultural pattern for the single person, but subtly exploited them and deprived them of a distinctly *communal* religious meaning for their single state. Yet, some of the most influential Protestants, strong men and women of prayer, have been single persons—Soren Kierkegaard, Dietrich Bonhoeffer, Anton Boisen, Kenneth Scott Latourette, to say nothing of the nineteenth and early twentieth century conception of the woman missionary, that the faithful, whether cleric or lay, have lost the "light-house," which could guide them in exercising their priesthood in the world. Pragmatism has blunted the edge of piety and, in doing so, has impaired the Church's effectiveness.

Admittedly, Protestantism has boasted a few mystics and, in the present critical era, interest in mysticism is on the upswing. Yet those classified as mystics, mostly poets, offer a rather tremulous witness to religious verities.[3] Blake, Wordsworth, Keats, Tennyson, Bronte, Yeats, Masefield, Emerson, Whitman, and others, for example, hardly emit in their writings the confident assurance of Bernard, Francis, Thomas á Kempis, and the army of greats produced by the Roman Catholic Church.

Perhaps this is as it should be, considering the times. Protestant mystics, at least, have laid aside the stereotypes of Catholic mysticism. They come at religious experience from new angles. Sometimes they come through with fresh insights. And always they have been mindful of the changing times to which religious experience must speak.

Ecumenical. The sizeable gap between Protestant this-worldly individualism and Catholic otherworldly ecclesiasticism has diminished markedly since World War II, thanks to the growth of appreciation for the entire Christian heritage on both sides coupled with the impact of secularization. The War itself de-

---

woman school teacher, and woman nurse as *necessarily* being single persons.

The struggle of the soul of such persons in the decision "to be or not to be" married has been the generative source of vast reaches of the private prayer life as recorded in our more recent Protestant life. One asks the question in his prayers: "Is the single life also a calling from God?" Only one's own prayers can answer this. The supportive community of Protestants is not often there. Consequently, Kierkegaard's word here is remarkably needed for the honest person at prayer.

serves much credit for this. In Nazi concentration camps,* for instance, ancient prejudices began to crumble when both sides realized they had to face a common foe with commitment to a common Lord. Out of this realization grew the Una Sancta movement, pioneered by Father Max Metzger, which prefigured the development of a Catholic ecumenical movement.

In the realm of personal devotion, the post-war years have ushered in a new era. Catholics and Protestants now visit freely in one another's churches. They hold joint services of worship. Protestants go on retreat in Catholic monasteries. Ministers offer counsel to one another, share ideas and insights, and do what they can to undergird all of Christendom in a trying era.

The way in which the threat of secularism has driven Christians closer together is seen clearly in the devotional literature of this era. Though the traditional varieties still hang on, the classics leave the old day far behind. The Lutheran Kierkegaard offers a striking analogy to the Catholic Pascal. Bonhoeffer and Delp, both martyrs to the Nazis, wrote and thought incredibly alike, so much so that it would be hard to say which was Protestant and which Catholic. The Jesuit Teilhard de Chardin caps off the whole process, for in his suggestive thought, the man of science and the man of faith have found the common circle within which they together may discuss the critical issues of life.

---

*Here, again, is the "prison motif" in the generation of the power of prayer. Remarkably enough, the concentration camps were the demonstration of one of the most persuasive of contemporary types of psychotherapy——logotherapy, as set forth by Viktor Frankl of Vienna in his book, *From Death Camp to Existentialism.* He found in the camp at Dachau the encounter with meaninglessness and the power of the human spirit in its struggle for meaning to lay hold of the ontological realities of life. Frankl is a Jew and is plain to say so. Yet, the devotional character of his book, *The Doctor and the Soul,* is reminiscent of the book of Psalms, the prayer book of Jew, Catholic, and Protestant.

Kierkegaard's Purity of Heart

The author. Soren Aabye Kierkegaard, born in Copenhagen, Denmark, in 1813, was the son of a well-to-do manufacturer, the last in a family of seven. A frail physical constitution, a brilliant mind, and the fact that he was born in the father's fifty-sixth year caused his father, Michael Pedersen, to dote on the child and to give hours to his entertainment and instruction. A man of great wit and imagination himself, the father cultivated his son's brilliant mind by taking him on imaginary trips around the room, describing passers-by, carriages, houses, and all, as if on a real journey. His devotion to Soren, not unexpectedly, established a bond between the two which erected a permanent scaffold for the great philosopher's understanding of religion.

In 1835 the young Kierkegaard experienced "the great earthquake," which momentarily disrupted the bond between him and his father. Before this he had had a number of things to unhinge his sensitive spirit. In 1834 both his mother and a sister had died. But the "earthquake" itself concerned his father, who, Soren discovered upon his return home from the University, suffered from the same melancholy which plagued him—unable to forgive himself because he had once cursed God. "I felt the stillness of death grow around me when I saw my father," he confessed in the *Journals,* "an unhappy man who was to outlive us all, a cross on the tomb of all his hopes."[4]

Badly shaken, Soren rebelled. He became a prodigal. Floundering about trying to determine "what God really wishes *me* to do," he directed his rebellion into three channels—a reaction against Christianity, aesthetic pursuits, and moral disintegration —which he represented in the figures of Faust, the Wandering Jew, and Don Juan. Yet in all of this he despised himself. "I have just returned from a party of which I was the life and soul;" he recorded in the *Journals* for March 1836, "wit poured from my lips, everyone laughed and admired me—but I went away— and the dash should be as long as the earth's orbit . . . and wanted to shoot myself."[5]

The cloud lifted a bit in May, 1837, when he met Regine Olsen, then only fourteen, with whom he immediately fell in love. Then, in May, 1838, he experienced a "conversion" connected with his reconciliation with his father.* May 19, 10:30 a.m., he noted, "There is an indescribable joy which enkindles us as inexplicably as the apostle's outburst comes gratuitously: . . . a heavenly refrain, as it were, suddenly breaks off our other song . . ."[6]

But Soren's father died in August. More than ever, he had to find God's will specifically for him. In accordance with his father's wishes but without a real sense of direction, he took the theological examination in 1840, passing *cum laude*. In September he became engaged to Regine Olsen. But this only increased his anxiety and deepened his inherited melancholy with

---

*Here again is the "father motif" in the life of the spirit in prayer. Erik Erikson has said that the mature person is one who has come to terms with his parents as persons for whom there is no substitute. In other words, he has *accepted* them and no longer seeks to "remake" them or to relate to them conditionally as if they would "get lost" and be no more of a problem to him. The reconciliation of Soren Kierkegaard to his father has this mark of psychological arrival, although from this point on his father was a vivid figure in his meditations.

Each person coming into the world does so *via* a mother and a father. They are representatives of God, and God is not an illusion projected forth on a grand scheme pictured after our parents. They draw their reality from him. Their creativity is a *derived* creativity. We are responsible to them, but they in turn are responsible to God. The breakthrough of realizing that parents are human, too, is the beginning of the real need for the true God. As long as we worship parents, either by negative absorption of our rejection of them or by positive absorption of our fixation upon them, we have major trouble in finding our prayers to be our own and real. Therefore, a face-to-face evaluation of our own relationships with our parents in conversation with God, as we know him in Christ, is a form of serious praying, a good place to start praying if you are having trouble knowing where to start.

the result that he broke the engagement less than a year later. Despite the loss of face and bitterness shown by her family, he saw no other alternative: his own personal limitations—physical, moral, and intellectual—and his sense of divine vocation would not allow it. Love of God compelled him.

Kierkegaard apparently began to get his bearings after this "event," *factum,* as he called it. He broke through to a new and deeper level of Christian faith—an acceptance of suffering as a part of his divine vocation. For a time, it is true, he still had some thoughts about becoming a country pastor. Attacked and caricatured from many sides, he must have had second thoughts about the cost of his resolution to be "a spy in the service of God." By January, 1847, however, he envisioned clearly wherein lay his calling—to disrupt the established order in Danish Christendom and to sound the demand of the gospel for absolute trust, loyalty, and devotion to God. The "boldness" to launch out in this task finally came in April, 1848. "My whole being is changed," he wrote in the *Journals* for April 19. "My reserve and self-isolation is broken—I must speak. Lord give thy grace."

A combination of financial problems, ill health, and whether to become a clergyman seem to have precipitated the final crisis. The complex series of events evoked a clear declaration of purpose in an essay on *The Point of View of My Work as an Author,* in which Kierkegaard avowed that all of his efforts had been divinely guided toward this end. Even though he had approached the question from an oblique direction, i.e., aesthetically, prior to 1846, "divine governance" had propelled him. No matter how others might interpret his work, he was, after all, a *religious* writer. Whereas, before he had been the Socratic gadfly, he now had to be the "witness," the *martyr* for the faith.

And a martyr he did become. At first it was "the martyrdom of laughter."* Absorbing his blows with courage, nevertheless,

---

Laughter as prayer. Genesis 17:17 tells us that Abraham was at prayer with God and God revealed to him that he would, by Sarah,

he stepped up his attacks against the twin evils of Danish Christendom—the anonymous press and a bourgeois Church. He criticized even Luther. For, though the great reformer should be thanked for his doctrine of faith, he held a one-sided view of the New Testament. His reaction to an overwrought asceticism, Kierkegaard charged, "brings forth the subtlest kind of worldliness and paganism." For three years, 1849-52, Kierkegaard kept himself in isolation in order to "train himself" in Christianity. He exercised admirable self-control as he refrained from direct attacks on the Danish church. One more attempt to preach flopped; even thinking about it overwhelmed him.

A further spiritual experience in June of 1852 brought to a climax Kierkegaard's Easter experience of 1848. "It is the 'imitation of Christ' that must now be introduced—" he noted in the *Journals* for June 19, "and I must be what I am, in being different from others."[7] At long last he had arrived at the point where he could accept the suffering he believed God required of every faithful man. The real man stepped forth. Denzil Patrick has rightly commented:

Kierkegaard may be presented as a mighty iconoclast, who smashed the complacency of his Church with thunderous blows; but that picture of him is incomplete. Behind the iconoclast lies the humble man of God. Behind the obvious psychological brain-storm of his

---

become the father of a son. Abraham then "fell upon his face and laughed. . . ." When he told Sarah what God had revealed to him, she laughed. Sarah was ashamed of having laughed, because, it seems, her laugh was a laugh of unbelief. I suppose this is one of the first instances of the "credibility gap." Soren Kierkegaard laughs the laugh of martyrdom, laughing in the face of his fate with irony, and yet this "offering up" kind of laughter was also a kind of prayer. One way of continuing to pray is to examine before God, without shame, the nature of the things we laugh at and the character of our laughter. As Shelley says in his *To A Skylark*, "Our sincerest laughter with some pain is fraught." Soren Kierkegaard's laughter was fraught with much pain.

latter days lies the hidden pneumatological calm of his dedicated life.[8]

Kierkegaard's last years brought upon his head the bitterest invectives of critics, but he remained resolute in his decision. The death of Bishop Mynster, his father's friend and a dedicated churchman, provided him an occasion to rip to shreds the comfortable exterior of Danish Christendom. Kierkegaard viciously pounced upon a eulogy of Mynster as "a witness to the truth" by his former teacher in the University of Copenhagen, Hans Martensen. When the wrath of all Copenhagen fell upon his head, he broadened his attack in a series of essays called *The Instant*. Almost to his dying day, he kept the church reeling from his blows. Nothing in the ecclesiastical system escaped his indictment—the clergy, marriage, confirmation, the whole panoply. On his deathbed, in fact, Kierkegaard demanded that a *layman* give him communion, for clergymen are "royal officials," and "royal officials are not related to Christianity."[9] His polemic was exaggerated, he knew; but a Church which had become the opposite of what God purposed for it needed a rude awakening. Engaged in this task, he died on November 11, 1855.

Purity of Heart. Purity of Heart stands in the very center of Kierkegaard's thought and helps unravel the mystery of his "task." Composed in 1846, the book brings to the surface an understanding of Christianity whose *personal* implications Kierkegaard himself did not yet comprehend fully. Yet, in time this understanding compelled him to don the martyr's robe he wore to the grave.

The one thing needful, Kierkegaard wrote in the greatest of his unpreached sermons or "edifying discourses" for the individual, is to will one thing, namely, the Good. To will anything but the Good is double-mindedness. All other desires merely bar us from what is essential, whether desire of variety and great moments, hope of reward, fear of punishment, egocentric service of the Good, or partial commitment to the Good. The price of willing one thing is *absolute* commitment—a willingness to suffer all for the sake of the Good. No matter what the situation may be or the station in life one may hold, to will the Good means to give all. The Good "demands neither more nor less than all, whether that is a mere bit or not is neither here nor there."*[10]

What all of this means from a practical point of view is that each person must be "that solitary individual." Luther, Kierkegaard complained, did a disservice when he tore down the papal edifices and did not at the same time call upon men to be individuals. One absolutely must *not* hide in the crowd (the mob) and excuse his failings. He must accept responsibility as that solitary individual who has willed the Good. He must use his cleverness to unmask every hypocrisy and subterfuge which shuns

---

*Kierkegaard's *Purity of Heart* reflects his ability as a psychologist. He perceived himself as a Christian psychologist in many of his writings. The underlying psychological theme of this devotional work is the probing of human *motivation* for commitment to God. The carbon of sham is burned off as he accelerates his examination of the human heart. Jeremiah said and asked: "The human heart is deceitful above all things and desperately corrupt; who can understand it?" He answers his question with a word from God: "I the Lord search the mind and try the heart, to give to every man according to his ways, according to the fruit of his doings."

The searching of the heart and its capacity to deceive itself is the concern of *Purity of Heart*. A refining process, removing the dross of duplicity, double-mindedness, and instability is at once a psychological exercise and a spiritual benefit. The mechanisms of defense—rationalization, displacement, isolation, undoing, reaction-formation, unconscious fantasy, etc.—all find a distinctly religious expression in this book. The psychotherapist, Karen Horney, in her book, *Our Inner Conflicts*, evaluates the deceptive qualities of neuroticism today in a way very akin to the mood and manner of Kierkegaard and actually gives him credit at many places in her writings for insight into the treatment of the neurotically uncommitted person of today.

the one needful thing.* In one's occupation and conduct, whatever it may be, he must constantly query his attitude and his method: Do I will one thing? "In eternity, the individual, yes, you, my listener, and I as individuals will each be asked solely about himself as an individual and about the individual details in his life."[11]

This concern for individuality holds the key to Kierkegaard's "rebellion" against philosophy, social custom, and, above all, religion. It explains his attack on Hegel, his open defiance of the rule which prohibited the cultured from talking to the hoi polloi, and his scathing indictment of the Danish church. It even helps to explain, I believe, some egocentric outbursts in praise of his own genius and against the stinging blasts of critics. Kierkegaard perhaps described himself best when he nicknamed himself "the stormy-petrel," the kind of bird who appears when storm clouds begin to gather. When the storm came, he did not flee. To the last he was "that solitary individual," not perfect, but knowing perfectly what God required of him.

Bonhoeffer's Letters and Papers

Subsequent generations owe Kierkegaard a huge debt, as he forecast prophetically, though his contemporaries failed for the most part to appreciate his sense of vocation, which was so closely tied to his oddities. Certain aspects of his thought have borne their finest fruit in the twentieth century, in fact: his concern for genuine discipleship, his critique of the established

---

*Anne Morrow Lindbergh says in her book, *Gift From the Sea,* that sham is the most fatiguing thing the human spirit has to endure. She says that she has decided to put away her mask. Kierkegaard is saying that the life of eternity is the unmasking of the self as we really are as an individual. We can no longer count on our roles as a hiding place, nor do we have to weary ourselves with the burden of social pretense in our prayers. God does not expect us to "put our best face forward" in talking with Him. Prayer is more

churches, his contempt for bourgeois religion, and his approach to reality (existentialism). In some of these matters he paved the way for Dietrich Bonhoeffer, the most influential voice in Christian theology during the past two decades.

The author. The backgrounds and careers of Kierkegaard and Bonhoeffer exhibit both remarkable parallels and remarkable contrasts. Like Kierkegaard, Bonhoeffer belonged to a socially and intellectually prominent family. His father, Karl Ludwig, was a distinguished neurologist who occupied the first chair of psychiatry at the University of Berlin. His mother, Paula, was the granddaughter of the famous Church historian, Karl von Hase. Dietrich himself, born in Breslau on February 4, 1906, as a twin, the sixth or seventh in a family of eight, grew up in enviable intellectual surroundings. After the family moved to Berlin in 1912, he played with the children of the famous historians Adolf von Harnack and Hans Delbrück.

In intellectual gifts and personal sensitivity, the two men also rank together. However, Bonhoeffer enjoyed a robust physical constitution and did not suffer from the melancholia and uncertainty which plagued Kierkegaard. At age sixteen, he decided to enter the ministry of the Lutheran church. With this goal in mind he enrolled in the University of Tuebingen, then after one year in the University of Berlin. A brilliant scholar, he awed the best minds on the theological faculty—Harnack, Adolf Deissmann, Hans Lietzmann, Ernest Sellin, Karl Holl, and Reinhold Seeberg. In 1927, at age twenty-one, he submitted his disserta-

---

often what we say under our breath to ourselves than we would like to admit that it is. We cannot really put distance between us and God. We only put distance between our fictitious selves and our real selves. All the while God is in touch with both. As Jacob Boehme has said, we cannot, by confessing our sins to God, thereby give him information about ourselves he does not already have. Yet in Christ we need not be afraid of His knowing us as we are already known. His love perfected casts out this fear.

tion for the licentiate in theology, entitled *Sanctorum communio,* which Karl Barth has called "a theological miracle."[12]

After a preaching mission of about one year in Barcelona, Spain, as vicar of a German-speaking congregation, Bonhoeffer returned to Berlin. As his inaugural address for admission to the teaching faculty, he prepared a second brilliant work entitled *Act and Being,* which reflected the influence of the Swiss theologian Karl Barth. Before undertaking his teaching duties, however, he accepted an invitation from Union Theological Seminary in New York to spend a year in the United States on the Sloan Fellowship, thus establishing his reputation in America as well as in Europe. When he returned to Berlin in the summer of 1931, he assumed a demanding load. Besides being a lecturer in theology, he served as chaplain of a technical college, leader of a confirmation class for fifty unruly boys whom another catechist had given up as hopeless, and Secretary of the Youth Commission for the World Alliance for International Friendship through the Churches. Despite these demands, he published a series of lectures entitled *Creation and Fall* in 1933.

Meanwhile, ominous clouds overshadowed Europe. The Nazis rose to power under Adolf Hitler on the crest of a giant wave of German nationalism. Two days after Hitler's installation as Chancellor of the Third Reich, Bonhoeffer, in a radio address which the authorities cut off the air before he finished, warned the German people about the dangers of the *Führer* concept. Now *persona non grata,* in October 1933 he took a leave of absence from his teaching duties and went to London, where he became pastor of two German-speaking congregations, thus signaling clearly his break with German Christians who supported Hitler.*

---

*The Nazi persecution fell with heavy hands upon Christian and non-Christian alike. The work of psychoanalysts was burned alongside that of Christians who broke with those who supported Hitler. Theodor Reik tells of bidding Sigmund Freud goodbye in Amster-

In 1935, in response to a plea from the anti-Nazi Confessing Church, the brilliant and dedicated theologian and Christian leader came back to his homeland to take over the reins of a seminary at Finkenwalde which would train pastors for the Confessing Church. Though Bonhoeffer was forbidden to continue teaching and the school closed by order of Heinrich Himmler in 1937, it continued a clandestine operation three years longer. In this same year, the German church situation uppermost in his mind, Bonhoeffer published his widely read exposition of the Sermon on the Mount, *The Cost of Discipleship*. In words reminiscent of Kierkegaard he denounced the doctrine of "cheap grace" which Lutherans gather around like vultures and called for discipleship, unswerving commitment to Christ.

Friends, anxious for his safety and knowing his value to the church, arranged for him to return to America in 1939. Bonhoeffer accepted an invitation to lecture at Union Theological Seminary. But he had hardly unpacked before his conscience drove him to return to Germany; he could not desert his people in an hour of crisis. Upon his return, with deep soul searching but convinced that as a Christian he had no alternative, he joined the resistance movement against Hitler.

---

dam as he left for London to flee from the Nazis. Freud told him that he had always liked him, because they had never had to pretend to each other. He told Reik that people "who belong together do not have to be glued together." The way in which the suffering of political persecution bound the most unlikely of companions together in suffering bespeaks of the ecumenicity of suffering. The poignant melancholy of a man like Freud who wanted a religionless faith is paradoxically reminiscent of the spirit of Bonhoeffer, although their philosophical presuppositions and faith commitments were vastly different. One wonders if John Baillie was right when he said that he was grateful for Freud in that Freud helped him to make a better confession of his sins to God. This is certainly true of the established results of the exploration of the unconscious which is in itself a form of prayer. One also gives thanks for Bonhoeffer in that he too enables us to make a *good* confession.

As a result of his activities in the underground, Bonhoeffer was arrested on April 5, 1943, and confined in Tegel Military Prison in Berlin. For the next two dreadful and uncertain years he served as counselor and friend to fellow-inmates and wrote. In September, 1944 the Gestapo discovered his connection with the abortive plot on Hitler's life on July 20. In October they moved him to the infamous Prinz Albrecht Strasse prison, later to Buchenwald, and then to Schönberg. By personal order of Hitler he was hanged at Flossenburg on April 9, 1945. Had he lived but a few days longer, he would have been liberated with others by the rapidly advancing American Army.

Letters and Papers from Prison. *Letters and Papers from Prison* (entitled *Prisoner of God* in the earlier American edition) consists of letters to his parents and various friends, brief essays, a few poems, and a wedding sermon written by Bonhoeffer during these fateful two years. Various nuances are hidden from the reader, obviously, in part because he lacked liberty to speak freely and in part because most of the material has a personal twist. Nonetheless, through the facade one can see a man who possessed in immense quantities depth of insight, commitment to the God revealed in Jesus Christ, pastoral concern for his people and particularly for his fellow prisoners, seriousness about life tempered by Christian optimism, involvement in and appreciation for life, honesty and courage in the face of present uncertainties, and hope for the future.

The letters to his parents and to his fiancée reveal unmistakably how sensitive he was toward others. Lest he make them anxious about his situation, he painted a halfway rosy picture of prison life, concealing from them his boredom, anxiety, and impatience. This was not merely a cover up, however; he used his time fruitfully in study and gave them a sense of satisfaction in supplying him with reading matter and food. He reminded them over and over how their love rendered the prison routine bearable, giving him some hope for the future.

The letters to his friend Eberhard Bethge, editor of the collected *Letters and Papers,* manifest the pastor, theologian, and man of faith. Bonhoeffer had cultivated his natural pastoral gifts in Spain and England as well as at home. Prison life, with the heavy demands it placed on the psyche, sharpened his eye to distinguish more precisely between genuine needs and sheer weakness. A man of aristocratic upbringing and temperament, Bonhoeffer detested cowardice and made short shrift of prisoners who tried to play on his sympathies. Yet he went out of his way to comfort and encourage those with authentic needs and took pride in the fact that the prisoners and even some of the staff looked upon him as their pastor.*

As a theologian, during this period Bonhoeffer took some halting steps beyond his earlier thinking. Gripped by the trauma of a world torn by strife, he grappled courageously with the question: "How can we reclaim for Christ a world which has come of age?"

In trying to answer this poser he reached no positive con-

---

*Bonhoeffer's forthrightness in Christian candor is a clean break with the "nicety" of much that passes for a devout life. Men and women of great tenderness are often also capable of genuine wrath. One can easily say this as a way of excusing his or her irascible temper, lack of self-control, and the snapping of nerves due to frustration, pain, and despair. Yet, on the other hand, this kind of self-restriction can also leave out the frank realization that all of us have our limits beyond which self-centered people cannot really push us without doing violence to our conviction that we *are* persons in our own right. Bonhoeffer, seeing the ravages upon the human spirit being made around him, feeling the scurrilousness of human nature at its worst, must have been driven beyond the level that any man or woman should be normally expected to contain his or her impatience. The Psalms express anger directly as a way of praying. Moses did so in Numbers 11. Our God is the kind of God that can "take it" when we express our anger. Do we dare believe that He loves us enough to let us be angry toward others, ourselves, and even Him? I think so.

clusions. He probed in the direction of a parlay between the Church and modern society in which the Church, by a new and "shocking" dialogue, again might capture the ear of modern man. We must stop thinking of God "as a stop-gap for the incompleteness of our knowledge." This merely allows Him to be edged farther and farther out of our existence. He must be brought into the very center of life, just as He was in the Incarnation. Hence, "in Christ there are no Christian problems." "The world's coming of age is then no longer an occasion for polemics and apologetics, but it is really better understood than it understands itself, namely on the basis of the Gospel, and in the light of Christ."[13]

The answer to this question therefore, involves a "non-religious" interpretation of Christianity. It may also signify the end of the Church as we now know it. The Christian must immerse himself in the life of the world, "live a 'worldly' life and so participate in the suffering of God." This is his repentance, his participation in Christ's messianic activities. He becomes "the man for others." For the Church, Bonhoeffer mused in an outline for a projected book, this entails a self-emptying.

The Church is her true self only when she exists for humanity. As a fresh start she should give away all her endowment to the poor and needy. The clergy should live solely on the free-will offerings of their congregations, or possibly engage in some secular calling. She must take her part in the social life of the world, not lording it over men, but helping and serving them. She must tell men, whatever their calling, what it means to live in Christ, to exist for others.*[14]

Notwithstanding his demand for "worldly holiness" for Christians and for the Church, Bonhoeffer himself perceived clearly

---

*Clergymen often lose their sense of identity because they are beholden to too many people. The Apostle Paul, said, "owe no man anything but to love him." This seems to be the mood of Bonhoeffer. Paul Tournier makes much of the power of gifts to place people into a bondage of the spirit in his little book, *The Meaning of Gifts.*

the need for personal devotion. Actually, this entails no contra-diction in his thought at all. The encounter between Church and world would necessitate individual Christian discipline in a new way. So Bonhoeffer was not ready to renounce his earlier appeal for discipleship, even if he had second thoughts about it. In fact, his own devotion grew with the years of imprisonment. He medi-tated on the Bible frequently, favoring the Psalms. "I am reading the Psalms daily, as I have done for years," he once informed his parents. "I know them and love them more than any other book in the Bible." Personal meditation steeled him against the tedium of seemingly endless confinement and furnished him with the courage to endure the harshness of it with a grace seldom sur-passed. "Bonhoeffer . . . was all humility and sweetness," Payne Best, a fellow prisoner in Schönberg, wrote later, "he always seemed to me to diffuse an atmosphere of happiness, of joy in every smallest event in life, and of deep gratitude for the mere fact that he was alive. . . . He was one of the very few men that I have ever met to whom his God was real and close to him."[15]

Alfred Delp's Prison Meditations

It is not surprising to find that *The Prison Meditations of Father Delp* possesses a remarkable likeness to *The Letters and Papers from Prison,* for both works were shaped in molds fash-ioned by the horrors of World War II. Alfred Delp, a Jesuit, had joined the Kreisau Circle, an anti-Nazi group which met secretly to plan for a new social order laid out along Christian lines after the war. With others he was seized by the Gestapo and jailed. An attempt was made to implicate him in the July plot on Hit-ler's life. Though able to prove his innocence on this charge, he

---

The appraisal of the "meaning of gifts," both those we receive and those we give, is a form of meditation and prayer. The distilling of our motives takes place most purely when we assess whether or not we should take the money of people and why. We find out who we are when we face frankly whose gifts we take.

had no chance against a kangaroo court. "The actual reason for my condemnation," he insisted, "was that I happened to be and chose to remain a Jesuit." Only thirty-seven years old, on February 2, 1945, about two months before Bonhoeffer, he was executed in Plotzensee prison.

From his prison cell Father Delp sized up the state of wartorn Europe with frank realism. German society—no, mankind—had suffered a shattering blow. Bombs and bullets had unmasked man for what he is. His shallowness and superficiality were laid bare. Even the Church has come up short. Is there any hope?

There is! In private diary entries; in Advent, Christmas, and Epiphany meditations; in brief essays; in a commentary on the Lord's Prayer and a pentecostal liturgy; and in his comments after he had been sentenced to die, Father Delp offers as man's hope a "God-conscious humanism." "God-conscious humanism" must replace that perverse pride which causes man to turn forces of good to destructive ends. Man must learn to control his passions and subordinate his preoccupation with self. "The essential requirement is that man must wake up to the truth about himself. He must rouse his consciousness of his own worth and dignity, of the divine and human potentialities within himself and at the same time he must master the undisciplined passions and forces which, in his name and by bemusing him with delight in his own ego, have made him what he is."[16]

What man needs, above all else, is to regain his freedom, which is potentially his as man. What he has lost by his egocentricity, he must regain by self-surrender and an open acknowledgment of God. God will not force Himself upon anyone; but He stands at the door knocking.* He comes to man ever and

---

*These two paragraphs underscore a paradox in the life of prayer. First we must rouse ourselves to our own worth and dignity, and at the same time we must enter the mood of prayer with a spirit of invitation that is, we ourselves must *invite* the Christ into our lives. He stands at the door and knocks, and if any man will hear Him,

again as the God of promise and fulfilment. In this lies man's
hope, for life is meaningless and futile without purpose and fulfilment. "It is God's alliance with man, his being on our side,
ranging himself with us, that corrects this state of meaningless
futility."[17] Life thus becomes "a continuous Advent," a continuous
movement toward an ultimate goal.

From man's immediate perspective, then, his view blurred by
time, happiness depends on an inward relationship with God,
who is present with us. The man of real faith has no doubt about
the outcome; he leaves everything in God's hands.

To Father Delp these last words had to be more than a hollow
boast. After his condemnation he confessed candidly that he did
not know whether he had steered the right course. "To be quite
honest I don't want to die, . . . But it has turned out otherwise."[18]
Yet, to the end he remained faithful to his understanding, dying
in hope. "I will honestly and patiently await God's will," he
said. "I will trust him till they come to fetch me. I will do my
best to ensure that this blessing, too, shall not find me broken
and in despair."[19]

Teilhard's Letters from a Traveller

Father Delp would have found much to his liking in the
thought of his fellow Jesuit Pierre Teilhard de Chardin, for the
latter sought to supply in a full blown philosophical system Fa-

---

open the door, and *let* Him in, He will come in and banquet with
him. This is a primary principle of the helping process of psychotherapy: the healing spirit never forces his way into the life of
another person. Yet he exercises the initiative of waiting at the door
to be invited into the other person's life. In this sense, the pastoral
counselor, the psychotherapist, or any helping person such as an
evangelist, does not bring good news by force but friendly persua-
sion. Prayer is the continuous invitation of the Spirit of God into
our lives: "Come, Holy Spirit, be Thou *the* Guest in my life. Fulfill
the promise of the Lord Jesus that Thou wouldst come and make
Thy home with us."

ther Delp's plea for a "God-conscious humanism." Teilhard's humanism stood at the center of a complete Christian evolutionary world view. The cosmos, he theorized, progresses continuously toward the "Omega point," that is, an ultimate unity. All levels of existence "converge" in the higher synthesis. This upward movement does not occur haphazardly, though it may appear to us to do so, but according to personal design. God, the Creator Spirit, who envelops the whole universe, insures the ordered movement of the whole. At the peak of this hierarchical structuring of things stands mankind, itself fragmented and incomplete, sinful, but moving toward the Omega point. Man represents the highest level of consciousness. Around him are structured concentrically in a definite pattern the elements of the universe. Man alone, Teilhard believed, could provide an intelligible explanation of the universe.

Human discord, so acute during Teilhard's entire lifetime, reflects par excellence the situation of the whole universe. Unlike many others in his day, however, the brilliant scientist and philosopher did not despair. He criticized harshly the prophets of gloom, the skeptics, and agnostics. He vocalized in opposition to this the strongest kind of optimism based on the Incarnation. In Christ, God restores the basic harmony of the universe. To use Paul's words, Christ "sums up all things in himself" (Col. 1:17). The Christian, therefore, must exercise both faith in our Lord who creates the world and faith in the world as animated by God, be a believer in the future of the world. Man's hope rests in God's "presenting Himself as the focus of salvation—not simply individual and 'super-natural salvation,' but collective and earth-embracing."[20] The unifying principle of all things is the divine love, summed up and made concrete in the universal Christ.

From an individual point of view faith in God and in His universe requires personal self-renunciation. One must envision his efforts as contributing to the work of God in bringing His creation toward its goal. For the Christian this means applying his energies to the forming of the body of Christ. "Because you are doing the best you can (even though you may sometimes fail)," Teilhard assured a friend, "you are forming your own self within the world, and you are helping the world form itself around you."[21] And he acted upon his own advice. "My whole spiritual life consists more and more in abandoning myself (actively) to the presence and action of God," he wrote his brothers in 1941. "To be in communion with Becoming has become the formula of my whole life."

Teilhard considered his massive efforts to work out a philosophy of the universe to be his "apostolate and mission." This philosophy, a "christifying" of evolution, was the end product of a lifelong spiritual and intellectual pilgrimage, which reached a point of crystalization in his major book, *The Phenomenon of Man*. To adopt such a position meant a radical break with the static theory of creation set forth in Church dogma. His spiritual biography, partially told in *Letters from a Traveller,* tells us what impelled him to take the risk of pioneering.

Teilhard descended from a distinguished and devout Catholic family. His father, Emmanuel, and mother, Berthe, a descendant of Voltaire, inculcated personal discipline and devotion in the home. Not surprisingly, they sent their gifted son to a Jesuit school. Teilhard did well in all subjects, earning several medals, but his real love was in "rocks." Though he subsequently joined the Society of Jesus, his love for the earth never diminished. "Teilhard was a son of the earth," Claude Cuénot has observed in his splendid biography, "and in earth's blind matter his being was rooted."[22] After completing his theological studies in 1912, he studied science in Paris. During World War I he continued his habit of making notes about the earth's makeup while serving as stretcher bearer at the front. Finally, after three years more at the Sorbonne, in 1922 he received the doctor's degree in the natural sciences. During these years, matter began "to take on the tint of life," resulting in Teilhard's quest, as he wrote in 1918, to be "the evangelist of Your Christ in the Universe."

Teilhard's scientific career, the bulk of which was spent in geological and paleontological research in China between 1923 and 1946, outfitted him with the data he needed to fashion his philosophy. By 1931 the main lines of the *Phenomenon of Man* had taken shape. However, his speculations thrust him far ahead of his contemporaries; though he published some essays of a strictly scientific nature, his philosophical works were kept under wraps until after his death in 1955. This censorship irritated him, his letters show, but he never broke his Jesuit vow of complete obedience. To a degree perhaps, as Cuénot has said, his attachment to the universe generated the sense of serenity and detachment which enabled him to persevere despite personal disappointment.

This same view of life assisted him in other ways as well. In his researches Teilhard endured the hardships of field expeditions without complaint, immersed in his quest of truth. He faced physical illness in his last years with the same optimism and faith he instilled in others. In 1947 he experienced a severe heart attack which virtually ended his field career. A year later his order forbade his taking a teaching position at the Collège de France, so he welcomed the opportunity to spend his last years in South Africa and the United States of America, which he called "practically my second fatherland." He died in New York City on April 10, Easter Sunday, 1955, after a second massive heart attack. A few hours earlier, he had told a friend, "I go to meet him who comes."[23]

His legacy, and that of the *Letters,* lies above all in his sounding a strong note of hope in an era of despair. The words "personalism" and "futurism" best summarize his concern. Against the background of the depersonalizing and dehumanizing of mankind which our age has wrought, they are words which Christians cannot say too often. Long ago, John the Seer said something not far removed. "I am the Alpha and the Omega, the first and the last, the beginning and the end." (Rev. 22:13) Somehow we must make modern man hear.

Selected Bibliography

Catholic Personal Piety

Graef, Hilda C. *Mystics of Our Times*. (London: Burns & Oates, 1961.)

Hugel, Friedrich von. *The Mystical Element of Religion*. Second edition. 2 vols. (London: J. M. Dent & Sons Ltd.; James Clarke & Co., Ltd., 1923.)

Protestant Personal Piety

The Protestant Mystics. Edited by Anne Fremantle. With an introduction by W. H. Auden. (Boston & Toronto: Little, Brown & Co., 1964.)

Wyon, Olive. *Living Springs: New Religious Movements in Western Europe*. (Philadelphia: Westminster Press, c. 1962.)

Kierkegaard

Purity of Heart. Translated by Douglas V. Steere. (New York: Harper Torchbooks, 1938.)

The Journals of Kierkegaard. Edited and with an introduction by Alexander Dru. (New York & Evanston: Harper Torchbooks, 1958.)

The Point of View for My Work as an Author: A Report to History. Edited with a preface by Benjamin Nelson. (New York: Harper Torchbooks, 1962.)

Lowrie, Walter. *A Short Life of Kierkegaard*. (Princeton, New Jersey: Princeton University Press, 1942.)

Patrick, Denzil G. M. *Pascal and Kierkegaard: A Study in the Strategy of Evangelism*. Vol. II. (London & Redhill: Lutterworth Press, 1947.)

Steere, Douglas V. *Doors into Life through Five Devotional Classics*. (New York: Harper & Bros. Publishers, 1948.)

Bonhoeffer

Letters and Papers from Prison. Edited by Eberhard Bethge.

Translated by Reginald H. Fuller. (New York: The Macmillan Co., 1953.)

The Cost of Discipleship. Translated by R. H. Fuller. (New York: The Macmillan Co., 1937.)

Life Together. Translated and with an introduction by John W. Doberstein. (New York & Evanston: Harper & Row, Publishers, 1954.)

Bethge, Eberhard. *Dietrich Bonhoeffer, Theologe, Christ, Zeitgenosse.* (München: Chr. Kaiser Verlag, 1967.)

Godsey, John D. *The Theology of Dietrich Bonhoeffer.* (Philadelphia: The Westminster Press, 1960.)

Marty, Martin E. (ed.). *The Place of Bonhoeffer: Problems and Possibilities in His Thought.* (New York: Association Press, 1962.)

Wedemeyer-Weller, Maria von. "The Other Letters From Prison," *Union Seminary Quarterly Review,* XXIII (Fall, 1967), 23-29.

Father Delp
The Prison Meditations of Father Alfred Delp. With an introduction by Thomas Merton. (New York: The Macmillan Co., 1963.)

Teilhard de Chardin
Letters from a Traveller, 1923-1955. (London: William Collins; New York: Harper & Row, 1962.)

The Making of a Mind: Letters from a Soldier-Priest, 1914-1919. Translated by René Hague. (New York: Harper & Row, Publishers, 1965.)

Le Milieu Divin: An Essay on the Interior Life. (London: William Collins Sons & Co., Ltd.; New York: Harper & Bros., 1957.)

The Phenomenon of Man. Translated by Bernard Wall. (New York: Harper & Bros., 1957.)

Cuénot, Claude. *Teilhard de Chardin: A Biographical Study.*

Translated by Vincent Colimore. Edited by René Hague. (Baltimore: Helicon, 1965.)

De Lubac, Henri, S. J. *Teilhard de Chardin: The Man and His Meaning.* Translated by René Hague. (London: Burns & Oates Ltd.; New York: Hawthorn Books, Inc., 1965.)

Speaight, Robert. *The Life of Teilhard de Chardin.* (New York & Evanston: Harper & Row, Publishers, 1967.)

PERSONAL DEVOTION IN
THE SPACE AGE

IX

Personal Devotion in The Space Age

Anyone who has read the classics described in the preceding chapters may wonder where his reading leaves him in terms of his own devotional habits. What do they teach us about personal worship? The substantial variety found in the classics allows no pat answers. Yet, considered as a whole, from Augustine to Bonhoeffer, they come through with one consistent message— *the need for some kind of spiritual discipline.*

Unfortunately, our generation does not like discipline. The very word "discipline" sounds too authoritarian. To be sure, we submit to all kinds of disciplines in other areas—work, study, government, athletics, even play. But, somehow, these fall into quite a different category than religion and devotion. These we can perform just as well, we reason, without established rules and patterns; in fact, much better. Regimentation may lead to stereotypes and artificiality of observance and hinder the Spirit.

This last statement may be quite true; heaven knows how many times it has happened! However, the typical non-regimented approach has not won any blue ribbons in Christian devotion either. We have borne ample witness to the shallowness of our personal piety by the patchy record we have achieved in various facets of Christian love such as race relations and aid to the poor. If these failings can't be blamed entirely on superficial Christianity, then where do we place the blame?

This matter of personal discipline is, in the last analysis, a matter of intention, just as William Law reminded his contemporaries. It requires a resolution to take one's relationship to God seriously. Now I'm not suggestiong by this that you use Law's devotional schedule, or anyone else's for that matter. You need to devise your own, one which will fit your personal situation.

The heart of all devotion is prayer. Quite frankly, I have to admit that I don't find prayer easy in our scientific age. Like many others, I've had to modify my perspective as I have become more literate scientifically. For example, where I once tried to visualize God "out there"—a twenty foot high grandfather with long white beard and flowing robes—now I can't. I have had to remember that God is nearer to us than we are to ourselves— that He is within me and those around me, within the happenings of His world. So, instead of laying aside all of my burdens and cares and trying to start with a clean slate, I begin where I am. I meditate upon the deepest concerns of my heart and mind, confident that God cares about those things as much as I do. In this way, as Bishop John A. T. Robinson has said, prayer rises *through* the world to God. God meets us in the mundane things of our lives—not in some far removed paradise which no human concern has ever entered.

Brother Lawrence's prayer to the "God of pots and pans" is chock-full of insight for the busy housewife, the common laborer, the assembly line operator, the mechanic, the pastor, the seminarian, or anyone else trapped in the routine of this day of machines. We need desperately to learn from Brother Lawrence that God is accessible anytime and anywhere. He stands ready to get involved in the outpouring of our energies for good in whatever measure we invite Him to. He is not "out there" but "here," wherever human life is lived.

With this understanding of God's operation in the world, I have found myself following no set routine of prayer, Bible reading, or other devotional acts. Basically, I am not cut out for that kind of regimentation in anything. My job permits a certain amount of freedom. Yet, I find momentary meditation in the midst of activities, many times a day, a help. For me this kind of praying amounts to putting myself in God's hands, so to speak, exercising a naive kind of trust that He will see me through the moment at hand. I utter no formulas. I simply resign myself, as I am at the moment, to Him, quietly meditating in mind and heart upon a special concern.

This sounds egocentric. But in reality it has been my way to empty myself. In moments of particular stress it has enabled me to pull myself together and to get my bearings again; momentarily, I forget myself as undiscovered spiritual resources well up from within.

In our increasingly complex and demanding society, every person needs periods of quiet for making a personal inventory. The greater the strain, the longer the period. Modern man suffers dehumanization and depersonalization, reduction to "thinghood" and deprivation of "personhood." At his job he is a "cog" in a machine. In the supermarket he is a "sale." On the street he is a moving "object." Wherever he goes, he is deprived of the sense of identity which his ego demands. Unless he can discover a place where he is "for real," he is lost.

The churches can furnish this essential *place*. *Their* survival, in fact, depends upon it. Through their public worship they may provide meaningful interludes in the midst of the clatter and din of daily activities. Worship services in the space age would benefit from many more periods of silence than we have been accustomed to. Too many of them offer not interruptions of the clatter and din but continuations. No wonder people seek "retreat" from the Church as much as from the world.

This is not to belittle the retreat. Longer periods away from the pressures of daily life are essential to the physical, mental, and spiritual well-being of more and more people. We prove this by our outings at the beach, in the woods, or in the backyard. Bodies and minds simply will not take the strain of living at breakneck speed all the time, as is evidenced by the sky-rocketing sale of alcohol, pep pills, and LSD. Many must have voluntary retreat or enforced retreat by hospitalization.

The classics offer some helpful insights about retreats—their values, their conduct, their purpose. Novices in faith, and all of us are, would do well to secure a guide, just like hunters do when they go into an unknown forest to hunt game. Let those who have been there before show the way. Yet, it would be foolish to follow the prescriptions of any classic exactly in our day, for the forest has surely changed some through the centuries. The times require the courage to experiment and adapt.

In their quest for religious vitality, many are turning to forms of mysticism. The oriental religions have begun to have a lot of appeal to Westerners. In the long run they probably will not prove overly attractive, unless put in the wealth affirming package sold so profusely by the Hindu holy man, Maharishi, mentor of the Beatles and certain big name Hollywood stars.

Possessing a strong positive attitude toward the things of this world, more and more of which science has placed in his control, the Westerner will undoubtedly find the mysticism of Francis of Assisi more to his liking. Francis' ecstatic flights reportedly produced a harmony with nature; his love extended to the whole of God's creation; union with God caused him to pour out his life in serving his fellow-man.

The mystical route obviously suits those of a particular temperament. Many would-be mystics, the use of LSD or other hallucination-inducing drugs notwithstanding, will not make the grade, even if they make a "trip." The current campus craze about mysticism represents a longing for certitude—the infallible revelation—in religious experience and a searching for authentic spiritual experience. Instead of being critical of such desires, the churches ought to channel them into streams which will not bring disappointment in the end.

Here is where open-ended discussion in small, informal groups can help. Religious experience, like personal experience of any kind, needs to be shared. Because it is intangible, the only means of validation is comparison. With what? The witness of Christians in other ages and the witness of our fellow Christians today.

Isn't this what Paul meant when he counseled that "speaking the truth in love, we are to grow up in every way into him who is the head, into Christ, from whom the whole body, joined and knit together by every joint with which it is supplied, when each part is working properly, makes bodily growth and upbuilds itself in love"? (Eph. 4: 15-16; RSV) Gathered together in the Spirit of Christ, we can indeed offer mutual help in this complex matter of living "in the Lord" while living in the world come of age.

The devotional classics represent a vast flower garden of Christian experience with life. Some will attract you personally, others may not. Somewhere in the garden, however, I am confident, you will find a blossom which repeatedly will bring new fragrance into the course of every day.

FOOTNOTES

Chapter One

1. See also William James' epochal study of *Varieties of Religious Experience.*
2. *Grace Abounding,* 129; ed. Roger Sharrock (Oxford: The Clarendon Press, 1962), p. 8.

Chapter Two

1. Tertullian, *On Prayer,* 25.
2. See Robert L. Simpson, *The Interpretation of Prayer in the Early Church* (Philadelphia: The Westminster Press, 1965).
3. For a critical sifting of the martyrologies, see E. C. E. Owen, *Some Authentic Acts of the Early Martyrs* (Oxford: The Clarendon Press, 1927).
4. For a standard collection, see M. R. James, *The Apocryphal New Testament* (Oxford: The Clarendon Press, 1924).
5. *On Baptism,* 17.
6. *The Sayings of the Fathers,* 1.1; in *The Desert Fathers.* Translated by Helen Waddell (London: Constable, 1936), p. 89.
7. See chs. 67-71.
8. *Prol.*; in *Ancient Christian Writers,* trans. Robert T. Meyer (Westminster, Maryland: The Newman Press; London: Longmans, Green & Co., 1950), X, 17.
9. Meyer, *op cit.,* X, 46.
10. Cf. a fine study of these in *The Confessions of St. Augustine,* Book VIII, edited and translated by C. S. C. Williams (Oxford: Basil Blackwell, 1953), pp. vii-xxvii.
11. Possidius, *Life of Augustine,* 3-4.
12. *Ibid.,* 5.
13. *Ibid.* 8.
14. Cf. Possidius, ch. 6, 15-16; and the fact that 13 of his 15 anti-Manichean writings appeared before 400.
15. Cf. Possidius, 9-14.
16. Cf. Possidius, 17.
17. Possidius, 28-30.
18. See *Saint Augustin. Confessions.* Texte établi et traduit par Pierre de Labriolle. Quatrième édition (Paris: Société d'édition "Les Belles Lettres," 1947), I, vii-ix.
19. Ps. 51. 3-5; RSV; cf. *Conf.* 1.7.
20. Ottley, *Studies in the Confessions of St. Augustine.*
21. *De contemptu mundi,* dial. i; in Ottley, *op. cit.,* p. 2.
22. Trans. Vernon J. Bourke. *The Fathers of the Church* (New York: Father of the Church, Inc., 1953), XXI, 36.
23. *Ibid.,* XXI, 304.
24. *Ibid.,* XXI, 7.
25. *Ibid.,* XXI, 48.
26. Cf. *Ibid.,* 7.20-21.
27. Ottley, *op cit.,* p. 2.
28. FC, *op cit.,* XXI, 83.
29. FC, *op cit.,* XXI, 89; see also 7.10.16, where Augustine confirms this prescription from his own experience.
30. Cf. 5.2.2.
31. FC, *op. cit.,* XXI, 180.

32. See particularly *Conf.*, 7.9.13-15, where he discusses the agreements and disagreements between Christianity and Neo-Platonism.
33. *Conf.* 8.7; trans. W. Watts, *Loeb Classical Library*, I, 439.
34. Cf. Ottley, *op. cit.*, p. 109.

Chapter Three

1. Gregory of Tours, *Hist. Ecc. Franc.*, 5.3; in G. G. Coulton, *Medieval Village, Manor, and Monastery* (New York: Harper and Row, Torchbooks, 1960), p. 107.
2. Cited by G. G. Coulton, *Ten Medieval Studies* (Boston: Beacon Press, 1906, 1959 reprint), pp. 112-3.
3. L. 84; *Piers the Plowman, A Critical Edition of the A-Version*, ed. Thomas A. Knott and David C. Fowler (Baltimore: Johns Hopkins, 1952), p. 69.
4. John of Joinville, *The History of St. Louis,* 2.16. Trans. Joan Evans (London, New York, Toronto: Oxford University Press, 1938), p. 22.
4a. 2.16.
4b. 2.145.
5. 1.3; Evans, p. 5.
6. William Ralph Inge, *Christian Mysticism.* 7th ed. (London: Methuen & Co., Ltd., 1933), p. 5.
7. *Enneads,* 6.9.11.
8. 86.9.7; Plotinus: *The Enneads,* tr. S. Mackenna. 2 ed. (London: Faber and Faber, Ltd., 1956), p. 621.
9. *Mystical Theology,* 3.
10. See the excellent discussion of E. Gilson, *The Mystical Theology of Saint Bernard,* tr. A. H. C. Downes (London: Sheed and Ward, 1940), pp. 108-18.
11. Ch. 31; *On the Song of Songs,* tr. and ed. by A Religious of C.S.M.V. (London: A. R. Mowbray & Co., Ltd., 1952), pp. 229-30.
12. *Soliloquy on the Earnest Money of the Soul,* tr. Kevin Herbert (Milwaukee: Marquette University Press, 1956).

Chapter Four

1. *Essential Works of Erasmus,* ed. W. T. H. Jackson (New York: Bantam Books, 1965), p. 396.
2. *Ibid.,* p. 409.
3. *Ibid.,* p. 416.
4. *Ibid.,* p. 419.
5. Quoted by David Knowles, *The English Mystical Tradition* (New York: Harper & Row, Publishers, 1961), p. 59.
6. 27; *Theologia Germanica,* introduction and notes by J. Bernhart (New York: Pantheon Books, Inc., 1949), translation of Susanna Winkworth.
7. 1.2; tr. Abbot Justin McCann (New York: Mentor, 1957), p. 18.
8. 3.55; McCann, p. 145.
9. 3.32; McCann, p. 113.
10. 3.57; McCann, p. 149.
11. 2.5; McCann, p. 57.
12. 2.3; McCann, p. 55.

Chapter Five

1. Tr. Anthony Mottola (New York: Image Books, 1964), pp. 140-1.
2. *Ascent of Mount Carmel,* 2.13; tr. E. Allison Peers (Garden City: Doubleday, 1958), p. 72.

3. *Life, p.* 11.
4. 14; Peers, p. 148.
5. *Life,* 18; Peers, p. 173.
6. *Interior Castle,* 5.1.

Chapter Six

1. *A Popular History of the Catholic Church* (Garden City: Doubleday Image Books, 1954), p. 196.
2. Cf. F. Charmot, S. J., *Ignatius Loyola and Francis de Sales, Two Masters One Spirituality.* Translated by Sister M. Renelle, S.S.N.D. (St. Louis: Herder, 1966). Charmot (p. 19), somewhat exaggeratedly, claims that "voluntarily, humbly, tenaciously, he made himself the disciple of St. Ignatius, followed him in everything, and often literally." He notes later (p. 24), however, that de Sales surpassed Ignatius "in culture, in the expression of the thought, and in its adaptation to lay and religious souls."
3. Pref.; *Introduction to the Devout Life,* translated by Michael Day. (London: J. M. Dent & Sons, Ltd., New York: E. P. Dutton & Co., 1961), p. 1.
4. 4.9; Day, p. 219.
5. *Pascal: His Life and Works;* tr. G. S. Fraser (London: Harvill Press, 1952).
6. Cf. J. Steinmann, *Pascal,* tr. M. Turnell (London: Burns & Oates, 1962), pp. 186ff.
7. See Mesnard, pp. 53ff.
8. In Steinmann, pp. 189-90.
9. See the splendid discussion of Pascal's apology by Denzil G. M. Patrick, *Pascal and Kierkegaard: A Study in the Strategy of Evangelism* (London and Redhill: Lutterworth Press, 1947), I, 159-223.
10. *Ibid.,* p. 170.
11. 17; tr. John Warrington; ed. Louis Lafuma (London: J. M. Dent & Sons, Ltd.; New York: E. P. Dutton & Co., Inc. 1960), p. 13.
12. 343; tr. Warrington.
13. 355; tr. Warrington, p. 98.
14. 394; tr. Warrington, p. 111.
15. 402; tr. Warrington, p. 113.
16. *Sol.* 2.1.1.
17. 602; tr. Warrington, p. 172.
18. First Conversation; (Fleming H. Revell Co., 1958), p. 13.
19. *Ibid.*
20. Second Letter; pp. 36-37.
21. *Ibid.,* p. 37.
22. *Ibid.,* pp. 37-8.
23. Second letter; p. 40.
24. Twelfth letter; p. 59.
25. Fourteenth letter; p. 62.

Chapter Seven

1. *Lancelot Andrewes,* 1555-1626 (London: S. P. C. K., 1958), p. 39.
2. See list of C. J. Stranks, *Anglican Devotion* (London: SCM Press, Ltd., 1961), p. 65.
3. H. Trevor Hughes, *The Piety of Jeremy Taylor* (London: Macmillan & Co., Ltd.; New York: St. Martin's Press, 1960), p. 155.
4. *Ibid.,* p. 23.
5. Stranks, p. 85.

6. 2.3; Kepler, p. 76.
7. *Grace Abounding*, 5.
8. *Bunyan Calling* (London: George Allen & Unwin Ltd., 1943), p. 50.
9. *Grace Abounding*, 20.
10. *Ibid.*, 37.
11. *Ibid.*, 269.
12. *Ibid.*, 327.
13. Brigid Brophy, Michael Levy, and Charles Osborne, *Fifty Works of English (and American) Literature We Could Do Without* (New York: Stein & Day, 1967).
14. See Willcocks, pp. 166-70, for an explanation of the critical problems.
15. Cited by Gerald Bullett, *The English Mystics* (London: Michael Joseph, 1950), pp. 132-3.
16. Bullett, p. 158.
17. Eric W. Baker, *A Herald of the Evangelical Revival* (London: Epworth Press, 1948), p. 189.
18. Ch. 1.
19. Ch. 2.
20. Ch. 4.
21. Ch. 10.
22. Ch. 15.
23. Ch. 17.
24. Ch. 18.
25. *The Journal of George Fox*, rev. ed. by John L. Nickalls (Cambridge: University Press, 1952), p. xlvii.
26. *Journal*, ch. 3 (New York: Corinth Books, 1961), p. 44.
27. *Journal*, 1; p. 8.
28. *Journal*, 12; p. 221.

Chapter Eight

1. See further Hilda C. Graef, *Mystics of Our Times* (London: Burns & Oates, 1961).
2. *The Journals of Kierkegaard*, translated, selected, and with an introduction by Alexander Dru (New York & Evanston: Harper Torchbooks, 1958), p. 130.
3. See further *The Protestant Mystics*, ed. Anne Fremantle.
4. *The Journals of Kierkegaard*, trans. by Alexander Dru (New York & Evanston: Harper Torchbooks, 1958), p. 39.
5. *Ibid.*, p. 51.
6. *Ibid.*, p. 59.
7. *Ibid.*, p. 216.
8. *Pascal and Kierkegaard: A Study in the Strategy of Evangelism* (London: Lutterworth Press, 1947), II, 130.
9. *Ibid.*, p. 155.
10. *Purity of Heart*, 8; trans. Douglas V. Steere (New York: Harper Torchbooks, 1938), p. 129.
11. *Ibid.*, p. 212.
12. A personal comment cited by John D. Godsey, *The Theology of Dietrich Bonhoeffer* (Philadelphia: Westminster Press, 1960), p. 21.
13. *Letters and Papers from Prison*, ed. Eberhard Bethge, tr. Reginald H. Fuller (New York: The Macmillan Co., 1953), p. 200.
14. *Ibid.*, p. 239.
15. *The Venlo Incident*, p. 180. Quoted by E. Bethge in *Letters and Papers from Prison*, p. 13f.
16. *The Prison Meditations of Father Delp*, with an introduction by

Thomas Merton (New York: The Macmillan Co.), p. 89.
17. *Ibid.*, p. 24.
18. *Ibid.*, p. 164.
19. *Ibid.*, p. 165.
20. *Letters from a Traveller,* 1923-1955 (London: William Collins; New York: Harper & Row, 1962), pp. 217-8.
21. *Ibid.*, p. 120.
22. *Teilhard de Chardin,* tr. Vincent Colimore (Baltimore: Helicon, 1958), p. 14.
23. *Ibid.*, p. 386.

INDEX

Adornment of the Spiritual Marriage, 93
Allport, Gordon, 179n
Andrewes, Lancelot, 135, 171-174, 190n
Angyal, Andras, 155n
Anthony, St., 18, 33, 36, 39-41
Are You Running With Me Jesus?, 144n
Arndt, Jacob, 166
Art of Counseling, The, 146n
Ascent of Mt. Carmel, 122
Athanasius, 37, 38, 39
Augustine, St., 18, 21, 22, 24, 32, 34, 37, 42-52, 55, 60, 70, 96, 99, 101, 145, 149, 156, 166, 191, 235

Baillie, John, 173n, 220n
Benedict, *Rule* of, 190
Bernard of Clairvaux, 70, 71, 72, 73, 74, 91, 94, 96, 101, 120, 145, 149, 166, 209
Berne, Eric, 174n
Boccaccio, 88, 116
Boehme, Jacob, 131, 166, 167, 174n, 186, 218n
Boehme, John, 99
Bonhoeffer, Dietrich, 21, 208n, 210, 217-224, 235
Boisen, Anton, 153n, 181n, 208n
Bonaventure, 91
Book of Margery Kempe, 96, 191
Boyd, Malcolm, 144n
Brothers of the Common Life, The, 87, 92, 93, 94, 166
Bunyan, John, 18, 21, 22, 24, 37n, 121n, 135, 171, 174, 179-185, 191

Calvin, John, 52n, 98, 112, 116, 128, 130, 131, 143, 165, 169
Christ and Selfhood 102n
Christ of the Indian Road, 143n
Christian Experience of the Holy Spirit, The, 143n
Christian Perfection, (F. Fénelon), 141
Christianity and Fear, 188n
Cloud of Unknowing, The, 95
Cohen, Herman, 206

Confessions, The, 20, 37, 42, 45-52, 55, 99, 191
Cost of Discipleship, The, 220
Dark Night of the Soul, The, 122
Decameron, 88, 116
Delp, Father Alfred, 210, 224-226
Dewey, John, 203n
Diary of Private Prayer, 173n
Disquisition on the Reformation of the Inner Man, 149
Doctor and the Soul, The, 210n

Eckhart, Meister, 45n, 92, 101, 166, 186
Erasmus, 88, 90, 94
Erikson, Erik, 40n, 129, 129n, 130n, 212n
Escape from Freedom, 29n
Existentialism and Religious Belief, 151n
Exploration of the Inner World, The, 153n

Fénelon, Francis, 141
Fire of Love, The, 94
Flame of Living Love, The, 122
Fosdick, Harry Emerson, 143n
Fox, George, 96, 135, 174, 191-192, 193n
Foucauld, Charles de, 206, 207
Francis de Sales, 135, 140, 142-147, 156, 176, 178
Francis of Assisi, 18, 19, 21, 22, 74-79, 94, 96, 120, 148n, 166, 209, 238
Franke, August Hermann, 98, 166, 168
Frankl, Viktor, 118n, 124n, 210n
Freud, Sigmund, 49n, 179n, 203n, 219n, 220n
Friends of God, The, 92, 93, 115, 166
From Death Camp to Existentialism, 210n
Fromm, Erich, 29n

Games People Play, The, 174n
Genuinely Human Existence, A, 102n
Gerard de Groote, 92, 93, 94, 99
German Theology, 21, 92, 96, 97-98, 130

Gift from the Sea, The, 174n, 217n
God and the Unconscious, 61n
Grace Abounding, 135, 182
Gregory the Great, 60, 96, 120
Groote, Gerard de, 92, 93, 94, 99
Guyon, Madame, 141, 186

Hammarskjöld, Dag, 45n, 173n
Harding, Esther, 183n
Hecker, Isaac Thomas, 206, 207
Hermann, Nicholas, (See Lawrence, Bro.)
Hilton, Walter, 95, 99
History of Medical Psychology, 62n
Holy Dying, 20, 135, 175, 176, 177
Holy Living, 20, 135, 175, 176, 177
Holy Spirit in Five Worlds, The, 193n
Horney, Karen, 69n, 187n, 216n
Hugo of St. Victor, 70, 73, 74, 91, 96, 120, 125

Identity and the Life Cycle, 40n
Imitation of Christ, 20, 21, 94, 96, 98-105, 119, 120, 179, 194
Inge, Dean William, 67
Interior Castle, 120
Interpersonal Theory of Psychiatry, 72n
Introduction to the Devout Life, 135, 140, 142-147, 176

James, William, 148n
Jansen, Cornelius, 142, 149
John of the Cross, 120-125, 127, 141
Jones, E. Stanley, 143n
Journal of George Fox, 96, 135, 191-192
Journal of John Woolman, 135, 192-195
Journals of S. Kiekegaard, 211, 213
Journey Into the Self, The, 183n
Julian of Norwich, 95
Jung, C. G., 42nd, 61n, 183n, 203n

Kempe, Margery, 94, 96
Kierkegaard, Søren, 148n, 208, 208n, 209n, 210, 211-217, 218

Law, William, 135, 147, 185-191, 235
Lawrence, Bro., 21, 135, 142, 156-160, 236
Lecky, Prescott, 51n, 52n
Letters and Papers from Prison, 20, 221-224
Letters from a Traveller, 20, 226-229
Libermann, Francis, 206
Life of St. Anthony, 37, 39-41, 43, 50
Life of Teresa of Avila, 120
Lindbergh, Anne Morrow, 174n, 217n
Little Flowers, The, 19, 20, 21, 77-79
Locke, John, 138n
Lonely Crowd, The, 30n
Loyola, Ignatius, 116, 117-120, 145
LSD: The Consciousness Expanding Drug, 68n
Luther, Martin, 18, 24, 86, 91, 98, 111, 112, 116, 128, 129, 129n, 130n, 131, 148n, 158, 165, 216

Markings, 45n, 17n
Marsh, L. C., 93n
Marx, Karl, 202, 202n, 204
May, Rollo, 146n
Meaning of Gifts, The, 223n
Merswin, Rulman, 92
McNeil, Stephen, 102n
Mill, John Stuart, 148n
Mirror of Perfection, The, 19, 20, 77-79
Modern Man in Search of a Soul, 61n
Molinos, Michael, 140, 141
Murphy, Gardner, 69n
Mystical Theology, 95

Neurosis and Human Growth, 187n
Neurosis and Treatment, 155n

Olmsted, Michael, 23n
On the Steps of Humility, 71
Organization Man, The, 61n
Out of the Depths, 153n
Our Inner Conflicts, 216

Pachomius, 33

Pascal, Blaise, 18, 21, 135, 142, 147-156, 160, 210
Pattern and Growth in Personality, 180n
Peale, Norman Vincent, 117n
Pensées, 20, 21, 135, 142, 151, 152-157
Pfister, Oskar, 188n
Pia Desideria, 135, 167
Pilgrim's Progress, The, 20, 37n, 121n, 135, 179, 183-185, 192
Plain Man's Pathway to Heaven, The, 180
Plotinus, 68, 68n, 69
Practice of Piety, The, 180
Practice of the Presence of God, The, 20, 135, 142, 158-160
Praise of Folly, The, 90
Prison Meditations of Father Delp, The, 224-226
Private Devotions, 135, 171, 173
Pseudo-Dionyius, 70, 95, 96, 120, 166
Psychotherapy and a Christian View of Man, preface note
Psychotherapy and Existentialism, 124n
Purity of Heart, 215-217

Radewyn, Florentius, 93, 94
Rank, Otto, 178n
Religious Factors in Mental Illness, 181n
Revelations of Divine Love, 95
Richard of St. Victor, 96
Roberts, David, preface note, 151n
Robinson, John A. T., 236
Robinson, H. Wheeler, 143n
Rolle, Richard, 94, 95
Ruysbroeck, John of, 92, 93, 101, 166

Sales, Francis de, 135, 140, 142-147, 156, 176, 178
Scale of Perfection, 95

Self-Consistency: A Theory of Personality, 52n
Serious Call to a Devout and Holy Life, A, 20, 135, 147, 185, 186, 188-191
Sherill, Louis, reface note
Short and Easy Method of Prayer, A, 141
Small Group, The, 23n
Soliloquy of the Soul, 99
Spener, Philip Jakob, 98, 135, 166, 167
Spiritual Canticle, The, 122
Spiritual Exercises, 117-120
Spiritual Guide, The, 141
Struggle of the Soul, The, preface note
Sullivan, Harry Stack, 72n
Suso, Henry, 92, 101, 159, 166

Table Talks, 129n, 131
Tauler, John, 92, 96, 98, 101, 159, 166, 186
Taylor, Jeremy, 21, 135, 174-179
Teilhard de Chardin, 210, 226-229
Teresa of Avila, 120-125, 127, 141
Teresa of Lisieux, 18
Thomas á Kempis, 92, 94, 99-105, 209
Tillich, Paul, 155n
Tournier, Paul, 223n

Way of Divine Love, The, 120, 187
Wesley, John, 18, 24, 147, 169, 187n, 188n, 192
White, Victor, 6n
Whyte, W. H., 61n
Woolman, John, 135, 192-194

Young Man Luther, 129

Zilboorg, Gregory, 62n
Zinzendorf, Nicholas von, 168, 169